CASS SERIES: STUDIES IN INTELLIGENCE
(Series Editors: Christopher Andrew and Michael I. Handel)

NOTHING SACRED

CASS SERIES: STUDIES IN INTELLIGENCE
(Series Editors: Christopher Andrew and Michael I. Handel)

Also in this series

Intelligence Investigations: How Ultra Changed History
by Ralph Bennett

Intelligence Analysis and Assessment
edited by David Charters, A. Stuart Farson and Glenn P. Hastedt

Codebreaker in the Far East
by Alan Stripp

War, Strategy and Intelligence
by Michael I. Handel

Controlling Intelligence
edited by Glenn P. Hastedt

Security and Intelligence in a Changing World:
New Perspectives for the 1990s
edited by A. Stuart Farson, David Stafford and
Wesley K. Wark

Spy Fiction, Spy Films and Real Intelligence
edited by Wesley K. Wark

From Information to Intrigue: Studies in Secret Service
Based on the Swedish Experience 1939–45
by C.G. McKay

Dieppe Revisited: A Documentary Investigation
by John Campbell

The Australian Security Intelligence Organization:
An Unofficial History
by Frank Cain

Intelligence and Strategy in the Second World War
edited by Michael I. Handel

Policing Politics: Security Intelligence and the
Liberal Democratic State
by Peter Gill

Espionage: Past, Present, Future?
edited by Wesley K. Wark

NOTHING SACRED

NAZI ESPIONAGE AGAINST THE VATICAN
1939–1945

DAVID ALVAREZ
and
ROBERT A. GRAHAM, SJ

FRANK CASS
LONDON • PORTLAND, OR

Published in 1997 in Great Britain by
FRANK CASS PUBLISHERS
Newbury House, 900 Eastern Avenue, London IG2 7HH

and in the United States of America by
FRANK CASS
c/o ISBS, 5804 N.E. Hassalo Street, Portland, Oregon 97213-3644

Website http://www.frankcass.com

Copyright © 1997 David Alvarez and Robert A. Graham, SJ

British Library Cataloguing in Publication Data
Alvarez, David
    Nothing sacred: Nazi espionage against the Vatican, 1939–1945
    1. World War, 1939–1945 – Secret service – Germany.
    2. World War, 1939–1945 – Secret service – Vatican City
    I. Title II. Graham, Robert A.
    940.5'48743

ISBN 0 7146 4744 6 (cloth)
ISBN 0 7146 4302 5 (paper)

Library of Congress Cataloging-in-Publication Data
Alvarez, David J.
   Nothing sacred: Nazi espionage against the Vatican, 1939–1945
David Alvarez and Robert A. Graham.
   p. cm.
   Includes bibliographical references and index.
   ISBN 0-7146-4744-6 (cloth) ISBN 0-7146-4302-5 (paper)
   1. World War, 1939–1945 – Secret service – Germany. 2. World War,
1939–1945 – Vatican City. I. Graham, Robert A. II. Title.
D810.S7A559   1997
940.54'8743–DC21
                                                     97–11657
                                                     CIP

Printed in Great Britain by
Bookcraft (Bath) Ltd, Midsomer Norton, Avon

For Donna,

D.A.

To the memory of Johannes Ullrich,

R.A.G.

Contents

Preface

Historians of intelligence have grown accustomed to hearing their subject described as the 'missing dimension' of history. In fact, since a British diplomatist first used that term more than a quarter of a century ago to characterize the limitations of traditional diplomatic and military history, historians have laboured mightily to expose that important dimension. In no area has that labour proved more productive than in the study of the Second World War. Spurred on by the release of documents long hidden from public scrutiny in classified military and intelligence archives, scholars have rewritten much of the history of that war by revealing the way in which intelligence (or its lack) influenced planning and operations on both the tactical and strategic level. For all of their contributions, however, these intelligence studies of the war have been marked by a certain imbalance. Historians have tended to approach the 'intelligence war' as if the only participants were the major belligerents. This focus on the principal actors and their interaction with each other is understandable given the centrality of these actors and their activity in the history of the war. It is also understandable in light of the fact that American, British and German archives have been, for historians, the richest and most accessible sources of information on the intelligence aspects of the war. A reliance upon these sources has further encouraged a rather narrow view of the field. As a result, we are now fairly knowledgeable about such subjects as the organization of the wartime German intelligence services, American and British codebreaking against Germany and Japan, Allied counterintelligence successes against German spies, and the role of intelligence in such operations as the Battle of Midway or the Battle of the Atlantic. On the other hand, we continue to know very little about the intelligence role, if any, of the minor belligerents and the neutral powers.

As players in the intelligence game, the neutrals have received little attention from historians other than that they provided a playing field on which Allied and Axis espionage services competed against each other. In fact, the neutrals were important intelligence targets in their own right. Spain and Turkey occupied strategic positions at either end of the Mediterranean and marshalled significant military forces. Ireland and Portugal (with its Azores and Cape Verde Islands) faced the vital Atlantic sea lanes. Portugal, Spain, Sweden and Turkey possessed important reserves of such strategic materials as chromium, iron ore, tungsten, and wolfram. Throughout the war Switzerland maintained its reputation as the financial and intelligence crossroads of the world. Since the actions of these neutrals could have a significant impact on the course of the war, their sympathies and plans were a constant source of concern and anxiety in Berlin, London, Moscow, Rome, Tokyo and Washington. Yet, the degree to which such anxiety was translated into intelligence operations against the various neutral powers is a subject that remains relatively neglected by historians.

And what of the Vatican? With a minuscule territory (109 acres – less than one-sixth the size of the Principality of Monaco), a comic-opera army of a few dozen colourfully uniformed halberdiers, a lack of any natural resources including water and food, a manufacturing sector limited to the production of religious mosaics, and an economy based on pious donations, museum entrance fees, and the sale of postage stamps, the Vatican, at first glance, would seem irrelevant to the belligerents and their intelligence agencies. In fact, the Vatican wielded influence in international affairs out of all proportion to its size, and that influence did not depend upon military or economic strength. As the home of the Pope and the central administration of the Roman Catholic Church, the Vatican was the symbolic capital of a world-wide religion, a source of international moral authority, and an object of respect and devotion for tens of millions of Catholics. No government could afford to ignore that authority or underestimate that devotion, especially in wartime when the sympathy or tacit support of the Supreme Pontiff might be worth any number of army divisions. During the war all of the major belligerents (with the exception of the Soviet Union) and most of the minor ones maintained diplomatic missions at the Vatican to press the righteousness of their cause and to solicit the support of the Pope and his advisers. At the same time, all of the major belligerents (including the Soviet Union) and many of the minor ones sought to determine the true sympathies of the papacy and to uncover and frustrate the intrigues of their opponents by maintaining intelligence coverage of the Vatican.

Intelligence on the Vatican was especially important for Germany. In 1933 the newly installed Nazi regime had negotiated a concordat with the Holy See in an effort to regularize church–state relations by adjusting certain disputes and clarifying mutual rights and responsibilities. Unfortunately, the accommodation disintegrated in the face of the persistent hostility and bad faith of the regime in Berlin. The legal protections supposedly assured by the concordat did not protect the Catholic Church in Germany from relentless persecution throughout the 1930s. For the Nazis, Roman Catholicism (along with Judaism, Communism and Freemasonry) was a 'Transnational Power' whose existence threatened the regime by asserting a claim on its adherents that transcended race, nationality and citizenship. The Catholic Church seemed a particularly dangerous threat not only because it affirmed that there was an authority higher than the state or because it controlled a network of cultural, educational and social institutions that challenged the Nazi party's effort to control all aspects of German organizational life, but also because the faithful were thought to be responsive to the authority and direction of a foreign leader, the Pope in the Vatican.

Before the war German intelligence operations against the Catholic Church focused primarily on uncovering the allegedly subversive activities of German Catholics and undermining the institutional structures, such as the Catholic press, which supported these activities in the Reich. With the invasion of Poland in September 1939 the focus shifted to Rome. Throughout the war it was axiomatic in Nazi party and intelligence circles that Pope Pius XII (who had been elected to the Throne of St Peter in March 1939) sympathized with the Allies and covertly assisted their cause. To expose and counter the pro-Allied machinations of the papacy, various elements of the German intelligence community intensified their coverage of the Vatican. Their primary targets were the Pope and his immediate circle, as well as the papal Secretariat of State, the

Vatican's foreign ministry whose senior officials were the Pontiff's closest collaborators during the war. Coverage of these targets might also produce useful collateral intelligence on any number of diplomatic, military and political subjects of interest to Berlin. German intelligence officers believed that the Pope sat at the centre of a vast web along whose strands flowed a stream of information from all parts of the world. By penetrating the Vatican, these officers hoped to tap into this valuable flow of information. German intelligence also targeted Allied diplomatic representatives who maintained their missions to the Pope even after Italy entered the war alongside Germany. These diplomats (especially the American, British and Polish representatives) were thought to exercise a pernicious influence over Pius as they constantly intrigued and propagandized against Germany. Islands of Allied activity deep in Axis territory, these diplomatic missions were also suspected of organizing espionage and sabotage operations from the sanctuary of Vatican City.

This study is an attempt to describe German intelligence operations against the Vatican during the Second World War. The authors hope that it will serve several useful purposes. The Vatican's role in the war remains a subject of controversy. Even among professional historians it is not uncommon to hear charges that the Catholic Church was comfortable with many aspects of Nazism and Fascism, that the Vatican successfully accommodated itself to the 'New Order' in Europe, and that Pope Pius (if only through his refusal to speak out against Nazi and Fascist crimes) condoned the activity of immoral regimes. This study will show that the Nazis considered the Catholic Church in general and the Vatican in particular to be their arch-enemies beyond any hope of accommodation, let alone collaboration. This study may also contribute to a more realistic appraisal of the wartime status of the Vatican. German intelligence accepted uncritically the popular view (still prevalent today) of the Vatican as a rich and powerful institution whose lines of information and influence reached into the most distant parts of the globe. While the potential influence of the papacy, then as well as now, was great, in practice the Vatican found itself, during the war, limited in its options and constrained in its freedom of action by any number of factors, not the least of which was the interference of German and other intelligence services. Finally, this study will examine how one of the major belligerents mobilized its intelligence services to attack the secrets of a neutral power. By focusing on the intelligence role of a small neutral, it may contribute to illuminating a 'missing dimension' of the history of the Second World War.

Many individuals contributed to the completion of this book. Archivists and librarians in Germany, Italy, the United Kingdom and the United States provided valuable advice and assistance. Among this group John Taylor of the National Archives and Records Administration in Washington deserves special mention for guiding the authors, as he has guided so many others, through the documentary record of America's wartime intelligence services. The staff of the Freedom of Information Office at the National Security Agency responded to every request for documents with patience and good humour. At Saint Mary's College of California, Pat Reitz, of the library's interlibrary loan desk, patiently tracked down obscure titles. Steve Sloane, then serving as a Dean at the College, expressed his confidence in this project by releasing one of the authors from some of his teaching responsibilities for a semester of research and writing. Wilber Chaffee, Monica Clyde, and Kathy Roper provided advice and encouragement. David Kahn and Owen Lock read portions of the manuscript and provided helpful comments. Bruce Handler brought the authors together and spurred their enthusiasm during those times when it seemed that this book would never see completion.

The Faculty Development Fund of Saint Mary's College and the California Province of the Society of Jesus provided financial support for the project.

The research for this book began over 20 years ago. Much of that research involved the testimony of American, British, German, Italian and Vatican officials who shared their memories of wartime events and personalities. Many of these individuals have not lived to see the publication of this book. The authors wish to acknowledge the valuable testimony of the following: Pentti Aalto, Federico Alesandrini, Cardinal Emanuel Cerejeira, Reverend Walter Ciszek, SJ, Edward Clancy, Ottfried Deubner, Giuseppe Dosi, General (ret.) Giulio Fettarappa-Sandri, Paul Franken, Wilhelm Hoettl, Dom Cyrill von Korvin-Krasinski, OSB, Reverend Robert Leiber, SJ, Archbishop Ambrogio Marchioni, Dom Augustine Mayer, OSB, Ernst Nienhaus, Cardinal Silvio Oddi, General (ret.) Eugenio Piccardo, Harold Tittmann, Fritz Wuchner and Costa Zoukitch.

Donna Kelley maintained her cheerfulness and optimism when her husband, one of the authors, often lost his. No one is happier to see its completion than she.

Postscript
As this manuscript went to press, Father Robert Graham succumbed to a sudden illness. His passing will be felt by his family and friends and all who value the pursuit of historical understanding.

1

Traditional Channels

Germany fought the Second World War with a large and disparate collection of intelligence organizations. At the height of the conflict more than 20 agencies, civilian and military, were collecting information for the German war effort. Some, like the 'Research Institute' of the Reich post office which untangled the electronically scrambled voice messages on the London–Washington radio-telephone link, were small and unknown to the public, while others, such as the massive Reich Security Administration (RSHA), were prominent institutions of the state. A few, like the Cipher Branch of the Armed Forces High Command, which broke the secret codes and ciphers of foreign governments, hunted the most jealously guarded secrets of both friend and foe, while yet others, such as the Press Bureau of the Foreign Ministry, harvested intelligence from the popular newspapers and magazines which were fixtures of any news-stand in Paris, Madrid, Stockholm, or Buenos Aires.

Among the members of the German intelligence community (many of which were created during or shortly before the war), two institutions had seniority. Traditionally, the foreign ministry claimed responsibility for foreign political and economic intelligence. Reports on political developments, diplomatic policies, and economic affairs in various countries flowed into the ministry's offices on the Wilhelmstrasse from German embassies, legations, and consulates around the world. The *Abwehr*, the espionage service of the Armed Forces High Command (OKW), concentrated on military intelligence. From offices in the various military districts inside Germany and, during the war, from stations in the capitals of neutral and friendly states the *Abwehr* collected information on the military capabilities

1

and plans of foreign powers. During the war competing intelligence agencies would successfully challenge the primacy of the foreign ministry and the *Abwehr*, but in the early days these two agencies were the main elements of Germany's intelligence offensive against all governments, including the Vatican.

FOREIGN MINISTRY

At the outbreak of the war in September 1939, Germany's principal source of information on the Vatican was the Reich embassy to the Holy See.[1] Berlin had every reason to expect much of its diplomatic mission to the Pope. With a staff of four, the embassy was not among the largest of the 34 diplomatic missions then accredited to the Holy See, but it was certainly among the most distinguished. Many governments considered the Vatican a minor diplomatic post and were content to treat their missions as sinecures for politically or socially deserving individuals who were pleased to enjoy the attractions of Italy without the distractions of a demanding post. As a result, the diplomatic corps accredited to the Pope partook of a certain rakish eccentricity. Many ambassadors could only rarely be found in Rome. Some, like those of Argentina and Peru, preferred the social attractions of other European capitals, while others, like the representatives of Estonia, Liberia and El Salvador, were simultaneously their country's ambassador to other countries and could more reasonably justify their residence in Paris or Brussels. Latvia's ambassador was detained in Riga by his responsibilities as his country's foreign minister and had not appeared in Rome for years. The Panamanian ambassador had simply disappeared one day in 1929 and was never seen again; his foreign ministry failed to notice or care about his absence. The Belgian ambassador quietly passed the time until he could claim his pension, while his colleague from Nicaragua drifted into senility. At papal ceremonies the staff of the legation of the ancient but tiny republic of San Marino outnumbered the delegations representing such great powers as Britain and Italy.[2] Of course, with more at stake, the embassies of the major powers were more conscientious in asserting their governments' interests at the Vatican but, even among these missions, the German embassy was distinguished by the professionalism of its staff and the stature of its ambassador.

2

Ambassador Diego von Bergen was an accomplished professional who found his posting to the Vatican to so complement his aptitudes and temperament that during the Weimar Republic he twice refused the office of foreign secretary and also declined the prestigious Paris embassy in order to remain in Rome. Ambassador since 1920, Bergen had a knowledge of the Vatican and its personalities unmatched by any of his colleagues in the diplomatic corps. His education in papal affairs began in 1906 when he was posted as a junior officer to his country's legation to the Holy See. His friendship with Pope Pius XII (Eugenio Pacelli) extended back to the First World War when he had been responsible for Vatican affairs in the foreign ministry and the then Monsignor Pacelli had been the papal nuncio (ambassador) in Germany. The friendship was further nurtured during the 1930s when the future Pope, then Cardinal Secretary of State, collaborated with the ambassador on various issues of church–state relations including the landmark Concordat (Treaty) of 1933 which was intended to regularize relations between the Nazi regime and the Catholic Church. The Vatican's frustration over Hitler's refusal to honour this concordat and its alarm over anti-Catholic measures in the 'new' Germany did nothing to lessen its respect for the German envoy. In the papal Secretariat of State (the Vatican's foreign ministry), Bergen's reputation for probity and good sense was so strong that his eventual retirement in 1943 was considered a calamity for German–Vatican relations.

Privileged by the special status of its chief and by the Germanophile inclinations of a Pontiff who admired German culture, spoke its language fluently, and surrounded himself with German staff, the Reich embassy was potentially a rich source of information on the papacy. For various reasons it never fully realized that potential during the war. In part, the embassy was constrained by factors beyond its control. With the onset of war, the secrecy which normally characterized the internal affairs of the papal Secretariat of State became even stricter. Concerned to avoid any questions about its neutrality, the Vatican adopted an attitude of correct but reserved relations with the belligerents. It became more difficult for Allied as well as Axis representatives to tease information from their contacts inside the Vatican. At one point the German embassy frankly informed Berlin that 'It is impossible to drag any information out of responsible sources', while the Japanese ambassador admitted to his superiors in Tokyo that 'Vatican officials do not tell me much'.[3] In Germany's case this reserve took on a particular chill as a result of policies in the Reich and in German-occupied territories which the Vatican considered either anti-Catholic or contrary to divine and natural law. The arrest and deportation of priests, the suppression or harassment of Catholic newspapers, and the dissemination of anti-Catholic propaganda were not policies conducive to warm relations. The German embassy also suffered from the effective loss of its leader. Socially and professionally Diego von Bergen was a product of the conservative milieu of the old imperial Germany. He had little enthusiasm for the new Germany of National Socialism whose personalities and policies he found increasingly distasteful. Disenchanted with the regime he was sworn to serve, plagued by ill-health, and increasingly weary of a mission whose principal task had become the defence of his government's anti-religious policies, the ambassador withdrew from the day-to-day operations of his embassy. Cables still went out over his signature and his presence was occasionally required at important ceremonial events in St Peter's Basilica or the Apostolic Palace, but increasingly Bergen left affairs to his deputy, embassy counsellor Fritz Menshausen, a competent career officer, but one whose experience and contacts fell far short of his superior's. By the second year of the war, the 68-year-old ambassador rarely appeared at the Vatican and seldom ventured beyond the walls of the Villa Bonaparte, the ambassadorial residence overlooking the Porta Pia.[4]

The German mission collected political intelligence from a variety of sources. The Vatican's daily newspaper, *L'Osservatore Romano*, was required reading for embassy officers who scrutinized its columns for signs of shifts in papal attitudes. Ambassador Bergen or Counsellor Menshausen regularly visited the papal Secretariat of State for conversations with the Cardinal Secretary of State, Luigi Maglione, and his deputies, Monsignors Domenico Tardini and Giovanni Montini. During these conversations the Germans would seek to discover the Vatican's attitude towards various developments and, through careful questioning, uncover some hint of what the Secretariat was learning from its nuncios in foreign capitals and from the other missions accredited to the Holy See. These contacts were potentially important sources of information, but all too frequently they were limited to presenting or receiving protests concerning the dismal state of church–state relations in the Reich. Additional information was gleaned from contacts with colleagues in other diplomatic missions to the Vatican, although the growth of the Allied coalition reduced the circle of accessible colleagues to the representatives of states associated with the Axis (Italy, Hungary, Japan, Rumania, Slovakia) and the neutrals which maintained relations with the Holy See (Ireland, Portugal, Spain). Occasional items of political interest would come from the German-speaking community in Rome, especially from priests like Bishop Alois Hudal, the Austrian rector of one of the German ecclesiastical colleges in Rome, who was a regular source of information for the embassy. Finally, there was the small army of informants, professional tipsters, journalists and purveyors of informal news services which served as a fertile field of information for any diplomat foolish or desperate enough to trust its reliability. Bergen usually viewed this group with a sceptical eye, but the embassy developed a particular relationship with one of their number, the shadowy Monsignor Enrico Pucci. This priest and sometime journalist held no official position in the Vatican, but prowled the corridors and reception rooms of the palace, noting the arrival of visitors and gossiping with the guards, ushers, messengers and chamberlains who were the natural denizens of these spaces. Whatever items of news or scandal he picked up from these contacts he sold in the always bustling market of real or spurious Vatican intelligence.[5]

The reports of the German embassy to the Vatican were generally rather pedestrian, but no more so than those from any diplomatic mission in any capital. Despite a tendency to exaggerate the papacy's sympathy for the Axis cause, the embassy, in the early years of the war, reported affairs at the Vatican as it saw them, although it did not always see them correctly. Under Ambassador Bergen it was not afraid to contest the fantasies or prejudices of officials in distant Berlin. In February 1941, for example, the embassy politely threw cold water on foreign minister Joachim von Ribbentrop's excitement over reports circulating in the Reich capital that the Pope had expressed optimism about an eventual German victory in the war. The embassy noted that it had attempted to check such reports and that in every case had discovered that they had been taken out of context or had been considerably and imaginatively modified in the telling. It was also prepared to acknowledge the limits of its information, as when in September 1941 it admitted that it was only partially informed about the mission to the Vatican of a Special Representative of President Franklin Roosevelt and could outline only its general purpose. Often, however, the embassy's reporting merely skimmed the surface of Vatican affairs and failed to notice what was hidden below. This was evident in its appreciation of the events surrounding the Pope's decision to send letters of sympathy to the King of Belgium, the Queen of the Netherlands, and the Grand Duchess of Luxembourg after the German invasion of their countries in May 1940. The embassy advised Berlin that the letters were intended neither as a political intervention nor as a protest against Germany's attack. Despite pressure from the Allies to pronounce a condemnation of German aggression, Pius had settled for polite expressions of sympathy for the heads of state as their countries faced the hardships of war.[6] The embassy, however, misperceived the nature of the Vatican's reaction to the attack. It was unaware that the German aggression against the three small neutrals had deeply offended the Holy Father and aroused much ill feeling in the Secretariat of State, which had drafted for Pius two versions of a public response which it urged the Pontiff to release. Both versions explicitly condemned the German action as unjust and illegal. Always cautious, Pius ultimately preferred the low-key response of a personal letter of condolence to the heads of state not, as the embassy implied, from any friendship for Germany or complacency in the face of international lawlessness, but from a fear of provoking political attacks, or worse, against the Vatican which was already subject to vilification by the Fascists for its allegedly pro-Allied sympathies. By simply accepting the letters at face value the embassy seriously underestimated the German invasion's negative impact at the Vatican.[7]

Occasionally there were outright intelligence failures. Some were merely embarrassing, as when the embassy was taken by surprise when the Vatican and Japan announced that they were establishing diplomatic relations. Others, however, were more serious. After the Japanese attack on Pearl Harbor brought the United States into the war, the embassy erroneously reported that the Vatican was now disillusioned with President Franklin D. Roosevelt, having decided that the President, insincere in his professed desire to avoid war, had deliberately manoeuvred his country into the conflict. In March 1942

Bergen informed Berlin that the Vatican had urged the South American Republics at the Rio de Janeiro Conference (January 1942) to resist American efforts to turn them against the Axis Powers and to align their diplomatic and military policies with those of Washington. In this case Bergen was a victim of 'blowback' from Axis propaganda which fabricated the story of papal opposition to American policy in order to torpedo the Conference. In fact, the Vatican had adopted an attitude towards the Conference of strict non-involvement, turning aside Italian and Ecuadorian suggestions that it should exert its influence on behalf of neutrality, and actually reprimanding the nuncio in La Paz for private comments to the Bolivian president which had been construed as endorsing neutrality.[8] The most serious lapse, however, was the embassy's failure to pick up any hint of the so-called 'Roman Conversations' of October 1939–January 1940 and April–May 1940, when Pope Pius served as a channel of communication between the British and opposition circles in Germany who were exploring possible conditions for peace between the Allies and a Germany freed from Hitler and Nazism. These contacts culminated in the 'May warnings' when Pius, informed by the German opposition of the imminent offensive in the west, warned Brussels and The Hague as well as the British, French and Belgian diplomatic missions at the Vatican. The conspirators went to great lengths to protect the secrecy of these conversations, but a surprising number of individuals in the German ecclesiastical community in Rome were aware of the conversations, if not their content, and two agents of German counterintelligence who visited Rome, one in the summer of 1940 and the other in the spring of 1941, rather quickly exposed the traces of the conspiratorial talks.

In July 1943, Diego von Bergen was recalled into retirement and Ernst von Weizsäcker, the state secretary in the foreign ministry, was appointed the Reich's new ambassador to the Holy See. For some time it had been apparent to Berlin that, physically and emotionally, the failing Bergen was no longer up to the job. His replacement by the number two man in the ministry was not, however, a sign of the Vatican's importance to Nazi foreign policy. Ribbentrop saw a chance to remove an able and independent deputy who had become an irritating contrast to the servile mediocrities with whom the arrogant foreign minister preferred to surround himself. For his part, Weizsäcker was disillusioned with the fatuous diplomacy of his superior, and eagerly sought the appointment in Rome. The assignment was attractive also because it offered a platform from which to launch a scheme which the state secretary had long been nurturing. Convinced that the continuation of the war would result in Germany's defeat and dismemberment, Weizsäcker saw a negotiated settlement as the only salvation for his country. He believed that the Vatican might serve as the mediator in such a settlement, but he knew that the leadership in Berlin would accept papal mediation only if it was convinced of the Pope's sympathy with Germany.[9]

Weizsäcker's dream of ending the war had a significant impact on the political reporting of the embassy. In order to enhance Berlin's confidence in the Vatican, the new ambassador deliberately distorted papal attitudes towards Germany, the war on the eastern front, and the prospects for a negotiated peace. His reports seriously exaggerated papal sympathy for Germany. They portrayed the Vatican as obsessed with the fear that Germany's defeat would result in the Bolshevization of Europe, convinced that only a strong and unified Germany could serve as a necessary bulwark against the Bolsheviks, and committed to inducing the Western Allies to negotiate a separate peace with Berlin as a preliminary to a common front against the threat from the east.[10] This was a caricature of Vatican attitudes. To be sure, the Pope and his advisers were under no illusions concerning the Soviet Union. They dismissed the glib assurances from Washington that Stalin was really a social democrat and that the anti-religious policies of his regime had been abandoned in favour of religious toleration. From the perspective of the papal palace, the Soviet Union was an implacable foe of the church and all that the church held dear, and there was every reason to worry about the westward extension of Soviet influence. Furthermore, papal officials considered the Allies' commitment to unconditional surrender a misguided policy which (since Germany would fight to the end rather than surrender unconditionally) would prolong the war, increase human misery, and leave a dangerous vacuum in central Europe by destroying Germany.[11] Nevertheless, the Vatican did not allow its anti-communism to influence its policy towards Berlin. Weizsäcker's reports that the Vatican desired a coalition of the Western Allies and Germany against the Soviet Union were complete fabrications. At no time did the Secretariat of State propose such a course to American or British representatives. When the ambassador suggested at the Vatican that London and Washington underestimated the importance of Germany as a bulwark against Bolshevism, papal officials did not rise to the bait. Indeed, on one occasion Cardinal Maglione responded to the envoy's warnings about the dangers of a Russian victory by noting, 'Unfortunately, the anti-religious policies of Germany have provoked anxieties just as serious.'[12] Comments such as these, which revealed a critical rather than sympathetic attitude towards Germany, were not included in Weizsäcker's reports for fear that they would make a bad impression on Berlin. As a result, the foreign ministry was seriously misinformed as to the true state of Vatican attitudes and policies.[13] Ironically, Weizsäcker's behaviour gave credence to the suspicions of foreign minister Joachim von Ribbentrop who, though ignorant of his ambassador's deliberate distortions, generally distrusted the reporting from his embassies. This distrust, combined with an ideological suspicion of the Catholic Church and all its works, made Ribbentrop and his associates in the Nazi hierarchy impervious to Weizsäcker's surprisingly naïve efforts to influence their perceptions of the Vatican.

Scrambling for position in a court where information was a currency which purchased status and influence, Ribbentrop was never satisfied with the routine political reporting of a diplomatic service whose commitment to National Socialism and the interests of its foreign minister was always suspect. From the days of the *Büro Ribbentrop*, that independent party office which he had established in 1934 in order to advance his claims as the principal foreign policy adviser of the Führer, Ribbentrop had been accustomed to seeking information from independent and, at times irregular sources. Many of these sources had been cultivated by Rudolf Likus, an old school chum, who collected the latest gossip and rumour circulating in Berlin's diplomatic and social circles. This news had been eagerly consumed by Ribbentrop during his tenure as ambassador in London when the ambitious courtier felt especially distant from the competition for Hitler's favour. When the former champagne salesman assumed direction of the foreign ministry in 1938, Likus was among the many *Büro* veterans who sailed into the Wilhelmstrasse in the wake of their chief.[14]

At the foreign ministry the loyal Likus continued to serve his patron as a personal adjutant and informal intelligence adviser. Although an individual of only modest attainments (one commentator dismissed him as 'semi-literate'), he was appointed, in 1940, chief of the second section in the ministry's *Abteilung Deutschland*. This assignment to *Deutschland II* formalized his role in the intelligence process since this section was responsible for liaison with the security and intelligence services.[15] In this capacity he became, in effect, the ministry's intelligence coordinator, passing on items obtained from the various intelligence offices of the Reich Security Administration, as well as news from personal contacts in German diplomatic missions and foreign embassies in Berlin and abroad. Berlin's diplomatic community provided the arena for what may have been Likus's greatest intelligence success: the partial penetration of the NKVD residency in the Soviet embassy through the recruitment of a Latvian journalist who was an agent of the Soviet intelligence service and who passed to Likus information on Russian espionage in Germany.[16] Although his attention focused primarily on Germany's principal adversaries, Britain and the Soviet Union, Likus always retained a special interest in the papacy and avidly collected information on Vatican diplomacy. Reports on activities inside the papal nunciature (embassy) in Berlin came regularly from a German journalist who moved in the circle of the nuncio, Archbishop Cesare Orsenigo, and from a patriotic German priest who served in the nunciature as an adviser on German and east European affairs, and who had been passing information to the German foreign ministry since his appointment to the nunciature in 1925. Information on events and personalities at the Vatican arrived in specially sealed envelopes from Harold Friedrich Leithe-Jasper, a press attaché at the German embassy to Italy. As Likus's man in Rome, Leithe-Jasper reported outside normal embassy channels and his information was used as a check on the reports filed by the German embassy to the Vatican.[17]

Likus had reason to be especially pleased with the reports from Rome. Radiating confidence and authority and bursting with enough detail about individuals, events, and dates to satisfy the most demanding policy-maker, these reports apparently emanated from a source very close to the 'terza loggia', the third floor of the Vatican palace that housed the offices of the Secretariat of State. Apparently SS Major Rudolf Likus (*Reichsführer* Heinrich Himmler had commissioned the spymaster in the Black Corps as a favour to Ribbentrop) had pulled off another intelligence coup by penetrating the secret heart of the papacy as effectively as he had penetrated the Soviet intelligence station in Berlin. The information supplied by 'our man in the Vatican' (*der am Vatikan tätig Gewährsmann*) was deemed so important that many of the reports were marked for Hitler's personal attention.

The material covered a range of intriguing diplomatic topics.[18] In September 1941, for example, intelligence from the Vatican included a report that President Franklin Roosevelt had asked Pope Pius to mediate between Tokyo and Washington in order to reduce tensions in the Far East; a prediction that Myron Taylor, President Roosevelt's Personal Representative to the Pope, would suggest to Pius that American Catholics should moderate their anti-communist sentiments in view of Moscow's struggle against Nazi Germany; a report that the Vatican's department for missionary affairs had reported to the Pope that the German invasion of the Soviet Union had solidified opinion in Japan against Russia; and news that the papal nuncios in Lisbon and Madrid had informed the Secretariat of State that Portugal had agreed to provide Britain and the United States with military access to its territory (including Portuguese possessions in the Atlantic, Africa and the Far East) in return for military support in the event of an attack by the Axis Powers. From the perspective of the Führer and his foreign minister, the most intriguing material was probably that dealing with the Vatican's reaction to Germany's invasion of the Soviet Union in June 1941. In the last half of 1941 the intelligence reaching Likus through his special channels suggested that Pope Pius followed Hitler's eastern adventure with interest and sympathy, and that the Pope was doing all in his power to support the 'crusade' against godless communism. In September, for example, Likus's source in the Vatican reported that the Secretariat of State had instructed the nuncio in Madrid to inform the Spanish bishops and clergy of the need to exhort Catholics to support the anti-Bolshevik policies of General Francisco Franco, including the Spanish leader's efforts to recruit a volunteer legion (the Blue Division) to fight alongside the Germans on the eastern front. Another report revealed that the apostolic delegate in Washington had been summoned to the White House to receive assurances from President Roosevelt that any new relationship between the United States and the Soviet Union would be limited to the pragmatic objective of keeping Russia in the war against Germany.[19] Since this policy would not alter America's basic anti-communism, the White House hoped that the Vatican would maintain its friendly attitude towards the United States and that American Catholics would continue to support President Roosevelt. A third report, from October 1941, maintained that the German government and the papal *Commissione Pro Russia* (Commission for Russia) had negotiated an agreement to re-establish the Catholic hierarchy in Russian territories occupied by German troops, and that with the assistance of the papal nunciature in Berlin the first steps towards installing Catholic bishops in Russian dioceses had already begun. The report included a list of Catholic bishops who would shortly return to their former dioceses in Russia.

The latter report should have set off alarm bells in the foreign ministry where word of an agreement with the Vatican on ecclesiastical affairs in occupied Russia would have been news to everyone including Ribbentrop. The posture of the Nazi regime towards the Catholic Church had long been one of unrelenting hostility, and the idea of any agreement with the Holy See in 1941 was unimaginable. For its part, the Vatican had experienced nothing but frustration and disappointment in the aftermath of the one agreement it *had* negotiated with the Third Reich, the Concordat of 1933, and it was not inclined to put much faith in further agreements with that regime even if the desire for accommodation had been present.[20] There were certainly no grounds for an accommodation over Russia. When Italy appealed to the Vatican to express support for the war against communism, Monsignor Domenico Tardini, the chief of the section for 'Extraordinary Affairs' in the Secretariat of State, informed the Italian ambassador: 'It [communism] is the worst, but not the only, enemy of the church. Nazism practised and still practises a real persecution of the church. The swastika is thus not the cross of the crusades.'[21] The papal Secretariat correctly understood that Germany had no intention of tolerating, let alone assisting, the expansion of Roman Catholicism in the Soviet Union. At a policy conference on 16 July 1941 to review the situation in Russia after almost a month of German advances, Hitler clearly stated that 'any missionary activity was absolutely out of the question'. That month Reinhard Heydrich, the head of the security service, circulated a report which maintained that the Vatican had prepared a plan to proselytize in Russia as part of a long-term policy to encircle the Reich with hostile Catholic states. According to Heydrich, the 'Tisserant Plan' (named for Cardinal Eugène Tisserant, the prefect of the Congregation for the Eastern Churches, the Vatican department responsible for ecclesiastical affairs in Russia) visualized a future eastern bloc composed of Catholic Croatia, Slovakia, and Russia to complement a western bloc of France, Italy, Portugal and Spain. To begin the arduous task of converting Russia, the Vatican planned to use the Catholic chaplains routinely attached to the Italian, Hungarian and Slovakian units on the eastern front, as well as those accompanying the 'Blue Division' of Spanish volunteers. The Vatican would also secretly infiltrate religious materials and specially trained priests into the Soviet Union. Heydrich argued that draconian measures were necessary to prevent the entry of priests into Russian territory occupied by German troops. In reality the Tisserant Plan existed only in the imagination of certain officers in the Nazi party and security apparatus who were obsessed with fears of Catholic conspiracies against the regime.[22] Nevertheless, measures were taken to block the alleged plot. In August the Armed Forces High Command (OKW) issued orders that 'The entry into the occupied territories in the East of non-military priests from the Reich or elsewhere is prohibited', and followed that directive with additional orders forbidding military chaplains from conducting services or 'religious propaganda' among the civilian population. The handful of bishops and priests who tried to enter Russia behind the German army were arrested and expelled. A priest seeking to enter occupied Minsk was actually executed by the German police.[23] Given these circumstances any intelligence source reporting a formal agreement between Berlin and the Vatican to support Catholicism in Russia was gravely misinformed or worse.

Generally, the quality of Likus's intelligence on the Vatican was poor. The occasional report might prove to be accurate, but the great majority were hopelessly unreliable. As we have seen, the reports concerning papal reaction to the attack on the Soviet Union were especially muddled. The Vatican did not come to an arrangement with Berlin on the evangelization of Russia. Nor did it urge the Spanish bishops and priests to rally behind the anti-Bolshevik policy of General Franco. At the very moment that the Vatican was supposedly encouraging Spanish Catholics in their anti-communist attitudes, it was setting in motion an effort to moderate such attitudes among American Catholics. The apostolic delegate in Washington did not receive an invitation to the White House in 1941 to discuss US–Soviet relations or any other subject for that matter; in fact the delegate did not meet the President at all that year.[24] The intelligence on other subjects was hardly more accurate. President Roosevelt never approached the Pope to mediate between Washington and Tokyo since outside mediation was never considered an option by Washington in its confrontation with Japan, and an approach to the Pope would have been, in any event, unacceptable to Roosevelt for domestic political reasons. Similarly, there was no Anglo-American-Portuguese accord in the late summer of 1941. As recently as that spring, Portugal was sufficiently suspicious of American intentions and protective of its neutrality that it objected to a visit to its Cape Verde Islands by American naval vessels. Lisbon would not agree to Allied bases on its territory until August 1943.[25]

Rather than running a precious source at the heart of the papacy, Rudolf Likus had become entangled in a web of fabrication and disinformation. Throughout the war the neutral capitals were notorious markets for all manner of mindless gossip, groundless rumour and calculated falsehood, and all too often Allied as well as Axis intelligence services discovered that they had invested in inflated or worthless shares. Because the secrecy and mystery which surrounded the Vatican made the collection of reliable intelligence on the papacy extremely difficult, the Vatican information exchange was especially volatile and speculative. For German intelligence the problem was compounded by the fact that Britain, through its 'black' propaganda organization, the Political Warfare Executive, flooded the market with false or misleading stories concerning the Pope, the Vatican and the Catholic Church. Broadcast by clandestine radio stations, introduced into legitimate news channels, or circulated by word of mouth, the stories ranged from the apparently minor but intriguing item, such as a report in May 1943 that a British Jesuit priest had recently returned to the Vatican from a visit to Madrid, to major revelations, such as a rumour in December 1940 that Mussolini had asked the Vatican to approach Britain about a separate peace for Italy.[26] One of London's most successful efforts at disinformation involved the fabrication and dissemination of a letter purportedly addressed to a priest in Stettin by a *Luftwaffe* officer, 'Colonel Werner Mölders', shortly before his death in combat. In this letter, which was read from the pulpit in many German parishes, the 'colonel' denounced religious persecution in Germany and revealed that most of his comrades-in-arms had abandoned their anti-clericalism and found consolation in the church. The Gestapo reacted violently to this letter; several priests were sent to concentration camps for publicizing it, and a reward of 100,000 marks was announced for information concerning the true source of the missive.[27]

Starved for information, Vatican watchers pounced upon even unfounded reports. The fabricated item concerning Mussolini's alleged interest in a separate peace reached Vichy and caused the French foreign ministry to instruct its ambassador to the Holy See to seek confirmation from the Cardinal Secretary of State. As late as February 1941 the Portuguese ambassador at the Vatican was reporting to Lisbon that representatives of the Italian army and royal court were meeting secretly inside the Vatican with the British minister, Sir Francis d'Arcy Osborne, and his American counterpart, Harold Tittmann.[28] All too often German authorities fell victim to such deceptions. In the case of the fictitious peace negotiations, German intelligence rushed to uncover details. Berlin actually received a report through the party intelligence service, the *Sicherheitsdienst* (SD), that the Pope had dispatched a certain 'Count Lednitzky' to the Balkans to investigate the possibility of a separate peace for Italy.[29] Of course, the elusive Count was no more real than the negotiations supposedly taking place inside the papal palace. Such disinformation caused no end of difficulties for German operatives in Rome. Driven to distraction by repeated requests to confirm reports that Pope Pius intended to abandon Rome for a more secure and sympathetic refuge, Ambassador von Bergen impatiently reminded his foreign ministry that in recent months alone the Pope had been authoritatively reported as being on the verge of moving to any number of locations including Switzerland, Spain, North America, Mexico, and even the Belgian Congo.[30]

British disinformation was not the only threat to German intelligence at the Vatican. The Germans also ran afoul of Virgilio Scattolini, perhaps the most brazen and successful fabricator of intelligence to emerge from the Second World War. A sometime journalist who had written for various Italian newspapers as well as the Vatican daily, *L'Osservatore Romano*, where he served briefly as a film critic, Scattolini had achieved minor notoriety in pre-war Italy for his licentious plays and novels. In 1939 the unscrupulous writer discovered that he could make more money by selling to the press accounts of political events and personalities in the Vatican. From the comfort of his apartment near the Spanish Steps, he concocted stories based upon a careful scrutiny of the papal audience schedule and a very large dose of fanciful detail concerning the alleged content and results of such audiences. Soon even the papal audiences became imaginary as he sought to 'improve' his reporting. The closed, secretive, and (to outsiders) mysterious world of the Vatican inadvertently abetted this confidence game by creating an audience of journalists, diplomats and intelligence officers hungry for any information about papal affairs, and by inhibiting any effort to confirm the veracity of the often dramatic reports through more informed sources. Scattolini's first customers were the Rome offices of United Press and Associated Press wire services which innocently distributed the bogus reports to such press outlets as the *New York Times, The Times* of London, and the *Neue Zürcher Zeitung* in Zurich. By 1940 the growing subscription list for his 'News Bulletin' (*Notiziario*) included the German embassy, the Rome office of the official German news service (*Deutsche Nachrichten Büro*), the Japanese embassy, the Japanese news agency *Domei*, and the Spanish paper *Ya*. Scattolini's lucrative business was temporarily suspended in 1942 when the Italian police questioned the industrious fabricator about the distribution of military information to foreign governments, but the *Notiziario* returned with the Allied liberation of Rome in June 1944 and its subscription list eventually grew to include banks, political groups, religious communities, businesses, embassies, and secret services. Among the latter, the most prominent victim of Scattolini's fertile imagination was the American Office of Strategic Services (OSS) which forwarded his reports to Washington where many received the special attention of President Roosevelt. The OSS did not begin to suspect their special source in the Vatican until early 1945 when the State Department noted that a report of a meeting between the American representative to the Pope, Myron Taylor, and his Japanese counterpart, Ken Harada, could not possibly be true. Despite this warning, the OSS continued to accept at least some of Scattolini's reports (codenamed VESSEL) until the end of the war.[31]

Clearly, Rudolf Likus was in good company when he fell for the fantasies of the artful fabricator in Rome. Still, the confusion and consternation in the German foreign ministry in the autumn of 1941 must have been great as there should have been earlier signs that Likus's intelligence from the Vatican was suspect. A more competent intelligence chief might have wondered why there was nothing from the German diplomatic missions in Lisbon and Madrid to corroborate the news of an Anglo-American–Portuguese defence agreement, or why the embassies in Tokyo and Washington knew nothing about papal mediation of US–Japanese differences. The absence of supporting evidence from the embassy to the Holy See should have been especially disturbing to Likus. From his reports to Berlin, Bergen was apparently unaware of any conversations between the United States and the Vatican on the subject of Japan, and it would have been news to him that Pope Pius had taken such a lively interest in promoting the recruitment of Spanish volunteers for service in the Russian campaign. In fact, the embassy had become increasingly suspicious of any information allegedly originating in the Secretariat of State. It was aware that as early as May 1940 *L'Osservatore Romano* had warned its readers that information falsely attributed to Vatican sources was being circulated in international press and diplomatic circles. The warning was repeated in November 1941. In the spring the embassy had cancelled its subscription to the *Notiziario* after more than a year of avid interest in the news bulletins. The cancellation was almost certainly related to a request from the ambassador, Diego von Bergen, that the Wilhelmstrasse provide him with details concerning the interception and decipherment of papal diplomatic telegrams. The request was unusual because the codebreaking unit inside the foreign ministry normally did not share its results directly with ambassadors. Specifically, Bergen requested the texts of messages allegedly transmitted by Vatican Radio to the apostolic delegate in London and to the Archbishop of Baltimore on 13 and 14 April, respectively. The ambassador explained to Berlin that he wanted to verify information supposedly coming to him from within the Vatican concerning communications of the papal Secretariat of State, information which he had increasing reason to distrust.[32] Since Scattolini apparently ran a lucrative sideline in alleged copies of papal diplomatic telegrams, it is likely that Ambassador Bergen had concluded that the consumers of the *Notiziario* were being led down the garden path.[33] If Ambassador Bergen's scepticism about sources claiming to report from inside the papal palace was brought to the attention of Rudolf Likus, it did nothing to undermine the credulous aide's confidence in his 'man in the Vatican'. Apparently Likus was not disconcerted by the absence of any information from the German embassy to the Holy See which could confirm his special intelligence. Of course, Likus may have felt nothing but pride at having found a source who provided a clear glimpse of events which remained a closed book to a professional diplomat who had observed the Vatican for over 20 years.

Likus's vacuous efforts to penetrate the Vatican were symptomatic of a deeper malaise, one marked by scattered and uncoordinated collection programmes and inadequate analysis, which enfeebled the intelligence efforts of the foreign ministry. The weaknesses of these efforts were dramatically revealed in the spring of 1941 when the Wilhelmstrasse failed to anticipate a successful coup by anti-German elements in Yugoslavia, which forced a surprised and angry Hitler to divert attention and resources from the preparations for the invasion of Russia. Embarrassed by this fiasco, Ribbentrop sought to improve his ministry's intelligence capabilities by creating a new unit to collect information outside the usual diplomatic channels. Formally constituted as the *Informationsstelle III* (Information Desk III), but commonly known as Inf III or the *Hencke Dienst* after its first director, the career functionary Andor Hencke, this unit soon had outposts in every German diplomatic mission. In each embassy an officer was designated the representative of the *Hencke Dienst*, and this officer was to seek information by cultivating journalists and businessmen, primarily in the local German community. Citizens of the Reich were encouraged to cooperate by promises to prevent their conscription into the army. Reports were forwarded periodically to the Wilhelmstrasse where Hencke's modest staff would collate and evaluate the information before passing it to Ribbentrop and any concerned desks in the foreign ministry.[34]

Although the hapless Likus continued periodically to forward Vatican intelligence to Ribbentrop's office, the *Hencke Dienst* gradually displaced Likus as a source of information on papal affairs. Indeed, the new intelligence unit considered the papacy sufficiently important to warrant two representatives in Rome: Harold Friedrich Leith-Jasper, a press attaché at the Reich embassy to Italy and a sometime contact for Rudolf Likus, and Carl von Clemm-Hohenberg, a shadowy individual loosely connected with the embassy as 'Special Representative for Economic Questions'. Soon after assuming his new office, Andor Hencke reminded his two representatives of the importance of information from the Vatican, and he assured them that in pursuit of such information money was no object. A visit to Rome by Ribbentrop in February 1943 provided additional impetus to the effort. The Reich foreign minister saw Benito Mussolini and Count Galeazzo Ciano, the Italian foreign minister, but he did not seek an audience with Pope Pius. It was a calculated snub which was actually received with some relief inside the Vatican. Relations between the Holy See and Germany were perpetually agitated by the anti-religious policies of the Nazi regime. Given the dismal state of German–Vatican relations a visit to the Pope by the volatile foreign minister would have been an awkward, if not stormy, occasion. Ribbentrop, however, did not completely ignore the Pope. On the contrary, he gave orders to intensify the intelligence coverage of the Vatican. In March, Clemm-Hohenberg reiterated the foreign minister's interest to Marschall Adolf von Bieberstein, who had just replaced Andor Hencke as the director of Inf III upon the latter's promotion to head the foreign ministry's political division:

> Minister Hencke said to me earlier on different occasions that it would be desirable to obtain more information from the Vatican, and that funds were available to create such a source. Now the foreign minister himself mentioned to me with some emphasis that he would like to get information about the English and American circles there. Money, even foreign currency, was available.[35]

While interest at the highest levels may have stimulated additional exertions on the part of Inf III's representatives in Rome, it did little to improve the foreign ministry's coverage of the papacy. To be sure, the intelligence collected by Inf III was, at least at the outset, marginally more accurate than that obtained by Rudolf Likus, but it is unlikely that it was much better than the information generated by the routine reports of the German embassy to the Holy See. In the autumn of 1942, Leithe-Jasper was able to identify for the *Hencke Dienst* the general outline of the current visit to the Vatican by Myron Taylor, President Roosevelt's Personal Representative to Pope Pius XII. He correctly reported that Taylor had worked to discourage Pius from launching any new peace initiative and that the American representative had explained to the Pope the Allies' vision of a post-war world. In another dispatch Leith-Jasper discounted rumours that the Pope was preparing a peace encyclical, and correctly predicted that the next papal message would deal only with general religious issues. Discounting rumours reaching Berlin from other capitals that the Pope would leave Rome in the face of Allied air attacks, several reports accurately predicted that Pius would never abandon the city. Another report noted that a few days after the crucial meeting of the Fascist Grand Council on the night of 24–25 July 1943 which would result in the removal of Mussolini from power, the Pope had received a member of the Council, Senator Luigi Federzoni, but the representative of Inf III erred in adding that the Pontiff had also received Dino Grandi and that the Cardinal Secretary of State, Luigi Maglione, had met with the new Italian police chief, Carmine Senise.[36]

Not every report was accurate. In their first months of work the Rome representatives of the *Hencke Dienst* exhibited a curious obsession with the activities of the Archbishop of New York, Francis Spellman, and a propensity to attribute to this prelate any number of intrigues at the Vatican on behalf of American interests. These reports were completely fanciful as was a report in December 1942 that the Holy See and the Soviet Union had signed an agreement to allow 20 Jesuit priests to enter Russia for religious activity. Efforts to collect intelligence from Allied diplomats residing in Vatican City were no more fruitful despite Ribbentrop's special interest in their activities. Indeed, in an attempt to get close to these diplomats, Inf III would be badly burned.

In March 1943, shortly after Ribbentrop's visit to the Eternal City, Friedrich von Clemm-Hohenberg informed Berlin that he had been approached by a 'reliable Italian' with a scheme to penetrate the very circles in the Vatican so dear to the German foreign minister. This Italian claimed to know a well-placed individual who was a friend of various cardinals, including the Cardinal Secretary of State, and who had easy access to Vatican City. This distinguished individual was the head of a ducal family, a member of the best Roman clubs, well-connected in Roman society especially among the so-called 'Black' nobility around the Pope, and a true Italian (fascist) patriot. Unfortunately, this man was in rather straitened circumstances.

> My contact emphasized again that the party in question is in every respect the right person to get behind the scenes on a social basis. He would need help to present himself appropriately, but could be trusted not to overdo it.

Clemm-Hohenberg's contact suggested that with the help of 50,000 lire the nobleman could present himself in circles which would prove a veritable gold-mine of intelligence. The German jumped at the opportunity. He convinced Berlin to release the necessary funds which were accepted on behalf of the 'duke' by his middleman, the equally anonymous 'reliable Italian'.

Despite his allegedly wide-ranging contacts inside the Vatican, Clemm-Hohenberg's poor but well-bred source concentrated most of his attention on Harold Tittmann, the American chargé d'affaires.[37] According to Clemm-Hohenberg's Italian contact, the 'duke' was able to insinuate himself into Tittmann's circle by presenting himself as an anti-fascist and an advocate of a separate peace with the Allies. The result was a steady stream of what appeared to be the most sensitive military information. In late March, for instance, the impoverished nobleman reported that the Allies were constructing 12 airbases in Libya from which to bomb southern Italy. This air offensive would prepare the way for landings in Calabria which had been selected over Sicily for logistical reasons. In April the source discovered that the Allies were also planning offensive operations in the eastern Mediterranean with landings in Greece, Cyprus and Rhodes. Inside the Vatican, the American and British representatives were reportedly spinning intrigues at dinner parties attended by papal officials and Italian anti-fascists. In June the nobleman warned that a Turkish emissary had arrived secretly in Rome for talks with the American and British diplomats with the result that Britain had agreed to assist Turkey in the event of an attack by the Soviet Union. The next month there was word of frequent exchanges between the British minister, Francis d'Arcy Osborne, and the papal Secretariat of State, and warnings that espionage activity had increased inside Vatican City. In August the cut-out, the 'reliable Italian', returned to

Clemm-Hohenberg with news that their aristocratic friend knew someone in the immediate entourage of Cardinal Secretary of State Maglione who would agree to supply information about the cardinal for 100,000 lire. The local representative of Inf. III urged his superiors at the foreign ministry to accept the offer. It is impossible from the available evidence to determine whether Berlin pursued this opportunity, but they would have been well advised not to do so, for it appears that Clemm-Hohenberg had been duped.

Except in matters so general and trivial as to be useless ('Tittmann has been meeting with his British counterpart', 'There has been much activity in the Secretariat of State'), the reports from the 'duke' were invariably wrong. For instance, the source warned of imminent Allied landings in Calabria, Cyprus, Rhodes, Greece, and various other places, but explicitly excluded Sicily, the one place where a landing would occur.[38] The tale of a secret emissary from Turkey and the negotiation of an Anglo-Turkish agreement was apocryphal; indeed, in the spring of 1943 relations between Britain and Turkey had actually deteriorated because of Ankara's refusal to bow to London's demands that it abandon its neutrality.[39] Finally, while the Vatican was aware of soundings by Italian diplomats and army officers on behalf of a change in government and a separate peace with the Allies, it scrupulously avoided any action that might compromise its neutrality. In the spring of 1943 the Vatican did not receive anti-fascist representatives, let alone invite them to cosy dinners with Allied diplomats.[40]

It is difficult to avoid the conclusion that the intelligence provided by the 'duke' was spurious. The nobleman himself was probably a phantom concocted by a confidence trickster to extort money from the eager but gullible Germans. Clemm-Hohenberg never met his aristocratic source, but dealt only with the Italian middleman who had made the original approach. Allegedly, the source had frequent contact with Harold Tittmann, but the American diplomat received very few visitors during his sojourn inside the Vatican (contact between the Allied diplomats in the Vatican and individuals living in Rome was discouraged by the fascist police) and did not include the head of a ducal family among his associates in this period.[41] Even if the source had managed to meet Tittmann frequently, he would have learned little of Allied intentions since the American diplomat, isolated and without a cipher in the heart of enemy territory, was not privy to important military information.[42] The intelligence so eagerly purchased for Inf III by Clemm-Hohenberg was almost certainly fabricated by the alleged middleman from the various rumours, gossip and news stories which were always circulating in the milieu of the Vatican.

The reports from the Vatican undoubtedly contributed to Inf III's poor reputation in the foreign ministry where the intelligence office was recognized as worthless by almost everyone but its patron, Ribbentrop. The dismissive response of Ambassador von Bergen when asked to confirm an early report from Harold Leithe-Jasper reveals the Vatican embassy's attitude towards the office: 'This [report] matches in content information already reaching me from obviously the same source, of the same days. I did not pass it on because numerous earlier reports from this same source have always proved to be fantasies.' The ambassador went on to say that anyone with knowledge of Vatican affairs can tell in most cases when such reports were 'drawn out of thin air'.[43] In the Wilhelmstrasse attitudes were no different. The chief of the press section considered Inf. III's information so trivial and unreliable that it was not worth the attention of the foreign minister, and even its first director, Andor Hencke, eventually admitted that the office, which was dissolved before the end of the war, 'attained no great importance'.[44] Hencke's words might well have served as the epitaph for the foreign ministry's entire intelligence effort against the Vatican.

THE *ABWEHR*

As a military intelligence service the *Abwehr* had little reason to interest itself in the Vatican. The papacy had no military significance and it is unlikely that questions about the armament of the Pope's Swiss Guard or the strength of the papal police would have interested even the most conscientious officer of the General Staff. Of course *Abwehr* officers were not limited to purely military information in their collection efforts, and through its *Ausland* section the *Abwehr* monitored foreign political developments for their potential impact on military affairs, but in general church affairs received very little attention. To be sure, a few patriotic priests, usually veterans of the Great War, served as part-time informants, passing on news from their ecclesiastical travels and contacts in other countries (one monk photographed the Swiss–German border while on hiking vacations), and an item on the papacy might occasionally reach *Abwehr* headquarters, as when the Munich office (*Abwehrstelle*) reported misleadingly on 18 July 1939 that Pope Pius was collaborating with Mussolini on a proposal to mediate the Polish crisis, but such reports remained the exception before the war.[45] The *Abwehr* representative in Rome, Colonel Otto Helfferich, an accomplished linguist and cultivated officer of the old school, was responsible primarily for maintaining liaison with Italian military intelligence in whose headquarters he had an office. At least in the early stages of the war Helfferich ran no agents of his own and merely passed to Berlin intelligence provided by the Italians. He had little interest in the Vatican and contented himself with reporting the occasional scrap of ecclesiastical gossip from the Roman cocktail circuit. Upon the outbreak of war, however, the papacy suddenly became an object of interest in certain offices at *Abwehr* headquarters on the *Tirpitz Ufer*. Senior officers called for seldomly used files and quietly discussed their meagre contents. An officer from the Munich station was ordered to Rome to improve coverage of the Vatican. The Vatican may have been an insignificant source of military intelligence, but it had suddenly become an important centre for conspiracy.

The history of the 'Roman Conversations' is well-known among historians of the German resistance.[46] In the last days of the Polish campaign, two *Abwehr* officers in the anti-Hitler resistance circle around General Ludwig Beck, Colonel Hans Oster, chief of the *Abwehr*'s Central Division, and Major Hans Dohnanyi, director of political affairs in the Central Division, conceived a plan to use Pope Pius XII to establish contact with Britain. The two officers, who led what amounted to an opposition cell in German military intelligence, believed that the Pope would provide a discreet and credible channel for determining London's attitude towards a change of regime in Berlin and the bases for a negotiated settlement of the war. To approach the Vatican and open the secret channel, the conspirators recruited Josef Müller, an anti-Nazi lawyer from Munich. Müller was well-known in ecclesiastical circles for his many business and legal services to the Catholic Church in Germany, and he was on friendly terms with two well-placed countrymen at the Vatican: Father Robert Leiber, SJ, the confidential assistant of Pope Pius, and Monsignor Ludwig Kaas, the former head of the defunct German Centre Party, then living in quiet exile as the administrator of St Peter's Basilica. To facilitate his mission and explain his frequent trips to Rome, Müller was inducted into the *Abwehr* as a lieutenant and assigned to the Munich *Abwehrstelle* ostensibly to report on political developments in Italy and at the Vatican.

Müller made his first trip to Rome in late September 1939 to consult with Monsignor Kaas about the best way to approach the Pope. Kaas directed his friend to Pius's assistant, Father Leiber, to whom the Munich lawyer explained the intentions of the opposition in Berlin. Leiber agreed to carry the request to the Pope. When Müller returned to Rome in mid-October, he learned from the papal aide that Pius had accepted the invitation to serve as intermediary with the British. Müller then embarked on a clandestine odyssey which over the following months would see him shuttle between Berlin and Rome with the various proposals, counterproposals, queries and clarifications of two parties wary of each other but probing in search of common ground. The lawyer never dealt directly with the Pope. Carrying instructions from Oster and Dohnanyi, he would arrive in Rome and go directly to the local *Abwehr* station which served as a liaison with Italian military intelligence. Using the office's secure line he would telephone Father Leiber with the simple message, 'I am here', to which the priest would respond with the time at which they would meet. Initially, all meetings were in Leiber's rooms at the Jesuit Gregorian University in central Rome, but later, for greater security, they shifted to the Jesuit church of San Bellarmino on the outskirts of the city. At these brief encounters Müller would explain the conspirators' position to Leiber who would, in turn, carry the message to Pius. The Pope would summon the British minister to the Holy See, Sir Francis D'Arcy Osborne, and pass on the information. Osborne would then send the message to the Foreign Office. London's response would reach Berlin through the reverse channel. During these frequent journeys along the Berlin–Munich–Rome line, Müller also acted as a courier for the German bishops by carrying to the Vatican reports of anti-Catholic persecution in Germany and Austria.[47]

Never more than exploratory, the Vatican exchanges did little more than nurture London's scepticism about the authenticity of the approach and reveal the conspirators' reluctance to abandon the territorial claims of a Greater Germany with as much readiness as they were prepared to abandon Adolf Hitler. Ultimately, the contacts proved irrelevant as the military conspirators could not bring themselves to act against the Nazi regime before the successful military operations in the west in the spring of 1940 solidified Hitler's support among the officer corps. In a desperate effort to demonstrate their good faith and forestall the operations against France, the Low Countries and Scandinavia, the resistance circle around Colonel Oster in the *Abwehr* leaked word of Hitler's intentions to the Pope in the expectation that the Holy Father would warn the intended victims. On several occasions Müller rushed to Rome with the latest dates for the frequently postponed offensive in the west and Pius discreetly passed warnings to the threatened governments.[48] The most dramatic and eventful warning was the final one in May 1940. Müller arrived in Rome on the first of the month with word that the attack in the west was imminent.[49] At the Pope's orders the Secretariat of State alerted the nuncios in Brussels and The Hague on 3 May and instructed them to warn the governments to which they were accredited. At an audience on 6 May with the Italian Crown Prince, Umberto, and his Belgian wife, Princess Marie, Pius spoke so urgently about the danger to the Low Countries that the princess promptly sent a special courier to warn her brother, the Belgian king. On Tuesday, 7 May, a senior official of the Secretariat of State informed the British and French representatives at the Vatican that Germany would attack the Low Countries before the week was out. Meanwhile, Father Leiber had arranged for a separate warning to Belgium. With the Pope's permission he informed a Belgian colleague at the Gregorian University of the serious news from Berlin, and the Belgian Jesuit rushed to tell his country's ambassador to the Holy See, Adrien Nieuwenhuys. The envoy was inclined to dismiss the message as alarmist, but changed his mind upon receiving confirmation from Father Hubert Noots, the respected Belgian Abbot General of the Premonstratensian Order who was a close friend of Josef Müller. On 2 May Nieuwenhuys sent a cipher telegram to Brussels: 'I have received same source as my report of 13 November, No. 163, information according to which aggression against Belgium and Holland decided for next week . . . I transmit this information without being able to check it, every sort of surprise being possible.' In response to a request from his foreign ministry for details, the ambassador asked Noots for more information. The Belgian monk met Müller (who remained unknown to the ambassador) and relayed his comments to Nieuwenhuys who, on 4 May, sent a second cipher telegram to Brussels informing his superiors that the warning came from a source 'who must draw his information from the General Staff of which he calls himself [an] emissary', and that this source confirmed that 'the Chancellor had irrevocably decided to invade Holland and Belgium, and . . . the signal for this attack will be given very soon without declaration of war'.[50] Both of Ambassador Nieuwenhuys' telegrams were intercepted and deciphered by the *Forschungsamt* ('Research Office'), a communications intelligence unit in Herman Göring's air ministry.

In agreeing to serve as a link between London and the anti-Hitler resistance, Pope Pius acted to hasten the end of the war and facilitate the removal of a vicious political regime which threatened to extend its anti-religious and inhuman sway over all of Europe. By collaborating in conversations which had as their purpose the subversion of a foreign government and by passing that government's military secrets to its opponents, Pius seriously compromised the traditional neutrality of the Vatican and jeopardized his personal position as well as that of the papacy. Since exposure could mean disaster, Pius took great care to protect the secrecy of his mediation. Little was committed to paper. Inside the Vatican knowledge of the exchanges was closely held; Pius's principal diplomatic advisers, the Cardinal Secretary of State, Luigi Maglione, and his under-secretaries, Monsignors Domenico Tardini and Giovanni Montini, were unaware of the Pope's secret activities. Father Leiber remained his only point of contact with the Germans, and the Pope dealt personally with the British representative, Osborne. When Osborne wished to visit the Holy Father he avoided the normal channels of the Secretariat of State in favour of a quiet approach to the Pope's *maestro di camera*, who knew nothing of the clandestine affair, but probably wondered why he had been instructed to admit without question the British diplomat even outside normal audience hours. Despite the Pope's efforts, a rather alarming number of people in Roman ecclesiastical circles became aware of Müller's real mission at the Vatican. Müller confided in an old friend, Monsignor Johannes Schönhöffer, a Bavarian priest in the Congregation for the Propagation of the Faith (the Vatican department for missionary affairs), who in turn discussed the situation with Monsignor Paul

Maria Krieg, the chaplain of the Pope's Swiss Guard. Father Ivo Zeiger, a Jesuit at the German-Hungarian College in Rome, knew something of the business, as did Augustine Mayer, a Benedictine monk teaching at his order's College of San Anselmo. Father Leiber felt obliged to inform his nominal superior, Father Vincent McCormick, SJ, the American rector of the Gregorian University, where Leiber was a professor, as well as the Superior General of the Jesuits, Father Wladimir Ledochowski, both of whom were uneasy about the risks of the operation. Hubert Noots, the Belgian Abbot General of the Premonstratensian Order, was another friend of Müller's who knew that the Bavarian lawyer was visiting the Vatican on behalf of an anti-Nazi conspiracy.[51] As the circle of those informed grew, so did the risk of discovery.

Herbert Keller was a Benedictine monk of the ancient Abbey of Beuron. Clever, ambitious and no more scrupulous than necessary, Keller had been briefly exiled by his order to a monastery in Palestine in the mid-1930s for using irregular methods to secure election as Prior of Beuron. Returning to Germany at the end of the decade, he became (with the knowledge of his religious superiors) an occasional informant for the Stuttgart office of the *Abwehr*. During this time he also passed information to the Nazi party's intelligence service, the *Sicherheitsdienst*, from whom he was able to extract special favours for his monastery as well as lavish allowances for his first-class travels throughout France, Germany and Switzerland. During these trips the good monk disguised his intelligence activities by claiming that he was collecting photostats of medieval manuscripts for his abbey's library.[52] Upon the outbreak of war Keller began to labour full-time for German intelligence. The *Abwehr* station in Stuttgart worked, in part, against Switzerland, and while on an assignment to that country Keller encountered a German acquaintance who, unbeknown to the monk, was a member of the German resistance. In the course of a convivial evening of brandy and cigars, this indiscreet individual confided to his drinking companion that Generals Beck and Halder were leading a military conspiracy to depose Hitler and that a certain Josef Müller, a member of the plot, was in regular contact with the Vatican to arrange a negotiated peace with the Allies.[53] Keller knew Müller and had nurtured a strong antipathy towards him ever since the lawyer had helped the Benedictines expose the political chicanery which had caused Keller to be exiled to Palestine. Hoping for revenge and an opportunity to impress his employers in Stuttgart, the monk hurried to Rome to uncover the trail of the conspiracy. Although his reputation was unsavoury enough for a senior official in the papal Secretariat of State to warn one of Keller's Roman contacts against close association with the adventurer, the industrious monk managed, in a few days, to discover the main outline of Müller's mission.[54] He returned to Stuttgart to report his findings to his *Abwehr* and SD controllers. Reinhard Heydrich, the chief of the RSHA (the parent organization of the SD), read the report when it reached Berlin and summoned the monk for a personal interview. Heydrich nurtured a violent antipathy to the Vatican which he suspected of constantly conspiring against the Nazi regime. He found the accusations against Müller especially interesting. The Nazi security chief had had his eye on Müller since 1936 when the Bavarian's legal work on behalf of the Catholic Church had first attracted the attention of the SD. Not only was Heydrich convinced that Müller was engaged in secret work for the Vatican, he also believed that the Munich lawyer was actually a disguised Jesuit who had, for purposes of cover, received from the Pope a special dispensation from his vows to allow him to marry and have children. Keller's report merely confirmed the security chief's suspicions. The Roman Conversations were on the verge of exposure. Disaster was averted when *Abwehr* chief Admiral Wilhelm Canaris, who had learned of Keller's charges from Arthur Nebe, the director of criminal police in Heydrich's police and security empire, intervened to protect the conspirators. He instructed Müller to prepare a report indicating that while in Rome he had uncovered evidence of a conspiracy directed by General Werner von Fritsch, who conveniently had died in the Polish campaign, and General Walter von Reichenau, a Hitler fanatic. In fact, neither of these officers had any connection with the opposition. As Canaris expected, when Hitler was told that Reichenau, one of his most loyal generals, was purportedly planning a coup, he dismissed the report as 'rubbish', thereby disarming Keller's accusations.

Unfortunately, the threat of exposure had been only temporarily diverted. Traces of the Roman Conversations were uncovered again in the summer of 1940. As we have seen, the warnings of attack which the Belgian ambassador at the Vatican had cabled to Brussels on 2 and 4 May had been intercepted and decrypted by the

Forschungsamt, the signals intelligence service working for Herman Göring in the air ministry. Outraged by this evidence of treason, Hitler had ordered the *Abwehr* to investigate the leak, a decision which Reinhard Heydrich likened to 'sending a goat to guard your garden'.[55] As if to confirm Heydrich's appraisal, Admiral Canaris promptly sent Josef Müller to Rome to conduct the 'investigation'. In consultation with Father Leiber, the Bavarian contrived a story in which the Italian foreign minister, Count Galeazzo Ciano, had learned of the planned offensive from a source in the entourage of his German counterpart, Joachim von Ribbentrop, and that the news had been carried to Ambassador Nieuwenhuys by a Belgian Jesuit, Father Monnens, who had since left Rome for central Africa. The conspirators hoped that this fabrication would provide a satisfactory explanation of the leak and deflect attention from Müller and his visits to the Vatican.[56]

Lieutenant Colonel Joachim Rohleder, the chief of the *Abwehr*'s counter-espionage section (*Abwehr III*) was not a member of the resistance circle. Upon learning of the intercepted telegrams, he had embarked on his own investigation. Rohleder noted that in his second telegram to Brussels the Belgian ambassador had mentioned that his source 'left Berlin 29 April, arrived in Rome 1 May and Friday evening [3 May] had a new discussion . . . with our compatriot'.[57] Reviewing the list of those who had crossed the frontier into Italy during this period, the colonel noticed the name of Josef Müller, who had entered Italy on 29 April and returned on 4 May. Rohleder contacted the Munich station (Müller's nominal post) to learn if the agent had gone to Rome on the days in question. Luckily, Müller had arranged with a friend, who was the *Abwehr III* officer in Munich, to report that he had been in Venice. The wily Bavarian had also gone to the trouble of securing from a friendly Italian customs officer an official rubber stamp which he used to smear the entry and exit dates on his passport.[58] Momentarily checked, but convinced that the solution to the mystery would eventually be found in Rome, Rohleder bided his time until he could find a way to penetrate the secrecy of the Vatican. His opportunity came when the *Abwehr* station in Stockholm added a peripatetic Silesian journalist to its roster of informants.

A Jewish convert to Catholicism, Gabriel Ascher had arrived in Rome in 1935 and soon secured a post as secretary to Father

Friedrich Muckermann, a German Jesuit known throughout Europe for his anti-Nazi polemics. Through Father Muckermann, Ascher was introduced to the world of ecclesiastical Rome, and soon the personable secretary was on friendly terms with abbots, superior generals of religious orders, and monsignors from the Vatican. Ascher accompanied Muckermann when the priest relocated to Austria in 1937, but after the *Anschluss* he resigned his post and went briefly to Switzerland before returning to Rome as the Vatican correspondent for the *Basler Nachrichten*. The prospect of new Aryanization laws in Italy convinced him to abandon Rome again, this time for Stockholm where he continued to submit articles on the Vatican to the Swiss newspaper and to the *New Catholic Herald* of London.[59]

In January 1941 Ascher was approached by Hans Wagner, the *Abwehr* chief in Stockholm. Wagner may have heard of Ascher's ecclesiastical connections in Rome, or he may have acted in response to certain cryptic letters which the journalist had written the previous October to two individuals, identified only as V and K, in Berlin. In both letters he indicated that he had learned from contacts in Britain that there was some sentiment for ending the war. It is possible that the letters were meant to renew an old relationship with German intelligence.[60] On the other hand, Ascher was in contact with Rennie Smith, the British Secretary of the anti-Nazi 'Friends of Europe', to whom he boasted of his connections at the Vatican. In what might have been an approach to British intelligence, he coyly offered to reveal at least some of these sources 'to a confidential person to be named in Stockholm'.[61] Whatever his game or his loyalties, it is clear that Ascher was recruited by Wagner to go to Rome for Rohleder's counter-espionage section.

Ascher left for Berlin on 29 April with a letter from the editor of the *Basler Nachrichten* identifying him as the paper's Vatican correspondent and a letter from the Catholic Archbishop of Stockholm, Johannes Erich Müller, describing him as 'an excellent man, a solid and conscientious Catholic, and an intelligent journalist who perfectly understands the attitude of the Holy See'. In Berlin he met Colonel Rohleder, who provided money for the mission to Rome, and Archbishop Cesare Orsenigo, the papal nuncio, who provided another letter of introduction, this one addressed to Monsignor Giovanni Montini, the 'Substitute' (under-secretary) in the Secretariat of State.[62] Arriving in Rome on 3 May, Ascher

31

proceeded to renew his old contacts in ecclesiastical circles. He called on Monsignor Montini at the Secretariat of State, and visited Father Leiber, Monsignor Kaas, and various members of religious orders. Many of these contacts were wary of the visitor from Stockholm, wondering how a Jew (though a convert) was able to secure permission to travel unmolested across Germany. Leiber asked a Swedish journalist about Ascher and was told that in Stockholm he was reputed to be a German informant. The Superior General of the Benedictines warned at least one of his aides in Rome to be careful in his conversations with the visitor.[63] Suspicion hardened into certainty by the end of June when Ascher had already left Rome. On 24 June Father Leiber alerted Monsignor Montini that confidential information from Berlin indicated that Ascher had reported to the Gestapo the substance of his conversations in Rome. The Pope's assistant concluded that the journalist was 'an extremely dangerous agent of the Gestapo'.[64]

Actually, Ascher was an extremely dangerous agent of the *Abwehr*. Despite the reserve with which he was received in Rome, Rohleder's agent was able to uncover the main lines of Josef Müller's mission to the Vatican, and he returned to Berlin convinced that the Bavarian lawyer had transmitted the warning of the western offensive. Finding Ascher's report 'logically convincing and conclusive', Rohleder carried the information to Admiral Canaris. Aware of the explosive nature of the report, the *Abwehr* chief told his counter-espionage officer that he considered the evidence too flimsy to warrant further action. The report was suppressed, although it would return to haunt Canaris, Oster, and Müller when it was uncovered, along with other incriminating documents, by the Gestapo during their investigation into the unsuccessful coup of 20 July 1944.[65] These documents provided the evidence that would lead Canaris, Oster, Dohnanyi, and others to the scaffold. Although arrested with other members of the Oster circle in April 1943 and subjected to relentless interrogation, Josef Müller kept his adversaries at bay through a combination of nerve, intelligence and good fortune. Among the principal German protagonists of the Roman Conversations, he was the only one to survive the investigations. As for Gabriel Ascher, he returned to Stockholm where the Swedish police monitored his contacts with the local *Abwehr* representatives. In April 1942 he was taken for questioning by the police. While no formal charges were brought against the journalist, the police applied for permission to expel him from Sweden. In mid-May, with the application pending, the authorities expressed concern over his mental condition and transferred him to a mental hospital, where he was to remain until the last months of the war.[66]

As operations, neither the Roman Conversations nor the subsequent inquiries into the travels of Josef Müller were intended to collect information about the Vatican. Despite all the activity, the *Abwehr* was producing very little real intelligence on the papacy. In fact, by the end of 1942 German military intelligence still had not established any systematic coverage of the papal enclave in Rome. At the outbreak of the war the *Tirpitz Ufer* had transferred an officer from Munich to Rome to establish such coverage, but he had been recalled (to justify Müller's frequent visits to the Vatican) so quickly that he demanded compensation for the apartment he had rented for the year. To explain Müller's trips to the Eternal City, Oster had contrived a cover story according to which the Munich lawyer was tapping his extensive circle of ecclesiastical contacts for information on papal affairs, but of course Müller never collected any intelligence that would be useful to the German government. As for the regular *Abwehr* station in Rome, it was primarily a liaison office for contacts with the Italian intelligence service. As a gesture of solidarity with his fellow dictator, Hitler had prohibited German intelligence from operating in Mussolini's Italy. The *Abwehr* chief in Rome, Colonel Helfferich, sometimes circumvented this prohibition by disguising his modest collection efforts inside Italy as operations targeted against other regions, such as Switzerland or North Africa, but he paid little attention to the Vatican. Only in early 1943 did the *Tirpitz Ufer* finally send an officer to Rome to work full-time on the papacy.

To any service except the *Abwehr* (which was notorious for its lax recruitment practices), Paul Franken would have seemed an unlikely recruit. Before the war he had been active in the Catholic social movement, and while completing a doctorate in history at Bonn had served as secretary-general of the Union of Catholic Students. Membership in this 'subversive' organization brought him to the attention of the Gestapo as did his interest in the Catholic trade union movement. He served two years (1937–39) in prison for political offences, and after his release was frequently recalled by the police for questioning. Though suspicious about his political

33

sympathies, the Gestapo did not uncover his connections with the anti-Nazi opposition. A protégé of the trade union leader Jakob Kaiser, Franken was the unionist's link with Konrad Adenauer, the former mayor of Cologne, who was tending his roses in apparent suburban retirement. In 1942 Kaiser, concerned about his associate's vulnerability, arranged for Franken to join the *Abwehr* which had become a centre for anti-Nazi resistance in the armed forces. Captain Bernhard Letterhaus, an *Abwehr* officer secretly connected with the Catholic trade union movement, sponsored Franken's candidacy, secured his assignment to the Cologne station, and arranged for him to be sent immediately to Rome on a mission to observe the Vatican.[67]

Upon his arrival in the Eternal City, Franken took a position as teacher in the German school on the Via Nomentana. He lost this cover when the school relocated to the Tyrol after the fall of Mussolini in July 1943, but he continued to occupy rooms in a clinic run by German nuns, the Grey Sisters, near the Basilica of Santa Maria Maggiore in central Rome. He maintained a low profile, avoiding those haunts where one would normally expect to encounter a German agent working against the Vatican: the Reich embassy to the Holy See, the offices of the German police representative in Rome, Major Herbert Kappler, and the residence of Bishop Alois Hudal, the rector of the German ecclesiastical college who was known as the 'Brown Bishop' for his pro-Nazi sympathies.[68] Franken's contacts were almost exclusively German priests working in Rome, most of whom had been close to Josef Müller: Monsignors Kaas, Krieg and Schönhöfer at the Vatican; the Jesuits Robert Leiber and Ivo Zeiger; from the religious orders, Hubert Noots, Abbot-General of the Premonstatensians, Pancratius Pfeiffer, Superior General of the Salvatorian Fathers, and Father Scholien, a well-known ethnologist who was a member of the Divine Word Fathers. From these sources Franken gathered the occasional item of political and military information and passed it to Berlin. On one occasion, for example, he reported information from Jesuit sources that in order to free more Russians for military service the Soviet Union was recruiting two million Chinese for labour in agriculture and industry.[69] Military items were scarce and always of third- or fourth-hand vintage. Such information rarely reached the Vatican, in part because ecclesiastics (with the possible exception of army chaplains) were rarely in a position to obtain military information, and in part because the papal Secretariat of State, fearful of compromising the Vatican's neutrality and aware that its communications were monitored by the belligerents, discouraged its nuncios from reporting military information in their dispatches.

Franken had more in common with Josef Müller than the same circle of friends. Like his *Abwehr* predecessor, Franken was a representative of the anti-Nazi opposition, but unlike Müller who was part of the conservative military opposition, his connections extended into the more liberal labour opposition which, in turn, was loosely part of the so-called 'Goerdeler Circle'.[70] His role was to pass to the Vatican information concerning the opposition's plans to remove Hitler and his minions and to seek opportunities for a negotiated settlement of the war. Once again, Monsignor Kaas and Father Leiber served as conduits for this information. Twice a week Kaas visited the clinic of the Grey Sisters for treatment of a stomach disorder, and before leaving he would call on Franken who lodged with the Sisters. Every Sunday morning the *Abwehr* officer would take coffee at Kaas' apartment inside the Vatican. Most Sundays Father Leiber would join his two countrymen, although occasionally he would invite Franken to his rooms at the Gregorian University. Since Kaas was in frequent contact with Sir Francis D'Arcy Osborne, the British minister to the Holy See who was then living in Vatican City, the monsignor was a potential channel to London. For his part, Leiber would listen and take notes as Franken explained the opposition's latest thoughts on the composition of the post-Hitler German cabinet or its plans for post-war Austria and the Sudetenland.[71] Leiber's notes were potentially incriminating documents, but when Franken expressed his concern the priest would always assure him that the notes were in safe hands. At one meeting in October 1943, Leiber calmed his friend by telling him that the previous night Pope Pius, having read the latest notes in Leiber's presence, had lit a candle and burned the pages, saying as he did so, 'You can tell him you saw the Pope burn the pages with his own hand.'[72]

The purpose of this clandestine activity is difficult to assess. In contrast to the earlier Roman Conversations, there could be no question of asking Pius again to risk his position by acting as an intermediary with the Allies. In their typically haphazard manner the fragmented opposition probably did not know (or could not decide) what it expected of the Pontiff. Franken's mission seems to have been limited to keeping the Pope informed of opposition efforts inside Germany and soliciting his comments and sympathies in the matter of plans for a post-Hitler Germany especially as those plans concerned frontier questions. On the pretence of reporting personally on important intelligence from the Vatican, the *Abwehr* officer would periodically return to Berlin for discussions with his contacts in anti-Nazi circles. In May 1944, shortly before the Allied seizure of Rome, Franken returned permanently to Germany. By this time the opposition cell in the *Abwehr* had been exposed and its leading members arrested, and the intelligence agency itself was about to be absorbed by the rival RSHA. Turning aside offers of shelter from sympathetic friends, Franken managed to disengage himself from the *Abwehr* without attracting the notice of the Gestapo and secured a new job as an interpreter for Italian 'guest workers' in the Rhineland. In the wake of the unsuccessful 'July 20 Plot', when a bomb planted at Hitler's daily staff meeting merely wounded the Führer, he quietly went to ground near Bonn and remained in hiding until the end of the war.[73]

Despite Paul Franken's departure from Rome, the *Abwehr* was able to maintain at least nominal coverage of the Vatican for, unknown to Franken, the agency had in Rome another agent reporting on the papacy. Wilhelm Möhnen was an inventive and industrious young man who managed to put his modest talents to use in wartime assignments in pleasant locales well out of harm's way.[74] A dealer in motorcycles with an avid interest in art, Möhnen had been conscripted into the army, but had been discharged after the successful French campaign on the grounds that his business was essential to the war effort. After a bomb destroyed his small business, thereby depriving him of a livelihood and an excuse for his civilian status, he cast about for a way to stay out of uniform, or at least out of the combat smock of a front-line soldier. Somehow he managed to talk himself into the *Abwehr* and in early 1941 was assigned to the service's Paris station. His job was to check that the manufacture of spare parts for military vehicles in the unoccupied zone did not violate the terms of the Franco-German armistice. While in France, Möhnen made the acquaintance of a German couple by the name of Graebner. Frau Graebner had recently returned from Rome where she had occasionally furnished the German air attaché, Lieutenant

Colonel Herbert Veltheim, with news about the Vatican. Frau Graebner was never more than a casual informant whose reports were probably a mélange of café gossip, newspaper stories and pure fabrication, and her employment by Veltheim suggests the dismal state of military intelligence operations against the Vatican. Her experience, however, suggested to Möhnen an opportunity just when one was needed. A new officer had taken command of Möhnen's section of the Paris *Abwehrstelle*. The new man had little interest in tracking vehicle parts and had made clear his intention to dispense with the former motorcycle salesman who was the chief tracker. To secure his continued employment by the *Abwehr*, Möhnen convinced his superiors that he could take over and expand Frau Graebner's earlier work in Rome. It may seem odd that the Paris station would assign one of its staff to work against the Vatican, but in the loose (not to say chaotic) administrative structure of the *Abwehr*, stations ran agents against any target they wished with little concern for coordination or duplication of effort.

After a series of brief visits to the Eternal City in the spring of 1942 to establish his credentials as a Vatican expert, Möhnen was assigned to the German embassy to Italy as an aide to Lieutenant Colonel Veltheim. His enthusiasm for art provided his first introduction to Vatican circles. At the time of his exploratory visits to Rome, he had made the acquaintance of Bruno Lohse who was in Paris as art agent for Herman Göring. Lohse was seeking fine paintings for the *Reichmarschal*'s private collection, and upon learning of Möhnen's interest in art and his imminent transfer to Rome, the dealer commissioned him to purchase any important paintings that might appear on the Italian market. Möhnen used this commission to secure an introduction to officials in the Vatican Museums. Once inside the Vatican's door, the amiable salesman was able to expand his circle of contacts until it came to include important personalities like Monsignor Kaas and Father Leiber.

Despite his posting to Rome, Möhnen remained administratively attached to the Paris *Abwehrstelle*, and he occasionally returned to France for leave and consultations with his superiors. During one such visit at the end of 1942, he encountered Marschall von Biberstein, an official of the German foreign ministry who would soon assume direction of Inf III, the ministry's intelligence section. The diplomat expressed great interest in Möhnen's contacts at the

Vatican and told the *Abwehr* agent that he hoped they could go into the matter more seriously at a future time. Möhnen probably dismissed the diplomat's words as an empty pleasantry and put the exchange out of his mind. In January 1943, while on leave in Germany, he received a summons to the Wilhelmstrasse for a meeting with Marschall von Biberstein. The recent Allied successes in North Africa and the looming disaster at Stalingrad had, apparently, further alarmed a few of the Führer's diplomats whose confidence in German victory was already shaky. Mainly these were able young men who had been recruited into the foreign ministry by Martin Luther, the ambitious director of the *Abteilung Deutschland,* which handled domestic affairs such as racial questions and relations with party organizations and the security services. Luther's circle of young technocrats had become disillusioned with the conduct of the war in general and the performance of their foreign minister, Joachim von Ribbentrop, in particular. As early as the autumn of 1942 one of their number, Walter Kieser, drafted a proposal for a negotiated settlement with the Western Allies on the basis of the reconstitution of Czechoslovakia and Poland, Germany's renunciation of any claim to European hegemony, and its commitment not to export National Socialism. Pressed by his subordinates, Luther carried this proposal to Ribbentrop, who carried it to Hitler, who rejected it out of hand. Subsequently, the peace faction in the foreign ministry concluded that the foreign minister (whom they considered an incompetent megalomaniac) was the principal obstacle to their plans and that his removal would enhance the morale and independence of the Wilhelmstrasse and weaken the hold of the fanatical Nazis on German foreign policy. They began to cooperate with Walter Schellenberg, the chief of foreign intelligence in the RSHA, who had concluded that a separate peace with the Western Allies was imperative if Germany were to survive the war. Schellenberg believed that Germany should explore the possibility of negotiations with London and Washington, but was convinced that the foreign minister, Ribbentrop, was too compromised in the eyes of the Americans and British to pursue any such *démarche*. With the tacit consent of SS chief Heinrich Himmler and the active cooperation of Martin Luther and his subordinates at the Wilhelmstrasse, Schellenberg sought to replace Ribbentrop and initiate peace feelers.[75] Marschall von Biberstein was apparently part of the anti-

Ribbentrop clique for he confidentially informed Möhnen that certain unnamed parties in the government believed that the time was ripe for a peace initiative and that Pope Pius was best placed to take such an initiative. According to Biberstein, Germany could never formally request papal intervention on behalf of peace, but a discreet, informal approach to the Vatican through unofficial but secure channels might encourage the Pontiff to use the occasion of his annual Easter message from Rome to appeal directly to Germany to accept negotiations.

Möhnen was an unlikely candidate for such a delicate mission, but ever eager to ingratiate himself with potentially useful patrons, he agreed to try to open a channel. Because of a dispute over his military status (from which dispute Lieutenant Colonel Veltheim had to extricate him) Möhnen did not return to Rome until April. He carried Biberstein's idea to Monsignor Kaas, but as was his practice in politically delicate situations the cautious monsignor passed him along to Father Leiber. The papal aide was dubious about the proposal for an Easter peace appeal which might all too easily be interpreted by Berlin as an Allied-inspired intrigue to undermine German morale and embarrass the Nazi regime. He promised, however, to inform the Pope of the matter.

The policy of Pius XII was to avoid direct peace proposals which were so pregnant with potential for misunderstanding unless he received a formal appeal from one of the belligerents.[76] An approach by a shadowy messenger of uncertain rank and credibility certainly did not qualify as a formal request; indeed, it bore all the signs of a possible provocation. Nevertheless, on Easter Sunday (15 April) the Pope addressed an open letter to his Cardinal Secretary of State, Luigi Maglione, in which the Pontiff called for prayers, especially by children, for the cessation of the conflict which 'not only brings slaughter to the armies but makes even peaceful cities run with fraternal blood'. This was a cryptic allusion to Germany's contemporary disasters, the capitulation at Stalingrad and the mounting Allied air offensive against German cities. The letter might have been interpreted as a cautious and indirect papal bid for the Reich to seek peace, but it was not the ringing peace appeal the Schellenberg–Luther group was seeking. In any event, by April the anti-Ribbentrop movement had collapsed after the foreign minister discovered its machinations and had Luther arrested and condemned to a concentration camp while some of his subordinates (but not Biberstein) were sent to the front.[77]

Having performed his mission for Marschall von Biberstein, the ever-industrious Möhnen set about making himself useful in any manner that would prevent his transfer to a combat unit. Since his assignment to Rome stemmed from his offer to his *Abwehr* superiors in Paris to collect intelligence on the Vatican, certain gestures had to be made in that direction. Möhnen, however, had no particular interest or aptitude for intelligence work; his offer to spy on the Vatican had been after all nothing more than an expedient to protect his job with military intelligence. Fortunately, his intelligence efforts were significantly augmented in the spring of 1943 when he managed to have an old friend from Munich, Hans Kühner, assigned to a propaganda unit in Rome and then detached as an interpreter to the office of the air attaché. Kühner knew Rome and the Romans well, and Möhnen used that knowledge to glean bits of café gossip and journalistic rumour which he then imaginatively arranged into 'intelligence reports' for Lieutenant Colonel Veltheim. Although these reports were not based on authentic Vatican sources and were more fanciful than accurate, the air attaché dutifully passed them to Berlin. Headquarters was probably thankful for any information from Rome it could get, especially after Benito Mussolini's removal from power in July when German intelligence found itself woefully short of intelligence resources in the Eternal City.

When the Germans occupied Rome after Italy signed an armistice with the Allies in September 1943, Möhnen's penetration into Vatican circles took a favourable turn. With the occupation the Vatican, which depended upon the city administration for the provision of water, gas, electricity and telephone services, encountered innumerable small but irritating problems whose resolution required discussions with the German authorities. Möhnen occasionally discussed these problems with Monsignor Kaas and these discussions led to his introduction to Prince Carlo Pacelli, the Pope's nephew, who supervised the Vatican's legal affairs in Rome, and Father Pancratius Pfeiffer, the Superior General of the Salvatorian Order and the Pope's unofficial liaison with the German occupation authorities. These rather elevated contacts stood the *Abwehr* agent in good stead when his nominal boss and patron, Lieutenant Colonel Veltheim, moved to northern Italy with most of the embassy staff to be close to the new government (the so-called Republic of Salò) which Mussolini, after his rescue by German commandos, had set up with Hitler's assistance. Undoubtedly impressed with his subordinate's new friends in the Vatican, Veltheim entrusted to Möhnen a bundle of blank forms, signed by him, which when completed and affixed to a building declared the premises off-limits to German personnel. This was a significant and potentially lucrative opportunity for a clever and not overly scrupulous young man who was now styling himself the 'assistant air attaché'. It certainly endeared him to his new contacts at the Vatican who were concerned to protect papal properties around Rome from search or seizure by the German police and military authorities.

In good standing with Vatican officials, Möhnen was unexpectedly summoned to Paris in January 1944 for discussions with his controllers. Anticipating further military reverses in Italy which might soon require the abandonment of Rome, the Paris *Abwehrstelle* had cast about for ways to protect the *Abwehr*'s rather skimpy intelligence assets in the Eternal City. The Vatican assumed a special importance in these plans. As a neutral state whose small territory was protected under international law, Vatican City offered an island of security in Rome, a potential safe haven for Germans should the Allies occupy the city. When Italy had entered the war in May 1940, the various Allied embassies to the Holy See had moved into Vatican City, and German intelligence always suspected (with little justification) that the Allies used this sanctuary as a secure base for espionage against the Axis. Perhaps Germany could turn the tables on the Allies. If the Allies seized Rome the German embassy to the Holy See would be allowed to move into papal territory, exchanging places with its Allied counterparts. Unfortunately, the *Abwehr* had never seen any reason to attach an officer to the embassy and it was unlikely that the mission, which would probably take only part of its staff into Vatican City and which, in any event, had always resisted the addition of intelligence officers to its personnel, would now provide diplomatic cover for an agent. Furthermore, it was unlikely that papal authorities would allow non-diplomatic personnel from the Axis powers refuge inside Vatican City. In such circumstances Möhnen's potential value as an agent increased dramatically. If he could use his contacts with influential Vatican personalities, particularly the Pope's nephew, Prince Carlo Pacelli, to receive special permission to live in the papal territory, then German military intelligence would have a man inside the Vatican, safely out of the reach of Allied security officers. If he could also receive some sort of papal identity card or safe-conduct pass that would allow him to go into Rome, then the agent might gather intelligence on Allied activities in and around the Eternal City as well as intelligence on papal affairs.

Möhnen eagerly accepted his new mission which promised to remove him permanently from the fighting and allow him to await the end of the war in secure and far from uncomfortable circumstances. The Paris *Abwehrstelle* provided him with special writing materials for clandestine communication with his controllers. These materials consisted of two match-like sticks which were to be used for writing on paper previously swabbed by a cotton ball soaked in a special chemical. On his way back to Rome, Möhnen called on his old patron, Lieutenant Colonel Veltheim, who was at the time in the north Italian town of Fasano, the headquarters of the German delegation to Mussolini's rump government. The *Luftwaffe* officer spoke about the need for accurate information on the attitudes and intentions of the Vatican as the war turned against the Axis. He instructed Möhnen to be especially alert for any indications of the Vatican's attitude towards the prospect of Allied landings in France; the intensification of the Allied air offensive against German cities; and possible strains in Anglo-American relations with the Soviet Union.

Möhnen returned to Rome in the last weeks of the German occupation. When German forces abandoned the city to the Allies on 4–5 June 1944, the *Abwehr*'s last representative in the Eternal City had not yet arranged his entry into Vatican City. With the prospect of arrest, interrogation and internment should he be discovered by Allied authorities, Möhnen cached his secret writing materials behind the bathroom cistern in the apartment of a friend on the Via Gregoriana and went into hiding. In his effort to gain sanctuary inside the Vatican he had already approached Father Pancratius Pfeiffer and the 'Brown Bishop', Alois Hudal, who served as the rector of the German College, but neither wished to intervene with papal authorities on his behalf. As a last resort he turned to Prince Carlo Pacelli and luckily his earlier contacts with the papal nephew paid off. The influential prince arranged for his German friend to be designated a political refugee and on 7 June Möhnen entered the safety of Vatican City. Seven days earlier the *Abwehr*, dismissed as ineffectual by the military command it professed to serve and rocked by the arrest of several of its senior officers for conspiring against the regime, was abolished and most of its intelligence functions and personnel transferred to the foreign intelligence section (Amt VI) of the RSHA.

Wilhelm Möhnen lived happily inside the Vatican for eight months. During that time he evidenced little concern for the fate of his old service or his future with the new. He sent reports to neither Lieutenant Colonel Veltheim nor to his superiors in Paris. Since he left his secret writing materials behind on the Via Gregoriana when he entered the Vatican, it is unlikely that he ever had any intention of filing intelligence reports. His controllers made at least one attempt to activate him during his Vatican sojourn. He received a letter from a former associate in the Paris *Abwehrstelle* who inquired about his condition and suggested he write to Otto Graebener, an old acquaintance from Paris, whose wife had preceded him as Veltheim's Vatican reporter. Möhnen did not respond. He probably considered the war over as far as he was concerned, although a more charitable judgement might be that he did not want to betray the good faith and charity of his Vatican sponsors who had accepted him as a refugee. Whatever the reason, Möhnen apparently abandoned all intelligence work once he established himself inside the Vatican. The erstwhile spy, however, found the papal city secure but rather dull. He soon began to make frequent sorties into Rome, although his refugee status did not extend beyond papal territory and he was subject to arrest and internment as an enemy citizen should he encounter Allied police patrols. Finally, he went out once too often. On 5 February 1945, as he approached the Spanish Steps in central Rome, he was arrested by American counter-intelligence agents who had been tipped-off about Möhnen's appearance by an anti-Nazi German who was cooperating with Allied authorities. German military intelligence had lost its last agent at the Vatican. Given that service's ineffectual and unprofessional efforts against the Vatican target, it is unlikely that anyone in Berlin even noticed the loss.

NOTES

1. Technically, the terms 'Holy See' and 'Vatican' refer to different institutional phenomena, but in practice they are used interchangeably.
2. Owen Chadwick, *Britain and the Vatican during the Second World War* (Cambridge: Cambridge University Press, 1986), p. 1.
3. National Archives and Records Administration (NARA), College Park, Record Group 457, MAGIC Diplomatic Summaries, 10 and 11 March 1943.
4. Chadwick, *Britain and the Vatican*, p.1.
5. Pucci was sufficiently trusted by the German embassy that they occasionally used him as a back channel to the Vatican. Pierre Blet, *et al.*, *Actes et Documents du Saint Siège relatifs à la Seconde Guerre Mondiale*, Vol. 5 (Vatican City: Editrice Vaticana, 1969), p. 679 (hereinafter cited as ADSS with volume and page number). Pucci did not work exclusively for the Germans. The records of the Italian secret police, for example, refer to the monsignor as 'our Palace informant'. John F. Pollard, *The Vatican and Italian Fascism, 1929–1932* (Cambridge: Cambridge University Press, 1985), p. 219, n. 6.
6. NARA. Microfilms of Captured German Records, T-120, Roll 314, 239432.
7. David Alvarez, 'The Vatican and Italian Belligerency' in D.W. Pike (ed.), *The Opening of the Second World War* (New York: Peter Lang, 1991), pp. 312–13.
8. ADSS. V, pp. 372, 389, 396; Kew: Public Record Office (PRO). Foreign Office Records (FO), 371/30340/A3930 and 371/30476/A1032.
9. Leonidas Hill, 'The Vatican Embassy of Ernst von Weizsäcker, 1943–1945', *Journal of Modern History*, 39, 2 (June 1967), pp. 142–4.
10. Robert A. Graham, SJ, 'La strana condotta di E. von Weizsäcker ambasciatore del Reich in Vaticano', *Civiltà Cattolica*, 2 (June 1970), pp. 455–71.
11. Hansjakob Stehle, *Eastern Politics of the Vatican, 1917–1979* (Athens, OH: Ohio University Press, 1981), Ch. 7.
12. ADSS. XI, p. 86.
13. R.A. Graham, 'La strana condotta di E. von Weizsäcker', p. 61. Weizsäcker's reports may also mislead scholars who are unaware of the ambassador's deliberate misrepresentations.
14. John Weitz, *Hitler's Diplomat: Joachim von Ribbentrop* (London: Weidenfeld & Nicolson, 1992), p. 121.
15. Christopher Browning, '*Unterstaatssekretaer* Martin Luther and the Ribbentrop Foreign Office', *Journal of Contemporary History*, 12 (April 1977), pp. 321–2. Browning suggests that Likus's intellectual limitations and his alcoholism limited his ability to direct his office, and that much of the work was done by his assistant, Werner Picot, who had recently served in the embassy to the Vatican.
16. James Barros and Richard Gregor, *Double Deception: Stalin, Hitler and the Invasion of Russia* (DeKalb: Northern Illinois University Press, 1995), p. 135. Hitler wrongly suspected the journalist of being a *triple* agent under Russian control.
17. Robert A. Graham, SJ, 'Come von Ribbentrop spiava il Vaticano', *Civiltà Cattolica*, 4 (Nov. 1982), p. 224; private information.
18. For a selection of the surviving reports, see NARA. T-120, Roll 34, 30951ff.
19. The Vatican accredits a nuncio to a government with which it has established formal diplomatic relations. An apostolic delegate is the Pope's representative to the bishops and faithful in a country with which the Vatican has no official relations. Delegates lack formal diplomatic status, but often act in a diplomatic capacity.
20. In the two years following the signing of the concordat the Vatican was compelled to address to the German government 34 notes of protest against violations of the agreement.
21. Quoted in H. Stehle, *Eastern Politics*, p. 208.
22. Far from having a plan to evangelize Russia the Vatican was unprepared to exploit any opportunity offered by the German invasion of Russia. When papal officials met in early July 1941 to consider whether to send several priests into western Russia to

investigate the state of religious life in long-closed areas such as the Ukraine, they were hard pressed to identify suitable candidates for the mission. Long after the war Cardinal Tisserant recalled that eventually eight priests were dispatched, although one of the surviving priests remembered that only four were sent. Robert A. Graham, SJ, 'Come e Perché Hitler Bloccó il Vaticano in Russia', *Civiltà Cattolica*, 4 (Nov. and Dec. 1972), pp. 241–52 and 435–42.

23. H. Stehle, *Eastern Politics*, pp. 217–19; NARA. T-120. Roll 314, 240059.
24. Gerald Fogarty, SJ, *The Vatican and the American Hierarchy* (Stuttgart: Hiersemann, 1982), pp. 271–8. There is no evidence in American or Vatican documents of any meeting between Archbishop Cicognani and President Roosevelt as described by Likus's informant. The White House logs indicate that Cicognani did not visit the President at all in 1941. Information from Raymond Teichman of the Franklin D. Roosevelt Library, Hyde Park, New York.
25. Robert Dallek, *Franklin D. Roosevelt and American Foreign Policy, 1932–1945* (New York: Oxford University Press, 1979), p. 262.
26. PRO. FO 898/69 (Sib L/376); FO 898/70 (Sibs for Italy). The invented stories were known to British propagandists as 'sibs' from the Latin *sibilare* (whisper).
27. Robert A. Graham, SJ, 'Il Vaticano nella guerra psicologica inglese, 1939–1945', *Civiltà Cattolica*, 1 (Jan. 1978), p. 115. Leading historians, unaware of the disinformation programme, have accepted the letter as authentic. See, for example, John Conway, *The Nazi Persecution of the Churches, 1933–1945* (New York: Basic Books, 1968), p. 288.
28. ADSS. IV, pp. 318, 377–8.
29. Bonn, Auswärtiges Amt (AA), Inland IIg, Italien 8 (ser. 850, 284044).
30. R.A. Graham, SJ, 'Il Vaticano nella guerra psicologica inglese, 1939–1945', p. 124.
31. Timothy Naftali, 'ARTIFICE: James Angleton and X-2 Operations in Italy', in G. Chalou (ed.), *The Secrets War: The Office of Strategic Services in World War II*, (Washington: National Archives and Records Administration, 1992), pp. 230–3. A subsequent evaluation of the Vatican reports by the CIA concluded that the reports had contributed to 'informing, misinforming and thoroughly confusing those individuals responsible for analyzing Vatican foreign policy during the period involved', and that the affair provided 'an unusual illustration of a paper-mill or fabrication operation'.

    For evidence that Soviet military intelligence may have been among Scattolini's victims, see Robert A. Graham, SJ, 'Il Vaticanista falsario: l'incredibile successo di Virgilio Scattolini', *Civiltà Cattolica*, 3 (Sept. 1973), pp. 467–78.
32. NA. T-120. Roll 314, 239806.
33. The archive of the Office of Strategic Services contains a large collection of cable summaries supposedly drawn from the files of the papal Secretariat of State in the last months of 1945. These telegrams include registry numbers and cipher designations which lend a spurious authenticity to the documents but which bear no relationship to the actual registration format used in the Secretariat of State. This collection came to the OSS through Scattolini's channels. Cf. NARA. RG 226. Entry 174, Box 1, folders 1-2 (JUX Memos).
34. David Kahn, *Hitler's Spies: German Military Intelligence in World War II* (New York: Macmillan, 1978) pp. 70–71; Information from Wilhelm Hoettl. During the war Wilhelm Hoettl was an intelligence officer in the RSHA.
35. AA. Politisches Archiv. Nachlässe Mackensen. Handakten. 'Kopien der Berichten der Deutschen Informationsstelle.'
36. Vatican records indicate that Pius met Senator Federzoni on 29 July, but there is no record of an audience with Grandi. On 27 July Cardinal Maglione recorded his intention to send someone to Senise to inquire into the welfare of Rachele Mussolini, the fallen dictator's wife. ADSS. Vol. VII, pp. 522, n. 6, 525.
37. As President Roosevelt's personal representative, Myron Taylor resided in the United States and made occasional visits to the Vatican. Tittmann, Taylor's special assistant,

remained in Rome and when Italy declared war on the United States after Pearl Harbor, he joined other Allied diplomats accredited to the Holy See who had moved into Vatican City.

38. Clemm-Hohenberg's source may have been caught up in the Allied deception operations surrounding the invasion of Sicily.
39. David Alvarez, *Bureaucracy and Cold War Diplomacy: The United States and Turkey, 1943–1946* (Thessaloniki: Institute for Balkan Studies, 1980), pp. 25ff.
40. O. Chadwick, *Britain and the Vatican*, pp. 247–8.
41. Information from Harold Tittmann. On the restrictions placed on Allied diplomats, see O. Chadwick, *Britain and the Vatican*, pp. 150ff.
42. For Tittmann's communications problems, see Ch. 5.
43. AA. Politisches Archiv. Serial 534. Vatikanische Beziehungen.
44. Quoted in D. Kahn, *Hitler's Spies*, p. 72.
45. NARA. T-77. Roll 1029, 6501666. In May the Pope had solicited Mussolini's support for a conference to discuss German-Polish tensions, and on 29 August His Holiness would make a last-minute appeal to *Il Duce* to intervene with Hitler on behalf of peace, but there were no efforts at collaboration in June or early July.
46. The standard account remains Harold C. Deutsch, *The Conspiracy against Hitler in the Twilight War* (Minneapolis: University of Minnesota Press, 1968); also O. Chadwick, *Britain and the Vatican*, pp. 86–100 and Klemens von Klemperer, *German Resistance against Hitler: The Search for Allies Abroad, 1938–1945* (Oxford: Oxford University Press, 1992), pp. 171ff.
47. H. Deutsch, *The Conspiracy*, p. 123.
48. Ibid., pp. 139ff. Oster also passed warnings to the Dutch military attaché in Berlin.
49. After returning to Berlin on 4 May, Müller kept Father Leiber informed of subsequent postponements by means of a telephone code.
50. H.C. Deutsch, *The Conspiracy*, pp. 340–2. Noots also sent word of the impending attack to the abbot of one of his order's monasteries in Belgium who proceeded to alert ecclesiastical circles including Jesuit authorities in Brussels who began to destroy confidential documents in anticipation of the arrival of the German secret police.
51. Ibid., pp. 125–8.
52. NARA. RG 238. Final Interrogation Report (CI-FIR), No. 123: Albert Hartl, Headquarters 7707 Military Intelligence Service Centre, 18–19.
53. This account of Keller's investigation is drawn from H.C. Deutsch, *The Conspiracy*, pp. 130–4.
54. Information from Augustine Mayer, OSB.
55. Domenico Bernabei, *Orchestra Nera* (Turin: ERI, 1991), p. 192.
56. H.C. Deutsch, *The Conspiracy*, pp. 345–6.
57. Ibid., p. 341.
58. Heinz Höhne, *Canaris* (Garden City: Doubleday, 1979) pp. 417–18.
59. Friedrich Muckermann, SJ, *In Kamp zwischen zwei Epochen*, edited by Nikolaus Junk, SJ, (Mainz: Mathias-Grunewald, 1973), p. 642; C.G. McKay, *From Information to Intrigue: Studies in Secret Service Based on the Swedish Experience, 1939–45* (London: Frank Cass, 1993), p. 168.
60. C.G. McKay, *From Information to Intrigue*, pp. 168–9.
61. PRO. FO 800/325.
62. Information concerning the letters of Archbishops Müller and Orsenigo provided by a confidential source. A minute from Montini's office dated November 1941 and attached to Orsenigo's letter says of Ascher: 'He is not a trustworthy person.'
63. Information from Robert Leiber, SJ and Cyrill von Korvin Krasinski, OSB.
64. Leiber to Montini, 24 June 1941. Copy in possession of the authors.
65. H. Höhne, *Canaris*, pp. 418–20.
66. C.G. McKay, *From Information to Intrigue*, p. 172.

67. Information from Paul Franken. At least once before Jakob Kaiser had tried to use the *Abwehr* as a refuge for anti-Nazis. In 1941, Josef Joos, a Catholic union leader, was arrested by the Gestapo. At Kaiser's instigation, sympathetic *Abwehr* officers contacted Joos and asked him if he would accept 'an important mission' in a foreign country. The suspicious prisoner refused the mysterious offer and two weeks later was sent to Dachau where he remained for the rest of the war.
68. Franken was not so inconspicuous that he escaped Kappler's notice. The Gestapo representative duly reported the *Abwehr* officer's activities to RSHA headquarters in Berlin. AA. Politisches Archiv. Inland IIg. 83. Italien. Berichtverzeichnisse des Pol. Att. in Rom. Ka-2302. Paul Franken.
69. Information from Paul Franken. The report concerning the employment of Chinese labour was received with scepticism by the Russian specialists in Foreign Armies East, the military intelligence section of the General Staff concerned with the eastern front. NARA. T-78. Roll 502, 6490858.
70. K. von Klemperer, *German Resistance*, p. 52. Carl Goerdeler, a former mayor of Leipzig and chancellor-designate in a post-Nazi Germany, was a civilian leader in the opposition.
71. Information from Paul Franken. Franken maintained that Monsignor Kaas reported their conversations to Osborne and to Harold Tittmann, the American representative at the Vatican. The authors have not been able to confirm this information.
72. The Pope's housekeeper confirmed that during the war Pius always kept a candle and matches on his desk 'because of possible blackouts'. Information from Mother Pasqualina.
73. Information from Paul Franken.
74. Unless otherwise indicated, information concerning Wilhelm Möhnen's intelligence work in Rome is drawn from Robert A. Graham, SJ, 'The Rise and Fall of a Secret Agent in the Vatican' (unpublished ms.).
75. Peter Black, *Ernst Kaltenbrunner: Ideological Soldier of the Third Reich* (Princeton: Princeton University Press, 1984), p. 181; Christopher Browning, '*Unterstaatssekretaer* Martin Luther and the Ribbentrop Foreign Office', pp. 313–44.
76. Pius probably recalled the dismal results of Pope Benedict XV's peace appeal in the third year of the First World War. The then Monsignor Eugenio Pacelli was serving as papal nuncio in Germany at the time of Benedict's appeal.
77. Heinz Höhne, *The Order of the Death's Head: The Story of Hitler's SS*, trans. by Richard Barry (New York: Coward-McCann, 1970), pp. 521–2.

2

Secret Police

In the labyrinth world of wartime German intelligence many agencies competed for influence and resources, but only one successfully challenged the traditional pre-eminence of the foreign ministry and the *Abwehr*. Formed in September 1939 by the amalgamation of various state and party police and intelligence organs, the *Reichssicherheitshauptamt* (Reich Security Administration, or RSHA) was a grim testimony to the ambition, industry, and ruthlessness of Heinrich Himmler, *Reichsführer* SS and Chief of the German Police, and his deputy, Reinhard Heydrich. Working within the Nazi party, they had created in 1932 a small security and intelligence unit, the *Sicherheitsdienst* (SD), which was responsible for protecting the party from real and imagined threats. With an eye for power and a knack for bureaucratic politics which would have dazzled Machiavelli, they aggressively asserted the prerogatives of their organization and extended its operations until it rivalled in scope and authority the security organs of the state. In 1936 Heydrich, who was already head of the SD, had been appointed to the new governmental post of chief of the Security Police Administration, an office responsible for the state's criminal and political police forces. The amalgamation of 1939 merely formalized Heydrich's control over all police agencies in the Reich and marked the final ascendancy of the party security apparatus over that of the state. It also created the most powerful intelligence agency in Germany.[1]

During the war the RSHA would exhibit a special interest in the Vatican, but in so doing it merely inherited and maintained a concern which had long been nourished by its progenitors in the Nazi intelligence and security apparatus. Almost from its founding, the

Sicherheitsdienst had been preoccupied with the Catholic Church. This preoccupation reflected, in part, a clear understanding in Nazi party circles that the church represented a threat to the ideological claims and political ambitions of their movement. By affirming the primacy of divine and natural law over human law, by teaching that there was an authority above the state, and by claiming the right to inform and guide the consciences of individuals, the church was always a rival for the 'hearts and minds' of the German people. Moreover the German church's extensive network of schools, newspapers, publishing houses, youth groups, confraternities and charitable institutions challenged the party's effort to extend its control over all aspects of German life. Under any conditions the Catholic Church's moral claims and its institutional vitality would have been troublesome to a regime with totalitarian aspirations, but the threat appeared all the more sinister to Nazi loyalists who believed that the primary allegiance of German Catholics was to the Pope in Rome who worked his will in Germany through a disciplined legion of clerical agents, most notably that dangerous corps of papal Janissaries, the Jesuits. The Catholic Church, then, joined the Communists, Jews, and Freemasons as one of the 'Transnational Powers' (*Uberstaatliche Mächte*) which were the mortal enemies of the National Socialist state.

The SD's approach to the Catholic Church was also influenced by the attitude of its chief, Reinhard Heydrich, who imagined the Pope hatching all manner of plots against the Nazi regime. Describing the security chief's hatred of the church, a one-time officer in his service commented, 'It was almost pathological in its intensity and sometimes caused this otherwise cold and calculating schemer to lose all sense of proportion and logic.'[2] Before the war Heydrich considered 'political Catholicism' the most dangerous threat to the regime. In his mind it represented a 'skilled and subtle attempt to undermine the unified political will of the German people', and he insisted that its destruction must take precedence over actions against Communists, Jews and Freemasons.[3] Heydrich was prepared to authorize extreme measures to ensure the destruction of this enemy. During the Röhm Putsch in June 1934, he personally added the name of Erich Klausener to the list of those marked for elimination. A former police director in the Prussian Interior Ministry and a leader in the Catholic Action movement who had publicly attacked Nazi policies in appearances before various Catholic assemblies, Klausener was the type of 'Catholic rabble-rouser' who fuelled the fear and enmity of the Nazi police chief.[4] For the chief of the SD the contest against the Catholic Church was a struggle to the death and he mobilized the resources under his command to ensure a German triumph in that struggle.

In 1933 the Vatican and Berlin had negotiated a concordat which regularized church–state relations in the Reich by detailing the rights and responsibilities of each party and by defining the legal status of the Catholic Church. By concluding an agreement with the new Nazi regime, the Vatican hoped to secure legal protection and freedom of action for its activities and institutions especially in the area of education. For the Nazis, however, the concordat was never more than a propaganda device to legitimize the new order and to curry favour among Catholics in Germany and around the world. They did not intend to allow a document to inhibit their plans to break the power of the church.[5] These plans proceeded along three lines. The first aimed at securing administrative control of the German Catholic Church by frightening or seducing the archbishops and bishops into subordination so that they would become little more than religious auxiliaries of the state. This goal required that the German hierarchy be isolated from the moral and institutional authority and support of the Vatican. The second line of attack was concerned with under-mining the popularity and moral influence of the church among German believers. This approach took the form of highly publicized 'morality trials' at which priests, nuns and monks were prosecuted for alleged sexual offences or violations of currency regulations. International religious orders such as the Benedictines and Franciscans were especially vulnerable to charges of currency violations since they often had to transfer funds between their headquarters in Rome and their various monasteries in Germany and other countries. The third line of attack against the German church concentrated on eliminating Catholic lay organizations which could provide an institutional base for anti-Nazi activity. This approach led to efforts to secularize Catholic schools, suppress Catholic newspapers and publishing houses, prohibit Catholic youth organizations, and restrict religious processions and pilgrimages.[6]

The intensity of the attacks against the church waxed and waned according to the shifting priorities of the regime, its political and military fortunes, and its perceptions of public opinion. The occasional relaxation of the anti-Catholic campaign, however, was only a tactical move and was never a sign of a substantial shift in the goals of the campaign. In the summer of 1941, for instance, when Hitler suspended the notorious euthanasia programme and slowed the struggle against the church in part because of the fiery sermons against euthanasia and the confiscation of church property preached by the popular Bishop of Münster, Clemens August von Galen, the Führer calmed his outraged subordinates who called for the execution of the outspoken prelate by promising them that the church question would be resolved at a more opportune moment. He assured them that 'It is all written down in my big book. The time will come when I shall settle my accounts with them.' Echoing the sentiments of his Führer, Heydrich loosed his intelligence agents against the church so that 'all proof of Church opposition to the state should be to hand on the day of reckoning', while Gestapo circles prepared for the day when all the Jesuits in Germany would be rounded-up and sent to concentration camps.[7]

To facilitate its assault against the Catholic Church the regime mobilized its police and security services. As early as 1933 the fledgling *Sicherheitsdienst* had established in its Munich offices a small intelligence unit targeted against the church. Under the direction of August Wilhelm Patin, a former priest and theologian who had the curious fortune to be related to both Heinrich Himmler and the Archbishop of Bamberg, this office was charged with gathering information on the organization of the church and its leading personalities. The scholarly Patin was suited by neither appetite nor aptitude for the role of intelligence officer, and when SD headquarters relocated to Berlin in 1934, the erstwhile cleric remained in Munich. In Berlin a certain Martin Wolf assumed direction of the 'Church Referat', but within the year that officer received a special assignment to investigate Bolshevik subversion in Germany and responsibility for the church desk fell to his assistant, Albert Hartl.

Albert Hartl was born in 1904 in the small Bavarian town of Rossholzen. His father, a liberal, free-thinking schoolteacher, always resented the Catholic Church's influence in Bavarian politics and society. In contrast, Albert's mother was a devout and strict Catholic who managed, when Albert was ten, to persuade her husband to allow their son to leave the local state school and enrol in an academy run by the Benedictine monks. Shortly after his father's death in 1916, Albert decided to become a priest, and for the next 13 years he pursued theological studies at the seminary in Freising and the university in Munich. As a seminarian Hartl excelled at his studies and participated actively in the Catholic youth movement. In 1929 he received ordination from the hands of Cardinal Michael von Faulhaber, the Archbishop of Munich, and subsequently began to teach religion in the local *gymnasium*. In 1931 he was appointed prefect of students at his alma mater, the seminary in Freising.[8]

Hartl conscientiously performed his academic duties and appeared to be a model cleric, but appearances were deceiving. Unsettled by the prospect of a lifetime of asceticism and celibacy, the young priest had already begun to question his vocation, and had also begun to associate with a group of conservative Bavarian priests who were adherents of the Nazi party. Shortly after his appointment as prefect at the Freising seminary, he became a paid informant for the SD office in Munich. In 1933 he denounced his best friend and superior at the seminary, Father Josef Rossberger, for anti-Hitler and anti-Nazi remarks. His testimony against Rossberger at the subsequent trial (which resulted in the priest's imprisonment for a year) caused a sensation in Munich and a scandal among Bavarian Catholics. Fearful of retaliation from his allegedly vengeful co-religionists, Hartl appealed to the chief of the SD, Reinhard Heydrich, who took him into protective custody. While under Nazi protection, Hartl renounced the priesthood and accepted an offer from Heydrich to join the SD. Within a month of transferring his loyalties the new recruit proved himself by collecting evidence against Nazi party members suspected of close connections with the Catholic Church, evidence which would be used, in some cases with deadly effect, during the Röhm Purges in the summer of 1934. The fledgling intelligence officer also applied his scholarly training to his new trade. At Himmler's direction Hartl began a study of the Inquisition in order to demean the Catholic Church by publicizing its alleged persecution of innocent victims. He also completed a study of the history and organization of the Jesuits for Himmler, who imagined that he could model his SS on that ascetic and disciplined religious order.[9]

When Hartl assumed its direction in 1935, the Church Referat was one of several desks in Amt II (domestic intelligence) of the *Sicherheitsdienst*. Since the small unit was responsible for monitoring all religious organizations and movements in Germany, its operations against the Catholic Church were relatively modest in scope. The ambitious new director set out to expand these operations and enhance his unit's (and his own) standing in the party security service. The field of church intelligence, however, was not unoccupied. The Gestapo, the state political police who at the time were administratively separate from the SD, already had its own church section which recruited low-level informants inside the German Catholic Church to collect evidence to justify confiscations of ecclesiastical property and support prosecutions against personalities and organizations at the infamous morality and currency trials. Hartl had little interest in such pedestrian investigations and was happy to leave what he considered petty police work to the Gestapo. He intended to work on an entirely different level. His unit would target the Catholic Church as a political threat to the party and the state and collect information about its anti-regime policies and subversive conspiracies. It would seek informants not among the sacristans, chaplains, and parish bookkeepers so attractive to the Gestapo's detectives, but among the bishops, diocesan administrators, and higher clergy who were the leaders and policy-makers of the German Catholic Church.[10]

Between 1935 and 1939 Albert Hartl relentlessly pursued his vision of a church intelligence unit. Every SD office in the Reich was assigned a special assistant for church affairs who had undergone a specific course of training at the SD school in Berlin. During the war such officers were also attached to police headquarters in the major occupied cities such as Paris, Brussels, Prague and Cracow. These officers were expected to read the local religious press, monitor church services and meetings, and cultivate a circle of contacts who were well placed to provide information about the higher levels of ecclesiastical affairs. To maintain the goodwill of such informants the officers were encouraged to be liberal in the distribution of fine food and wine and expensive gifts. At RSHA headquarters Hartl and his assistants processed the reports of the field officers and prepared regular reports on church affairs for distribution to the party chancellery and the propaganda, interior and foreign ministries. In response to specific inquiries from its 'customers', the Church Referat also prepared special reports on such topics as the financial assets of the Catholic Church, the influence of the Jesuits in Japan, and the Catholic press in western Europe. Whenever the Vatican appointed a new bishop or a university hired a scholar to fill a chair in Catholic theology, Hartl's office compiled a detailed biography of the individual.

By the outbreak of the war Amt II's Church Referat had developed extensive intelligence coverage of the German Catholic Church. Although useful information could be gleaned from the careful study of Catholic newspapers and journals, human sources provided the most important intelligence. One of Hartl's best sources was Josef Roth, the chief of the Catholic department in the Reich ministry for church affairs. A priest and former professor of theology in Munich, Roth had been an early convert to National Socialism and had advised Hitler on religious questions even before the Nazi leader came to power. Roth's official position brought him into close contact with leading Catholic personalities in Germany. He met regularly with bishops or their representatives to discuss the endless controversies over the application of the concordat of 1933 or to explain the regime's latest action against the church. He controlled the issuance of foreign exchange for individuals and groups travelling to Rome on ecclesiastical business, as well as for German theologians travelling abroad to conferences or seminars, and he made an effort to meet such travellers upon their return to discuss the results of their trips. From such contacts Roth received a stream of information concerning the affairs of the church at home and abroad. Hartl considered Roth such an important source that he ran him personally, meeting the department chief from the church ministry daily, often for a leisurely lunch in one of Berlin's more select restaurants.

In his efforts to penetrate the German church, Hartl actively recruited informants from among the Catholic clergy. His effort was enhanced by the presence on his staff of several renegade or apostate priests and monks who maintained contacts in ecclesiastical circles and who were aware of foibles or weaknesses that might make a particular priest a likely target for recruitment. Religious orders, especially the Benedictines, seem to have been a fertile field for Hartl's spotters. Karl Schaefer, a former monk who eventually became an SS general, maintained close connections with abbeys in western Germany and passed on information from these sources.

Peter Beham was a Benedictine monk who had administered the financial affairs of his order's monasteries in Bavaria before leaving his monastic community in 1937. He subsequently joined the SD where he specialized in intelligence on church finances. Another Benedictine, Hermann Keller, worked in ecclesiastical circles in France, Italy and Switzerland for the security service. In 1940 he uncovered the so-called 'Roman Conversations' in which elements of the German resistance used the Vatican as a channel of communication to the British, and later in the war he would be an important source for the SD office in Paris. In discussing the contributions of Schaefer, Beham and Keller with Allied interrogators after the war, Hartl would also claim that the abbots of several monasteries in Germany cooperated with their local SD offices.[11] It is unlikely, however, that most monastic sources (whose value as informants was, after all, seriously limited by their residence in monasteries) were in a position to report information of anything other than local interest. Potentially more significant were informants among the diocesan clergy who interacted more freely with civilian society and who were directly involved in the administration of the German church. Hartl boasted that he had 20–30 clerical sources in each German diocese, but most of these contacts were probably parish priests or chaplains to convents and hospitals who could report little beyond rumours and common gossip. As late as the end of 1941, after several years of building intelligence networks inside the Catholic Church, Berlin was still urging its regional offices in Germany to expand and improve their range of contacts. Headquarters was especially critical of the reliance on common priests who had no access to important ecclesiastical secrets, and it ordered its outstations to penetrate the offices of the bishops and the secretariat of the national bishops' conference.[12]

Despite Berlin's dissatisfaction, some well-placed sources had already been recruited. After the war Hartl would claim that by placing agents inside various diocesan offices he was able to secure copies of the confidential correspondence between the bishops and Rome, as well as informed reports on the political attitudes of the German bishops. Furthermore, since 1938 the security service had been able to obtain the confidential proceedings of the German bishops' conference held each year in Fulda. At these important meetings the bishops discussed the state of the German church, debated strategies to counterattacks by the regime, reviewed finances, and discussed directives from the Vatican. Access to the minutes of these meetings gave German domestic intelligence an authoritative insight into the administration of the German church and the Vatican's plans for that church.[13] From the available evidence it is impossible to identify the source who provided the security service with copies of the bishops' confidential minutes. Within the conference secretariat and the various diocesan administrations a number of private secretaries, advisers and printers would have had access to such material and one of these functionaries might have passed documents to his local SD office. Of course the penetration of the hierarchy may have reached much higher. The bishops, as a matter of course, would have sent the minutes of their annual Fulda conferences to the papal nunciature in Berlin where the SD had recruited an informant from among the nuncio's small staff. In addition to this unnamed informant, Hartl also had access to the nunciature through his friend Peter Werhun, the 'apostolic administrator' for Ukrainian Catholics. Father Werhun lived in Berlin where he was a confidant of the nuncio, Archbishop Cesare Orsenigo, and an adviser to the nunciature on Russian affairs.[14] It is also possible that the minutes of the Fulda conferences were leaked by one of the bishops. After the war both Hartl and Alfred Schimmel, the Gestapo's church specialist in Munich, reported that an auxiliary bishop in a Bavarian diocese had been blackmailed into cooperating with the security service. The accusations against this individual were eventually rejected by a post-war denazification court, but the possibility that a bishop may have been suborned cannot be entirely discounted.

Hartl also recruited informants from the Catholic faculties of German and Austrian universities. He was quite proud of his professorial sources, but these historians and theologians usually had little access to the ecclesiastical secrets most avidly sought by the SD. Mainly they contributed academic analyses of various problems in church–state relations and passed on the current gossip on the university circuit. At Charles University in Prague, for example, Professor Eduard Winter, an apostate priest who had been active in the Sudeten nationalist movement, supplied the SD with translations of church-related articles from various Slavonic-language publications. Sebastian Merkle, a professor of history at Würzburg who was decorated for his services to the Reich, was a keen student of papal diplomatic history and provided insights into Vatican policies on the basis of his studies and his contacts with other scholars. A former Catholic theologian at the University of Frankfurt, Dr Heinrich Nelis, contributed information gleaned from his extensive contacts in church circles in Germany, Belgium and Holland. Before the war he often attended ecclesiastical conferences in western Europe on behalf of the SD. A theologian at the University of Breslau carried out research for the security service and collected ecclesiastical intelligence from the academic circuit, as did a theologian at Vienna University, while a third professor, a theologian on the faculty of Freiburg, provided information on the activities of the local archbishop.[15] Professor Josef Mayer, a priest from the theological faculty at Paderborn, proved useful when Hartl was ordered by his superiors to secure a theological brief on the morality of euthanasia as the regime prepared to implement such a programme among so-called mental defectives. The amenable priest prepared for the SD a long, pseudo-scholarly report which purported to prove that in the past the Catholic Church had systematically done away with the insane through such practices as witch-burnings and starvation in prison cells, and that current theological thinking did not entirely rule out the application of euthanasia. Hartl was pleased with this analysis which provided a moral fig leaf for the intended crimes against humanity and 'cleared up the matter theoretically'.[16] As a reward for his services to the SD, Dr Mayer was sent to Rome in the summer of 1943 ostensibly to research the life of the Renaissance humanist Juan Luis Vives, but primarily to survey Vatican affairs for German intelligence in the politically uncertain weeks following Mussolini's fall from power. After his later disgrace, Hartl would boast that while in the Eternal City Mayer learned from his Vatican sources that Marshal Pietro Badoglio had agreed, as part of a secret arrangement to proclaim an armistice and take Italy out of the war, to allow American paratroopers to seize several airfields around Rome as a preliminary to clearing the city of all German forces. Radioed to Berlin by the Reich embassy in Rome, this information supposedly allowed the German high command to occupy the airfields and foil the plan.[17] Whatever the merits of his other services to the SD, Mayer's alleged intelligence coup in Rome does not withstand scrutiny. According to Hartl, the Vatican had learned of the arrangements for an air-drop from a theologian who had been present at the secret planning sessions. This is highly improbable. Furthermore, by all accounts the German embassy was completely surprised by the announcement of the Italian armistice on 8 September and, thus, could not have radioed advance word of the air-drops to Berlin. The Allied operation was cancelled because of Italian prevarication and timidity, not because the German military command had been alerted to the landings. German troops had not pre-emptively occupied the airfields; indeed, on 8 September General Maxwell Taylor, an Allied envoy who had secretly entered Rome, returned to his headquarters by flying from one of the airfields supposedly occupied by the forewarned Germans.

Between 1935 and 1939 Hartl established himself as the SD's pre-eminent specialist on church affairs, and under his direction the intelligence networks of Amt II's Church Referat reached into the highest levels of the German Catholic Church. In his spare time he managed to supplement his police pay and achieve a certain literary notoriety by writing (under the pen name 'Anton Holzner') a series of virulently anti-Catholic books. His status changed, however, with the outbreak of war. In September 1939 Hitler approved the amalgamation of the *Sicherheitsdienst* with the Gestapo and the criminal police to form a new organization, the Reich Security Administration under Reinhard Heydrich. As a result of this reorganization, Hartl's Church Referat was at first placed in the new organization's Amt VII (ideological affairs), but within a year was reshuffled into Amt IV (Gestapo). As we have seen, the Gestapo had its own Church Referat under one Erich Roth, and the transfer of Hartl's group immediately raised questions of jurisdiction and authority. Integration was not an alternative since Heydrich had decreed that the two units should remain separate and that their chiefs should report independently to Amt IV's chief, Heinrich Müller.[18] In practice the two units arranged an informal division of labour. Roth's group focused on 'executive functions', such as the investigation of political crimes allegedly committed by church personalities and organizations, while Hartl's personnel collected more general intelligence on church activities and policies.

At first the two units collaborated effectively. A conference of all Gestapo church specialists which convened at the service's headquarters on the Prinz-Albrechtstrasse in late September 1941 ('Uniform: Brown shirt and trousers worn with jackboots') probably marked the high-point of cooperation. Called to review intelligence and police operations against the churches and consider new tactics for the attack against religious organizations, the conference had a lengthy agenda which included such items as 'Intelligence tasks in the conflict with Political Catholicism in the Reich', 'Vatican world politics and our intelligence tasks', and 'Security Police measures for combating the political churches'.[19] Gestapo chief Heinrich Müller opened the meeting with a keynote address which reiterated the threat posed to the National Socialist regime by the churches ('these extremely dangerous opponents'). He emphasized that with the onset of war the church issue had to be approached not only as a police problem but also as an intelligence problem. 'The political churches perform the same role', Müller argued, 'as the Spartacists and Marxists in 1918. For this attitude the political churches must be made to pay. Therefore we must apply all the means at our disposal to gather material and in this way checkmate the political church enemy.' Albert Hartl followed his chief to the conference podium to review the recent attitude of all 'political churches', but especially the Catholic Church, towards Nazism. For Hartl this attitude was reflected in Pope Pius XI's encyclical, *Mit brennender Sorge* (1937), which 'summoned the whole world to fight against the Third Reich'. In the past the regime had responded to such provocations with an uncompromising attitude and severe police reprisals, but the time for such measures had passed. The threat now required an intensification of intelligence operations against the Catholic Church and all other 'political churches'. Hartl concluded:

> Our ultimate goal is the extirpation of all Christianity. But this goal can only be realized step by step. Our immediate task is to maintain absolutely the ground already gained on the church front and to carry out defensive measures against the stubborn assaults of the clergy and others, pending the time of the new great offensive. This calls necessarily for the intensification of intelligence activity in the investigation and surveillance of Catholicism and the other political churches. It is therefore necessary to regularly collect material on the tactics and methods of the church, as enemies of the state, in order to be

able to lay this probative background (originals, photocopies and so forth) before the Führer at the opportune time.

The next speaker was *SS-Sturmbannführer* Erich Roth, Hartl's colleague in church affairs in Amt IV, who reviewed current police measures against the churches. Under secret orders recently circulated by the Party Chancery, the Gestapo was to curtail arrests, confiscations, and other punitive actions in favour of gathering compromising evidence against ecclesiastical personalities and organizations. Roth frankly stated the ultimate goal: 'the destruction of the churches to be brought about by the collection of material obtained through intelligence activities, which will, at a given time, be produced as evidence for the charge of treasonable activities during the German fight for existence'. Following Roth, several speakers elaborated on the intelligence tasks in the conflict with the Catholic Church. *SS-Untersturmführer* Emil Jacobs reminded his audience that every church organization, no matter how innocuous, was always at the service of the Vatican, which was actively hostile to Germany. According to Jacobs,

> Our task in this sphere is to uncover the means by which the individual dioceses send their messages to Rome, to uncover differences of opinion among the bishops, with each other, with the Pope, with the nunciature and so forth, in order to evaluate them properly.

Next *SS-Obersturmführer* Heinz Kunze described the clever machinations by which the Catholic Church sought to circumvent the Nazis' anti-clerical measures and avoid police surveillance. He also detailed the particular threat posed to the regime by the intelligence service of the Vatican. On this subject the *Obersturmführer* gave vent to the obsessive fantasies which passed for received wisdom inside the RSHA in the matter of the Vatican. He believed, as did most of the leadership of his service, that the Catholic Church was in its very nature a huge intelligence organization of world-wide scope. For Kunze, 'Every Catholic is practically speaking an instrument of this intelligence operation.' The smallest item of information passed from the devout lay person to his pastor, from the pastor to the local dean, from the dean to the bishop, and from the bishop to Rome. The religious orders, especially the Jesuits, played an important role in this traffic in information by secretly collecting and evaluating anti-Nazi material on behalf of the Vatican. According to Kunze, the Pope was personally involved in this intelligence work:

> The Pope himself has other intelligence possibilities. He has at his direct disposal agents committed to the Vatican who are, in some cases, officials of various states who are at the same time in the secret service of the Vatican.

Kunze also attached sinister significance to the work of the international Catholic press agencies, especially those working from the Netherlands, whose reports on political and religious repression inside the Reich, he admitted, were mostly accurate. Military information harmful to Germany had also turned up in police searches of these agencies in occupied Belgium and Holland in 1940. Even if such organizations had been dissolved and their directors arrested, the anti-German work continued elsewhere. The speaker concluded that the espionage threat from the Vatican and from Catholic organizations in Germany and the occupied territories required a stronger effort by the security and intelligence services.

The myth that the Vatican controlled a vast intelligence organization was, at the time, commonly accepted by even the most experienced observers of world affairs, but it appeared in an especially exaggerated form in the leadership of the RSHA where it was an article of faith that the Pope's minions were everywhere and that no secret was secure from them.[20] Albert Hartl, for instance, was certain that bishops, priests, monks and nuns systematically collected information on behalf of the Vatican, as did a small army of Catholic aristocrats, professors, politicians and industrialists who placed allegiance to the Pope above loyalty to their country. He credited Vatican intelligence with an astonishing list of achievements on behalf of the papacy including the resumption of secret relations with the Soviet Union through the efforts of one of the Pope's best agents, Wilhelm von Braun; the clandestine infiltration of Jesuits into the Russian Orthodox Church; the establishment of contacts with the Tibetan Dalai Lama; and the cultivation of close contacts with Japanese industrialists, the Bank of Japan and the Japanese Admiralty.[21] In fact these breathtaking accomplishments were entirely fanciful. While it is true that Wilhelm von Braun (a wealthy convert and sometime seminarian who had spent the Great War in a Russian prison camp and who would die in a German concentration camp in 1941) was a middleman in the tentative and short-lived contacts between the Vatican and the Bolshevik regime in 1921, he was actually an agent of the Russians rather than the papacy.[22] The Jesuits did not infiltrate any priests into the Russian Orthodox Church, nor did secret papal agents brave the Himalayas to establish relations with the Dalai Lama. As for Japan, the Vatican was always poorly informed about affairs in that empire, especially during the war when the papal delegate in Tokyo was isolated and seriously constrained in his ability to communicate with Rome.

Equally illusory was the vast and industrious network of lay and clerical informants who diligently kept the Pope informed of the smallest item of news. For political information the Vatican depended almost exclusively on its nuncios and the diplomatic corps accredited to the Holy See. Aside from purely ecclesiastical information it received little news from the clergy and faithful of the world. To be sure, church law required all bishops to inform the Vatican of conditions in their dioceses. Every five years each bishop had to visit Rome and personally submit a report on his diocese. These reports, however, focused on specifically religious matters, such as the number of Catholic schools or the state of religious observance, while generally ignoring political and economic subjects. Conceived to provide the Vatican with a comprehensive view of the church, these procedures collapsed under the dislocations of a world war at the very time that they were most needed. As for the vaunted network of loyal and compliant clergy and faithful, it was a chimera. Occasionally the Secretariat of State would receive an item of information from a concerned Catholic, but such cases were uncommon. While accepting the authority of the Pope in matters of faith and morals, Catholics had little or no sense of political allegiance to the Vatican. They thought of themselves as *German* Catholics or *Spanish* Catholics with the emphasis as much on the national as on the religious identity. Most saw little conflict between the interests of their country and the interests of their religion, and most were no more inclined to pass information to Rome than they were to pass information to another state. Indeed, it probably would not have occurred to them to report anything to the Vatican. For their part papal officials (for whom, after all, the church was an instrument for the salvation of souls rather than an intelligence organization) never systematically sought to use the faithful for intelligence purposes. Even had they so wished, there was no way for the hopelessly understaffed and overburdened papal administration (which lacked the resources to establish even a rudimentary diplomatic courier system) to mobilize and coordinate the efforts of millions of potential agents. During the war, the Holy See made modest efforts to improve its access to information; Vatican Radio, for example, began to monitor and transcribe foreign news broadcasts and circulated the texts to the Pope and the Cardinal Secretary of State. Despite such efforts, experienced observers, like the French ambassador to the Holy See, Count Wladimir d'Ormesson, and his British counterpart, Francis d'Arcy Osborne, were shocked at how poorly informed the Vatican actually was about international affairs. At one point during the war Osborne was surprised to discover that for their news of world events the Pope and his Secretariat of State depended primarily on the daily summaries of BBC broadcasts provided by the British legation.[23]

Despite the appearance of amity and cooperation among the church specialists, Hartl's position had been considerably compromised by his transfer to Amt IV. His once patronizing attitude toward the Gestapo and its work had not gone unnoticed by the secret police officers who were now his colleagues. He also found himself constantly at odds with his new chief, Heinrich Müller, who ridiculed his deputy's propensity for long analytical studies of church policy and organization. Once the Gestapo chief bluntly told Hartl, 'That is very fine what you write, but they are pure doctoral studies. What can I do with that? It serves no purpose because I cannot arrest or hold anyone with this.'[24] Müller's hostility towards his deputy represented more than differences over methods; he also suspected the former priest of being a secret Jesuit and a double-agent for the Vatican. For his part Hartl did little to endear himself to his associates who were irritated by his boastfulness and scandalized by his constant sexual indiscretions with the female personnel of the RSHA. He was working on a programme to collect documentary material from sequestered ecclesiastical archives in Poland, Holland and Yugoslavia for a 'Black Book' on the allegedly subversive conduct of the Catholic bishops and the anti-German attitude of the Vatican when the axe fell. A clumsy attempt to seduce the wife of a senior SS officer on the

Berlin–Vienna express in December 1941 proved his undoing. Müller gleefully recommended his demotion to the ranks and assignment to an extermination squad in the east, but Heydrich decided merely to transfer him to the police command in Kiev with the task of reporting on civilian morale in the Ukraine.[25] In 1943 Walter Schellenberg, the director of Amt VI (foreign intelligence) in the RSHA, would recall Hartl from Russia to serve as a roving informant on church matters, but the man who had effectively created the regime's church intelligence capability would never again hold an important position in German intelligence.

Even if he had avoided disgrace, Hartl's domination of the church intelligence apparatus would have been challenged as Germany's requirements in that area changed. Throughout the 1930s the 'church problem' had been defined primarily as one of internal security. Thus when the Nazi party first created a church intelligence unit it had placed it in the domestic intelligence section (Amt II) of the *Sicherheitsdienst*. The Catholic Church in particular was seen as a threat to the Nazi regime, and the principal task of the church specialists in the SD had been the infiltration of the ecclesiastical and lay institutions of the German Church in search of information concerning political opposition and subversion. Typically, before the war, when Hartl convened conferences of church specialists to review operations and set intelligence priorities, the discussion of the Catholic target emphasized the need to collect more information on diocesan finances, religious orders (especially the Jesuits), and the surviving Catholic lay organizations in Germany. There was little interest in the church as a foreign intelligence problem.[26] Of course there had always been an implicit external component to the alleged threat from the church in so far as the Nazi leadership believed that German Catholics responded to direction from the Vatican. Reinhard Heydrich in particular was convinced that the Vatican was the arch-enemy of National Socialism, a conviction which was only reinforced when, on Palm Sunday 1937, German bishops read from their cathedral pulpits a new papal encyclical, *Mit brennender Sorge*, in which Pius XI criticized Germany's persistent violations of the concordat of 1933, and explicitly condemned the worship of race and state. In response to such provocations the SD occasionally made gestures during the 1930s towards extending its coverage to include the Vatican, usually by instituting operations to uncover the clandestine communication channels which connected the Vatican with the German bishops, but throughout the decade the principal focus remained the Catholic Church inside Germany.

The conclave to elect a successor to Pius XI, who died on 10 February 1939, was a rare occasion when the pre-war *Sicherheitsdienst* reached beyond the borders of Germany to spy on the Catholic Church. As the cardinals gathered in Rome from around the world to elect a new Pope the European chancelleries hummed with activity as the various governments sought to anticipate the outcome of the election and not a few worked discreetly to influence it. By the time of his death, Pius had become a resolute opponent of the Nazi regime, and as Europe staggered from crisis to crisis in the last year of peace the question of which cardinal would replace the old Pontiff mattered greatly to Britain, France, Germany, Italy and Poland. On the very day of the Pope's death the French Foreign Minister approached the British ambassador in Paris with the suggestion that London and Paris cooperate to secure the election of Cardinal Eugenio Pacelli, the late Pope's Secretary of State, whom the British and French assumed would continue the policy of firmness towards Germany. Oddly, Pacelli was also the favourite candidate of the experienced German ambassador to the Holy See, Diego von Bergen, who believed that the former nuncio to Germany, a known Germanophile who surrounded himself with German advisers and housekeepers, would seek a reconciliation between the Vatican and the Reich.[27]

With so much riding on the outcome of this papal election it was particularly important to assess the sentiments and inclinations of the cardinal electors as a preliminary to canvassing for (or against) a particular candidate. Normally this task would be left to the Reich embassy to the Holy See which would identify the leading candidates and evaluate their support within the College of Cardinals, but in this election the *Sicherheitsdienst* seized an opportunity to play an independent intelligence role. Upon the death of Pius XI, a sometime informant for the SD, Taras Borodajkewycz, volunteered to go to Rome to observe the conclave for his controllers. Vienna-born of Ukrainian parents, Borodajkewycz had briefly studied theology and claimed close connections in ecclesiastical circles. The SD accepted this offer with alacrity and dispatched Borodajkewycz to Rome with a generous expense account. The erstwhile theologian's precious connections apparently failed him for his reports to Berlin proved completely unreliable. His prediction that Cardinal Idlefonso Schuster, the Archbishop of Milan, would be chosen to succeed Pius XI was hopelessly wide of the mark. Indeed, the imprudent archbishop, who had often embarrassed the Vatican and his colleagues by his public support for Mussolini, was the one cardinal who had no chance of election.[28]

While Borodajkewycz did no more than misinform the SD, a second source nearly fleeced them of a small fortune. Shortly after the death of Pius XI, Albert Hartl learned from a contact, who claimed to report from inside the Vatican, that in return for a secret payment of three million gold marks a majority of the cardinals could be persuaded to support a candidate favourable to Germany: either Cardinal Maurilio Fossati of Turin or Cardinal Elia Dalla Costa of Florence. Hartl reported this offer to Heinrich Himmler who immediately carried the information to Hitler. The Führer solicited the advice of Hartl and Josef Roth, the director for Catholic affairs in the Reich Ministry for the Churches. Although Roth believed that Berlin should pay the bribe, Hitler accepted the recommendation of the unusually cautious SD specialist who took the proposal seriously but argued that Germany should not risk such a blatant interference in a papal election.[29]

It was just as well the offer was refused for the approach was almost certainly a ploy by a confidence trickster to extort a fortune from the German government. On its face the proposal was absurd, and it is a sign of how poorly the Nazi regime understood the papacy that the proposal went as far (and as high) as it did. The days when a papal election could be purchased were long past. Though differing in intelligence, piety and sophistication, the 62 members of the College of Cardinals were conscientious trustees of the Church, sensitive to their responsibilities before history and before their God. If one or two weak individuals might have succumbed to the temptation of gold, it is impossible to imagine that 42 cardinals (the two-thirds majority then necessary to elect a Pope) would have collaborated in the subversion of the conclave. Furthermore, if so many prelates had been prepared to sell their votes, the various embassies accredited to the Vatican would surely have heard at least whispers of the fact; after all, anyone seeking a bribe must make his interest and availability known, no matter how discreetly. The diplomatic dispatches from Rome (including those of the German embassy) contain not a hint that the election might be purchased. When British and French diplomats considered ways to influence the outcome, bribery was not even mentioned as an option, less because of moral scruples than because of that method's sheer implausibility. Finally, the two supposedly amenable cardinals offered by the intermediary to Germany in return for the secret payment would have raised eyebrows in intelligence offices better informed than those of the gullible SD. In the past neither had exhibited any particular sympathy for Germany or the Nazi cause. Though respected by his peers, Cardinal Fossati of Turin was never a serious candidate for the Throne of St Peter, and his attitude towards totalitarian regimes was, if anything, distinctly cool. The fascist prefect in Turin took it for granted that Mussolini's government would oppose any effort to elect Fossati, and complained to Rome that, at a requiem mass for Pius XI, the cardinal had preached in favour of such annoyances as the peace of Christ, the independent rights of the family over the state, and the importance of a free Catholic Action movement. Later, after Germany's invasion of Poland, Fossati would express pro-Allied sentiments and in a public statement understood by all to refer to Hitler blame the war on the 'arrogance and pride of one man'.[30] The Florentine cardinal, Dalla Costa, was more of an enigma. Ascetic, pious, and a man of prayer, Dalla Costa maintained a cold and austere demeanour which endeared him to few. His political sympathies were a mystery even to professional observers. As Archbishop of Florence he maintained good relations with the fascist authorities, but the French ambassador at the Vatican, who did not consider him a desirable candidate, reported that his rectitude and rigidity might well make him 'a more bitter adversary to governments with a totalitarian morality than a politique [sic] Pope with liberal and democratic ideas'.[31] His reputation for holiness and erudition made him an attractive candidate to those (like some in Italy and Germany) who hoped for a non-political Pope after the politically embattled Pius XI, and he would receive several votes on the first ballot in the conclave which would eventually elect Cardinal Pacelli.

After the outbreak of war in September 1939 the SD's coverage of the Vatican remained minimal, consisting of little more than brief reports of the comings and goings of political and ecclesiastical personalities. For Reinhard Heydrich and the church specialists in the RSHA the Catholic Church remained primarily an internal threat to the security of the Nazi regime and the unity of the German people, and during the early months of the war the intelligence effort against this threat continued to emphasize penetration of the administrative, financial and communication structures of the German Church. Gradually, however, the Vatican began to loom larger in intelligence planning. A directive from Heydrich in April 1940 identifying current intelligence priorities exemplified the shifting focus. The intelligence chief ordered his church specialists to focus on the following:

- Indications that the German bishops were using the diplomatic pouch of the Berlin nunciature to communicate with the Vatican.

- Identification of the secret couriers and courier routes used by the German bishops and introduction of trusted agents into these communication channels.

- Exploitation for intelligence purposes of tensions between the German bishops and the papal nuncio, among the bishops themselves, and between the bishops and the lower clergy, as well as the exploitation of all personal weaknesses of individual bishops.

- Interception of the bishops' quinquennial reports to the Vatican.

- Identification of prospective candidates for the German episcopacy.

- Recruitment of reliable agents in every diocesan chancery with particular attention to the penetration of diocesan archives.[32]

Supplementary directives in the following months would expand the list of intelligence priorities to include the identification of German priests and members of religious orders employed at the Vatican, and the surveillance of German theological students destined for studies in papal institutes in Rome. Heydrich was especially keen about the latter subject because he planned to plant agents in one or more of the papal institutes in the guise of students.[33]

The increasing interest in the Vatican was part of a more general reorientation in the intelligence priorities of the RSHA. During the

1930s, Heydrich had been too preoccupied with consolidating his control over the police and security apparatus to devote much attention to foreign intelligence, but with the onset of war the importance of foreign intelligence rose dramatically and the ambitious security chief realized that power would accrue to whomever controlled the flow of such material. Unfortunately, in September 1939 the SD had neither the organizational capacity nor the administrative authority to move decisively into the field of foreign intelligence. The SD had a small foreign (*Ausland*) section under Heinz Jost, but it sent no officers abroad and limited its activity to running a handful of low-level informants from SD stations along Germany's frontiers. After the invasion of Poland, the *Ausland* section became Amt VI (foreign intelligence) in the new RSHA and it began to expand its operations, a process that accelerated in June 1941 with the replacement of the lacklustre Jost by Walter Schellenberg, an ambitious and energetic young officer (at 31 he was the youngest department chief in the RSHA) who, as a university student in Bonn, had attracted the attention of SS talent spotters with his anti-clerical lectures to local audiences.[34] Parallel with his efforts to improve his organizational apparatus, Heydrich sought to establish his bureaucratic rights in the area of foreign intelligence collection. He was especially eager to establish secure operational bases abroad by placing his intelligence officers on the diplomatic staffs of the various German embassies and legations. This plan encountered resistance from the foreign ministry which rightly suspected the RSHA of seeking to intrude into the area of foreign political intelligence, a realm traditionally the preserve of the professional diplomats. Heydrich was not deterred by this resistance from an institution for which he had little love and less respect. His animus against the Wilhelmstrasse dated back to 1933 and the Second International Disarmament Conference at Geneva when he served briefly on the German delegation as a police and security expert. Snubbed by the career diplomats on the delegation and repulsed by the 'shabby compromises' of international diplomacy, he developed an abiding contempt for the Wilhelmstrasse and its personnel.[35] Not surprisingly, he also had little faith in the foreign ministry's ability to satisfy Germany's wartime requirements for foreign intelligence. In October 1939, after much bureaucratic manoeuvring, Heydrich secured Ribbentrop's reluctant agreement to assign RSHA officers to certain German diplomatic missions as 'police attachés'. Ostensibly these officers, most of whom were drawn from the Gestapo, were to act as liaison officers to the police services of the host country and to cooperate with those services in criminal matters of mutual interest. Their clandestine mission, however, was to recruit informants for intelligence purposes. They reported directly to RSHA headquarters in Berlin without reference to their nominal superior, the local German ambassador, although intelligence relating to diplomatic matters would be passed by the RSHA to the foreign ministry for evaluation and approval. Later, after SD agents bungled an attempt to overthrow the government of Rumania, Ribbentrop secured for his ambassadors the right to review all police attaché reports before their transmission to Berlin. In practice Heydrich's officers often ignored this requirement and continued to bypass the ambassadors, a practice facilitated by the fact that many of the attachés had separate radio links with Berlin and were not dependent upon embassy communication channels.[36]

Although the Pope had a small police force for patrol and traffic control inside Vatican City, even Heydrich realized that it would be impossible to post a police attaché to the Reich embassy to the Holy See. Nevertheless, the security chief wanted an intelligence officer assigned to the embassy which had proven particularly insensitive to the needs of the RSHA. The ambassador, Diego von Bergen, had useful contacts inside the Curia, but he refused to approach these contacts on behalf of the RSHA. Heydrich also had difficulty securing access to Bergen's reports to the foreign ministry. Heydrich eventually concluded that the ambassador lacked the energy and political commitment to pursue effective intelligence coverage of the Vatican.[37] In January 1941 he wrote to Ribbentrop:

> I have the intention of discussing with Minister Luther [Martin Luther, under-secretary and director of the ministry's 'Deutschland' section] a very necessary intelligence apparatus against the Vatican. I ask therefore that you give directions for the eventual assignment (under some guise or another) of an experienced man at the Vatican embassy and also for a certain change of personnel having relations with Vatican elements.[38]

The foreign minister undoubtedly considered this rather arrogant proposal an unwarranted intrusion into the affairs of his department, and nothing was done. Indeed, the Wilhelmstrasse resisted any effort by the RSHA to expand its intelligence operations to include the Vatican. Within a month of Heydrich's impertinent letter, Amt IV (Gestapo) asked the foreign ministry for a diplomatic passport for Albert Hartl, its specialist on Catholic affairs. The Gestapo was sending Hartl on a temporary mission to Rome to discuss with the police attaché at the embassy to Italy possible intelligence operations against the Vatican. The ministry politely declined to issue the passport 'because Foreign Minister Ribbentrop has reserved to himself all matters concerning the Vatican'.[39]

After these setbacks Heydrich changed his tactics. If he could not yet place a man inside the Vatican embassy, he would prepare the ground for a later attempt while gaining access to Bergen's reports by placing a man inside the Wilhelmstrasse. In early 1942 the RSHA leader convinced the foreign ministry that the competent head of its Vatican desk, Richard Haidlen, be replaced with an officer more amenable to the security service. In February 1942, the under-secretary at the ministry noted:

> The party chancellery and Bormann himself, as well as the SD are understandably very interested in the activity of this desk, and Obergruppenführer Heydrich has also shown a special personal interest in the matter. For this reason I have for a long time regarded it very urgent to remove Herr Haidlen and to replace him with a suitable person who understands and safeguards foreign policy interests but who at the same time has some understanding of the wishes of the party and the interests of the SD.[40]

The new Vatican desk officer was Werner Picot who had served briefly at the embassy to the Holy See. More recently, he had been assigned to the ministry's 'Deutschland' division where he had worked on the desk responsible for liaison with the security and intelligence services. Picot was clearly Heydrich's man. Upon taking up his new duties in the spring of 1942 he wrote to his friend, Herbert Kappler, in Rome to assure the police attaché that he would do all he could to realize Heydrich's wishes in regard to intelligence coverage of the Vatican. To underline his commitment to this task, he added, 'On the wishes of Obergruppenführer Heydrich, I will speak with Schellenberg [Amt VI chief] in the next few days about everything that concerns further collaboration in this area.'[41] Subsequently, Picot made several trips to

Rome where he busied himself with meetings at the embassy to the Holy See and formal calls at the Vatican. His real business, however, is apparent from his notes on a visit in November 1942: 'I concerned myself with intelligence matters relating to the Vatican.'[42]

In the absence of an RSHA officer inside the Vatican embassy, the principal burden of establishing intelligence coverage of the Vatican fell upon the police attaché at the embassy to Italy. A fanatical Nazi who proudly wore a steel ring decorated with the Death's Head and swastikas and inscribed 'To Herbert from his Himmler', *SS-Obersturmbannführer* Herbert Kappler held that post and that of Gestapo representative in Rome from 1939 until the German evacuation of the city in 1944. An electrician by training, Kappler joined the SS in 1932 and entered the police service of Württemberg the following year. In 1937 he became the first non-Prussian to graduate from the *Sicherheitspolizei* leadership school. Kappler quickly demonstrated a talent for secret police activity. His work against the remaining vestiges of liberal sentiment in post-*Anschluss* Austria caught the attention of his superiors in Berlin, and he was chosen to be in the first group of police attachés posted to German diplomatic missions. He was temporarily recalled to Berlin to participate in the interrogation of Major Richard Stevens and Captain Sigismund Payne Best, British intelligence officers who had been lured into a German trap on the Dutch frontier in the famous 'Venlo Incident' in November 1939. Kappler's nominal chief in Rome, Ambassador Hans Georg von Mackensen, a dignified, if unimaginative, diplomat of the old school, preferred to keep his new attaché and his distasteful activities at a distance, so Kappler set up shop not in the embassy but in a new building, originally intended for the embassy's cultural section, at 20 Via Tasso, an address that would become notorious among Romans as a synonym for police terror.[43]

As police attaché, Kappler advised the ambassador on security affairs, liaised with the Italian police on criminal matters of joint interest, exchanged information with Arturo Bocchini, the director of the fascist political police, and maintained surveillance of German emigrés resident in Rome. Many of these emigrés were ecclesiastics, some of whom had responsible positions inside Vatican City, such as Father Robert Leiber, the confidential assistant to the Pope, and Monsignor Ludwig Kaas, the former leader of the Catholic Centre Party in Germany then living in honourable exile as the administrator of St Peter's Basilica. Out of loyalty to his fellow dictator, Benito Mussolini, Hitler had forbidden espionage against Italy, but this prohibition did not extend to the papacy, so Kappler ran a handful of informants who helped him keep an eye on German ecclesiastics in the Eternal City and monitor events at the Vatican. Although the police attaché would eventually recruit a significant agent inside the Vatican (Chapter 4), his sources were in general low-level informants of modest position and access.

He inherited his first agent, a misguided young man who had volunteered his services to Germany in 1938 after reading Hitler's political testament, *Mein Kampf*, and learning there the 'truth' about the nefarious political influence of the churches. At the time of his offer this individual was an assistant to a German professor at the Gregorian, the Jesuit university in Rome, but he had previously worked as a secretary for Father Friedrich Muckermann, a German Jesuit and Catholic polemicist who was an active and articulate opponent of the Nazis. Muckermann had eluded the Gestapo in 1934 by escaping to Holland. Subsequently, he continued his attacks against Hitler and his regime from refuges in Italy, Austria (until the *Anschluss*), and Switzerland. The former secretary provided the German police with information about his former employer and his circle of anti-Nazi intellectuals and ecclesiastics.[44] Of course this material was entirely retrospective in nature since by 1938 the informant was no longer in Father Muckermann's employment. By the time Kappler took him on in 1939 his utility was reduced to passing on common-room gossip from the university and surreptitiously opening letters entrusted to him for mailing by professors. Since the Jesuits were well aware of the vigilance of Italian postal censors, it is unlikely that the mail of the Gregorian faculty provided much in the way of intelligence.[45] Another informant was the vice-rector of the Teutonicum, a residence for German ecclesiastics which was actually located just inside Vatican City. This priest had become a harsh critic of papal affairs and an apologist for the Nazis. He was relatively well placed to report to Kappler on the residents in his institution and to observe the comings and goings at the Vatican, but in 1940 he was recalled to Germany by his archbishop, Cardinal Michael von Faulhaber of Munich, at the instigation of Monsignor Kaas who was concerned about the rector's pro-Nazi sentiments.[46] A third informant was a German national,

Frau Kuehn-Stein Hausen, a researcher who occasionally worked at the Vatican Archives and passed on items of gossip picked up across the reading desks or in the cloakroom.[47] This source would have lost even her limited usefulness when, after the German occupation of Rome in September 1943, the Vatican closed its archive and library until the liberation of the city by the Allies. Kappler probably supplemented these meagre sources with information on the Vatican secured through his liaison arrangements with the Italian police who kept the Vatican under a close and effective surveillance which included taps on the phone lines running in and out of Vatican City.

Kappler's effort against the Vatican received a boost in early 1942 when Amt VI, the foreign intelligence division of the RSHA and the successor to SD *Ausland*, assigned one of its officers, Helmut Loos, to serve as a special assistant to the police attaché. Kappler was by training and temperament a policeman, and his various responsibilities allowed him little time for espionage activities. Loos was specifically responsible for organizing intelligence coverage of the Vatican. He came to Rome from Amt VI's Vatican desk where he had attracted the attention of his superiors by directing what seemed to be the RSHA's best penetration of the Vatican. In 1940 he recruited Alfred von Kageneck, the Catholic scion of minor German nobility, to go to Rome on behalf of German intelligence. In May Kageneck visited Rome and had several conversations with Father Leiber, the Pope's confidential assistant and a friend of the Kageneck family. Loos's agent returned from Rome with information about Pope Pius's attitude towards Germany and the relative influence in Rome of the various German cardinals and bishops. During another visit in August, Kageneck gathered information from Leiber on the Vatican's reaction to Ribbentrop's recent visit to the Italian capital and the chances of a *détente* in German–Vatican relations. A third mission in February 1941 resulted in information on the Pope's possible intention to transfer the papacy to a neutral country for the duration of the war, while a fourth trip in October of the same year produced intelligence on the Vatican's attitude towards Germany's war against the Soviet Union. In Berlin Amt VI was jubilant over material which seemingly originated in the highest levels of the papacy, and Loos's reputation as an agent runner soared. Loos and his superiors, however, were unaware that on his first trip to Rome in May 1940 Kageneck had confessed to Father Leiber his connections with German intelligence and the clandestine purpose of his visit. The Jesuit consulted the Pope and the Superior General of the Jesuits, Father Wladimir Ledochowski, and they agreed to allow the papal assistant on this and subsequent occasions to provide carefully selected information to his family friend. There can be little doubt that the Vatican used the unwitting Kageneck as a 'back channel' to put across to German intelligence a particular view of papal attitudes and policies, and that throughout the operation Loos's star agent was effectively under Vatican control.[48]

The scope of Kappler's coverage of the Vatican is suggested by the intelligence reports submitted by his office to Berlin and passed on to the foreign ministry by the RSHA. In the period February–December 1942 (apparently there were no reports in January) the Wilhelmstrasse received 37 reports on the Vatican from the police attaché's office at the Rome embassy.[49] The material covered the organization of the papal Curia, prominent ecclesiastical personalities, Vatican communications channels, and papal policies especially with regard to Russia and eastern Europe. Specific reports dealt with such topics as: Vatican eastern policy (four reports between February and June); *La Civiltà Cattolica* (a Jesuit journal of opinion); alleged papal message to Latin America; German soldiers at papal audiences; Vatican intelligence channels; the Jesuit Father [Gustav] Wetter (Pontifical Oriental Institute); Monsignor Ludwig Kaas; the Congregation [department] of Rites; Vatican rumours.

It is difficult to attribute these reports to any particular source. Some certainly came from Kappler's star agent, Alexander Kurtna, who had been recruited in early 1942 (Chapter 4); some probably originated with Italian liaison or reflected current gossip from diplomatic circles in Rome. The Rome bureau of the German news service, DNB, routinely passed to Kappler's office any items of potential interest concerning the Vatican and Italian affairs in general. The odd item of information may have been contributed by the network put together by Helmut Loos, although his informants proved singularly disappointing. Apparently none had direct access to the Vatican. The small group included Charles Bewley, a one-time officer in the Irish diplomatic service who had served as Ireland's ambassador to the Vatican and Germany before retiring to Italy after his resignation from the latter post. The Anglophobic Bewley was a familiar face in Roman diplomatic circles and passed to the Via Tasso information concerning Anglo-Vatican relations. Loos also received reports from Werner von der Schulenberg, a former army officer with literary pretensions who had retired to the Italian capital to promote Italo-German cultural relations and who collected gossip from Roman intellectual and aristocratic circles. After the war a one-time employee of Kappler dismissed such sources as 'for the most part corrupt, greedy and given to extravagant living'. Schulenberg in particular was constantly begging Kappler's office for money to underwrite his position in local society.[50]

The RSHA's coverage of the Vatican did not depend solely upon the operations of its police attaché in Rome. The Vatican's diplomatic network of nunciatures and delegations as well as the communications channels that connected this network with the papal Secretariat of State were inviting targets. As we have seen, the nunciature in Berlin was penetrated by the RSHA as was the nunciature in Slovakia. The former was a potentially useful penetration not only because it provided access to the attitudes and intentions of the nuncio, Archbishop Cesare Orsenigo, but also because with the closure of the nunciatures in German-occupied Belgium, Holland, Poland and the Baltic States, the Berlin nunciature had become a focal point for reports from the bishops and other church authorities in these regions. In another important operation the individual who served in Munich as a mail drop and collection centre for some of the Vatican's clandestine correspondence with the Baltic region allowed Amt VI officers to photograph the letters passing through his hands.[51]

The RSHA also occasionally employed the services of individuals whose professional or personal relations brought them into contact with important ecclesiastical figures. One such individual was a Czech Catholic who apparently possessed impeccable aristocratic and ecclesiastic credentials. His identity remains unknown (we shall call him 'Bravo'), but he seems to have been related to Cardinal Franz von Bauer who died in 1915.[52] He certainly had a wide circle of friends in European ecclesiastical circles. With the financial support of Amt VI he travelled frequently to Rome, Vienna, Prague, Bratislava, Budapest and Bucharest, nurturing these friendships and collecting information for his sponsors in Berlin. To ensure his welcome and enhance his credibility, he would occasionally pass to his clerical friends information about church and political affairs in Germany and the occupied territories which ostensibly he had picked up on his travels, but which in fact had been fed to him by Amt VI.[53] Bravo was on especially good terms with Hubert Noots, the Belgian Abbot-General of the Premonstratensian religious order which had monasteries throughout Europe. Noots was of particular interest to German intelligence because he was well-connected at the Vatican and because he was suspected (correctly) of involvement in the leak of Reich secrets which led to a warning to Belgium of the imminent German invasion in May 1940. The abbot wrote frequently to his Czech friend about Roman affairs and personalities, and Bravo promptly passed all the letters to Amt VI. Bravo was also friendly with the papal chargé d'affaires in Slovakia, Archbishop Giuseppe Burzio. In July 1944, for example, he called on his friend at the nunciature in the Slovakian capital, Bratislava. The visit began with the papal diplomat handing Bravo a letter from Abbot Noots which the Belgian (anticipating the Czech's visit to Bratislava) had managed to include in the most recent Vatican pouch to Burzio. The circumstances surrounding the arrival of this letter provided an opening for Bravo to inquire about Burzio's communications with the Vatican. The papal chargé explained that since the Vatican had no couriers of its own, he sent his dispatches to the nuncio in Switzerland by means of the diplomatic pouch of the Slovakian government whose couriers made the Berne run about once a month. In cases of extreme urgency Burzio said that a message would be carried to Berne by a junior officer of the nunciature. He thought that from Berne the dispatches were carried to Rome by Swiss or Spanish diplomatic couriers. The diplomat admonished his friend for not bringing a letter for Abbot Noots since the nunciature's mail was to go out that very day.[54] In the course of a pleasant conversation which lasted several hours Burzio also revealed to his attentive visitor that with the recent capture of Rome by the Allies the Vatican's relations with London and Washington had improved; that he did not expect the Holy Father to intervene with the Allies on behalf of a negotiated settlement of the war; and that he would not be surprised if the Vatican opened contacts with the Soviet Union now that large numbers of Catholics faced the prospect of Russian occupation in Poland and the Baltic States. Little did the loquacious papal diplomat suspect that his remarks would find their way to RSHA files in Berlin.

Johannes Denk, a gregarious East Prussian, was another of the occasional sources who proved useful to German intelligence. Too old for military service (he was 53 at the outbreak of the war), he accepted special assignments on behalf of the foreign ministry and the RSHA. In 1940, for example, the Wilhelmstrasse sent him to South Africa in the futile expectation (he got only as far as Portuguese East Africa) that he could establish contact with pro-German organizations in the Union of South Africa and bolster anti-British sentiment in the area. Denk's work for the RSHA is more obscure, but in 1943 Ernst Kaltenbrunner, Heydrich's successor as head of that organization, described the East Prussian as 'one of our reliable and tested agents'.[55] Denk was acquainted with several German bishops and probably reported on his contacts with these prelates. In November 1943 he was sent by Amt IV (Gestapo) on a special mission to Rome to seek an interview with Pope Pius. Denk had known the Pope during the First World War when the Pontiff had been the nuncio in Germany, and the Gestapo hoped that Pius would open his door and his heart to an old friend. Denk also offered his services as a secret courier to Archbishop Orsenigo, the nuncio in Berlin, and Cardinal Adolf Bertram, the Archbishop of Breslau, neither of whom was aware of their friend's connection with the Gestapo, and both of whom jumped at the chance to use Denk to circumvent the surveillance they knew to be in place on their normal communication channels.[56] One might safely guess that the letters entrusted to the secret messenger by these prelates were examined by the Gestapo before the courier set out for Italy. Upon his arrival in Rome, Denk learned that his credentials as an old friend from Munich days and a special messenger from Orsenigo and Bertram were sufficient to secure for him the unusual privilege of a one-hour private audience with the Pope. He had been directed by Berlin to lead the conversation into several areas of interest to German intelligence including the Vatican's appraisal of the current military and political situation and the Pope's attitude towards the National Socialist regime.

Denk's report of the conversation could not have encouraged his controllers in Berlin.[57] Pius saw no possibility of a negotiated peace and was convinced that Germany would lose the war in the face of the Allies' overwhelming material superiority. As for German–Vatican relations, the Holy Father reminded his visitor that the Catholic Church had, wherever possible, sought to adjust its differences with National Socialism, but that the Nazis had shown no inclination to reverse their policy of hostility towards the Church and religion.

When Ernst Kaltenbrunner, the SS and police commander in Vienna, was appointed chief of the RSHA after Reinhard Heydrich's assassination in Prague by the Czech resistance in June 1942, there was a shift in the organization's approach to the Vatican. Under Heydrich the organization had pursued an aggressive anti-clerical policy. This policy assumed that the Catholic Church in general, and the Vatican in particular, represented a serious threat to the Reich and had to be combated and destroyed. The stolid Kaltenbrunner did not share his predecessor's anti-Catholic obsession, and he believed that a more pragmatic approach might prove productive. Improved relations with the Church and increased contacts with the Vatican would be useful should Berlin need to establish a credible channel to the Western Allies as a preliminary to seeking a negotiated peace, an eventuality which the new police and intelligence chief considered increasingly likely by 1943.[58]

The new attitude at the top was presaged by changes in Amt VI, the foreign intelligence staff. Shortly after Kaltenbrunner's appointment, Walter Schellenberg, the head of Amt VI, selected Wilhelm Hoettl, a 28-year-old Austrian, to direct Amt VI E, the section responsible for south-eastern Europe which included the Italian and Vatican desks. The young Viennese had already had a tumultuous career in German intelligence. A student of Balkan history at the University of Vienna, Hoettl had been active in right-wing student associations which before the *Anschluss* were little more than fronts for National Socialist groups. During that period he passed information about Catholic professors and student clubs to the Nazi organization in the Austrian capital. After the *Anschluss* he formally joined the SD where he was assigned to the Catholic desk of Section II (domestic intelligence) in the Vienna office. The young intelligence officer was not in sympathy with the anti-church attitudes which were so popular in his office, and after a short time he transferred into the foreign intelligence section where he continued to specialize in Catholic affairs. In this new post he cultivated Catholic intellectuals and aristocrats in Austria and Bohemia-Moravia. These contacts would lead to his disgrace.

In late 1941 Hoettl's superiors in Vienna denounced him to Berlin as ideologically unreliable. Specifically, they accused him of exceeding his authority, employing ideologically unreliable (i.e.

Catholic) agents, and revealing Reich secrets to foreigners. The charges were the result of an initiative upon which Hoettl had embarked in 1941 on the advice of two of his aristocratic contacts. Prince Karl Anton Rohan, the descendant of an ancient family with roots in France and strong connections in Britain, and Count Karl Khuen-Belasi-Lützow, a Moravian landowner who was well known in Roman society through his wife, the daughter of a former Austrian ambassador to the Vatican, were zealous promoters of a west European coalition against the Soviet Union. They considered such a coalition, which they believed to be in the interests of Britain, France, Germany and Italy, the possible basis of a negotiated peace, and they believed that the Vatican was the appropriate channel for presenting the scheme to London and Paris. Prince Rohan conceived the idea of approaching the Vatican through Father Wladimir Ledochowski, the Superior General of the Jesuits. The prince had an estate near the ancestral home of the Ledochowskis (an aristocratic Polish family in reduced circumstances; Father Ledochowski, who, as a youth, had been a page at the Hapsburg court, was a Count although he never used the title) and the families knew each other. After the fall of France, Rohan discussed his plan with various contacts in Rome and then broached the scheme to Hoettl. The young officer had already decided that more could be gained at the Vatican through cooperation than antagonism, and he eagerly seized upon the prince's plan and pressed it on his superiors. His memos, however, remained unanswered. According to Hoettl, Count Khuen and his wife visited Rome in the spring of 1941 and talked with Father Ledochowski. On the basis of their account of this conversation, Hoettl concluded that the Jesuit Superior General, a known opponent of Bolshevism, would be prepared to pursue a measure of cooperation with German intelligence against the Soviet Union. The excited Amt VI officer saw an opportunity for Germany to exchange information with the Jesuits (an organization whose intelligence capabilities were greatly exaggerated by the RSHA), perhaps as a first step towards a new policy of church–state collaboration which, in turn, might contribute to an understanding with the West against Russia. The whole plan was, of course, extremely improbable. Whatever his motives, Count Khuen certainly exaggerated Father Ledochowski's interest in cooperating with German intelligence. While strongly anti-communist, the Polish Jesuit had no love for the

Nazi regime which had decimated his homeland and continued to persecute his church. For his part, Hitler had no intention of collaborating with the Vatican on anything, especially a compromise peace in the West.[59]

After the war Hoettl would claim that a Gestapo agent inside the papal nunciature in Berlin intercepted a letter to him from Ledochowski and that this letter provided a pretext for those in the RSHA opposed to a German–Vatican *détente* to secure his disgrace.[60] He vigorously defended himself by maintaining that an interest in policy towards the Catholic Church was itself no sign of ideological unreliability, that it was appropriate for a church specialist to cultivate contacts among the Catholic aristocracy, and that the approach to the Jesuits was a legitimate intelligence initiative and one known to his then superior, Heinz Jost. Such arguments proved futile. In February 1942 Hoettl was demoted and transferred to a *Waffen-SS* unit in the Balkans where he languished (editing the unit's newspaper) until rehabilitated and recalled to Berlin in 1943 by Walter Schellenberg.

Hoettl found a sympathetic superior in Schellenberg. The Amt VI chief was interested in church affairs and he shared his subordinate's interest in cultivating the papacy as a potential channel to the Western Allies. Always the pragmatist, Schellenberg had concluded as early as the summer of 1942 that Germany could not win the war and that its best chance was to reach out to London and Washington in search of a negotiated settlement. Eventually he would receive Himmler's and Kaltenbrunner's tacit consent to open contacts with the west.[61] Since the Vatican was a prospective channel for such contacts, Hoettl's new assignment took on added significance. The new head of Amt VI E (south-eastern Europe) had no sooner assumed his duties than he set off, in April 1943, to meet intelligence officers and inspect facilities in Croatia, Slovakia and Italy. A second trip in July took him to Rome for a month. During the visits to Italy he met with the German ambassador to the Holy See, Ernst von Weizsäcker, reviewed current operations against the papacy with Herbert Kappler and Helmut Loos, and interviewed some of the informants working for Germany in Vatican circles. During the summer visit he supervised the installation of a radio transmitter on the roof of Kappler's building in order to free the Gestapo and Amt VI officers on the Via Tasso from dependence upon embassy communication facilities. Despite his interest in church affairs, Hoettl did little to intensify operations against the Vatican, probably because he feared a provocation that might further alienate the papacy and spoil any chance of seeking its sympathetic intervention with London and Washington. His most notable initiative was a quiet agreement with Weizsäcker to align his intelligence reports on the Vatican with those submitted by the ambassador in order to improve the Vatican's image in Berlin by convincing Nazi leaders that the Holy See sympathized with Germany and recognized the importance of maintaining the Reich as a bulwark against the Soviet Union.[62] This collaboration in disinformation was short-lived since Hoettl left Berlin (and his role in church affairs) in late 1943 when most of Amt VI's Balkan operations were relocated to Vienna. Responsibility for Italy shifted from Amt VI E (south-eastern Europe) to Amt VI B (Western Europe) where the Vatican desk fell to one Alfred Reissman, an unimaginative officer with little understanding of Vatican affairs.[63] This hapless functionary would preside over the comic-opera Georgian Convent Affair (Chapter 3) and the effective collapse of his office's intelligence effort against the Vatican when the German withdrawal from Rome in June 1944 caused his few agents to go permanently to ground or into Allied prisons and internment camps.

Any review of the RSHA's operations against the Vatican must include a consideration of Hitler's purported plan to kidnap the Pope. The nature of this plan, indeed the very fact of its existence, remains uncertain. Concern about the territorial integrity of Vatican City and the personal security of the Pontiff had distracted papal officials as early as the first year of the war, although the initial concerns reflected uncertainty about Mussolini's intentions rather than Hitler's. Tension between the Palazzo Apostolico and the Palazzo Venezia increased in the spring of 1940 as *Il Duce* prepared to take Italy into the war alongside Germany. Fascist spokesmen assailed Pius for his pacific and allegedly pro-Allied attitude. Editions of *L'Osservatore Romano* were seized by the police and its vendors assaulted by thugs. The papal limousine carrying the Holy Father to mass at a Roman church was mobbed by fascist youths shouting 'Death to the Pope!' Tensions peaked in early May when Italian intelligence intercepted and deciphered the telegrams sent by the Secretariat of State to Brussels and The Hague warning of the imminent German invasion. A crisis was averted, but papal authorities were reminded of how exposed and vulnerable the Vatican would be in the face of a determined and ruthless enemy.[64]

Another scare the following year fuelled the anxieties. In May 1941 the Secretariat of State learned from a reliable source (probably in the Italian foreign ministry) that at a meeting with Count Galeazzo Ciano the previous month in Vienna, Joachim von Ribbentrop had suggested that Italy should remove the Pope from Rome since 'in the new Europe there would be no place for the papacy'. The Italian foreign minister had parried this proposal by suggesting instead that his government seek to isolate and control the Holy Father inside Vatican City. The Vatican was sufficiently alarmed by this sign of danger that the Cardinal Secretary of State, Luigi Maglione, summoned the Italian ambassador for an interview at which the envoy questioned the accuracy of the report. To emphasize his personal concern, Pope Pius sent Father Giacomo Salza, a chaplain in the Italian army and an acquaintance of Mussolini, to *Il Duce* who also denied the story. Meanwhile, another priest was dispatched to seek information from the chief of the political police, Carmine Senise, who assured the papal agent that the Vatican had nothing to fear. Such assurances, however, did not completely assuage Vatican concerns. On 8 May Cardinal Maglione convened a special meeting of the Congregation for Extraordinary Ecclesiastical Affairs (a committee of cardinals with diplomatic experience who advised the Cardinal Secretary of State on foreign policy matters) to consider contingency plans to confer special ecclesiastical powers on certain nuncios in the event that the Vatican was no longer in a position to communicate freely with its representatives abroad.[65]

In subsequent months the Vatican received further disturbing reports. A German official attending Holy Week ceremonies in the Sistine Chapel had been heard to remark, 'The ceremonies have been very interesting, but this is the last time for them. Next year they won't be celebrated again.' This individual made it clear that he did not expect the Pope to be in the Vatican the following year. In June Count Alfred von Kageneck, a sometime representative of German intelligence, had told certain friends in Rome that Berlin was preparing plans to expel the papacy from Europe. At the end of the year Prince Otto von Bismarck, a senior officer in the German embassy to Italy, had publicly remarked, 'Oh, the Vatican. That's a museum which one of these years we'll be able to visit for the price of a ten lire ticket.' Similar sentiments were attributed to Kurt von Tannstein, the first secretary at the embassy to the Holy See.[66] Throughout 1942 rumours that Germany was preparing to invade Vatican City, seize the archives and expel or kidnap the Pope were so common in Rome that Ambassador Diego von Bergen felt compelled to alert the Wilhelmstrasse to the situation.[67] The rumours continued into 1943 and reached a crescendo with the fall of Mussolini in July. Fears that the Germans would occupy the Italian capital including Vatican City were so great that the Vatican implemented certain of its contingency plans. Key staff in the Secretariat of State were ordered to keep a suitcase packed at all times in anticipation of a sudden evacuation. Sensitive diplomatic documents were hidden in obscure corners and secret recesses of the archives, and the Pope's personal files were hidden under the marble floors of the papal palace. Allied diplomats confined within Vatican City burned confidential papers, while rumours spread throughout Rome that the Archbishop of Lisbon, Cardinal Emanuel Cerejeira, had been summoned by the Pope who explained that in the event of his arrest by the Germans he would resign the papacy and that Cardinal Cerejeira should convene in Lisbon a conclave of the remaining cardinals to elect a new Pope.[68] On 4 August Cardinal Maglione called a meeting of all the cardinals residing in Rome to review the political situation in Italy and discuss the threat to the Vatican. He warned his audience that official Italian circles feared that German troops were moving to seize Rome, invade the Vatican, and carry the Pope to Munich. By September the threat appeared so imminent that the commandant of the Pope's Swiss Guards, Baron Heinrich Pfyffer von Altishofen, was informed orally of Pius's wish that his men offer no resistance when the Germans entered Vatican City. The Pontiff undoubtedly wished to avoid a repetition of the tragic events of 6 May 1527 when, during the so-called Sack of Rome, 147 Swiss died covering the escape of Pope Clement VII from the German and Spanish troops of the Duke of Bourbon. The Baron, the 10th in his family to command the Swiss Guards since 1652, mindful of the traditions of the Guard and bound by the oath sworn by new recruits on the anniversary of their corps' famous sacrifice on behalf of Pope Clement to 'faithfully, loyally and honourably serve the Supreme Pontiff and his legitimate successors, . . . sacrificing if necessary also my life to defend them', insisted that the order be committed to writing.[69] Although the Germans occupied

Rome without violating papal territory, the fears persisted. On 25 September the British Minister to the Vatican, Osborne, warned the Foreign Office:

> Most of my colleagues have destroyed their cyphers but I do not propose to do so unless you instruct me to, although in the event of German violation of Vatican territory there might not be time to do so . . . Probably most dangerous moment will be when Allied forces are approaching Rome.[70]

At the end of the year a source close to Italian intelligence warned the Secretariat of State that Herbert Kappler, the German police chief and Gestapo representative in Rome, had prepared a plan to seize Vatican City and that SS detachments were assembling in Rome for the operation.[71]

Was there a plot to seize the Pope? Clearly the Vatican took the threat seriously. Hitler was certainly prepared to order the removal to Germany of recalcitrant or inconvenient foreign leaders as evidenced by his treatment of such figures as Admiral Miklós Horthy, the Hungarian regent, and Marshal Philippe Pétain, the leader of Vichy France. Several Nazi officials testified that Hitler had indeed intended to act against the Vatican but had been dissuaded by his advisers. Walter Schellenberg, for example, asserted in his memoirs that Josef Goebbels and Martin Bormann supported a plan to remove the Pope to Germany, but that he convinced Heinrich Himmler to block the plan. For his part, Goebbels recorded in his diary that, upon learning of Mussolini's removal from power by the Fascist Grand Council, Hitler proposed to seize Rome and the Vatican, and that the Führer had only been dissuaded by his (Goebbels') arguments that an action against the papacy would make a terrible impression on world opinion. After the war General Karl Wolff, SS commander in Italy, claimed that he had been summoned to Hitler's headquarters in September 1943 and told by the Führer himself to prepare plans to occupy the Vatican, confiscate its archives, and transport the Pope to the tiny principality of Liechtenstein. Wolff claimed that he persuaded Hitler to postpone action by arguing that the Italians would be irremediably alienated by the arrest of the Holy Father, and that in any event time was required to collect specialists in Latin and Greek to examine the archives.[72]

With so much smoke in the air, one may be forgiven for assuming that somewhere in those clouds there must be a fire. Unfortunately, while the presence of smoke has often been noted, the actual flames have eluded discovery. Historians have yet to uncover a single piece of contemporary evidence indicating that Hitler, Himmler, Bormann, or any other authority had any serious intention, let alone plan, to invade Vatican City and carry off Pope Pius XII. As for all the smoke, the recollections are post-war and suspiciously self-serving; the rumours and warnings second- or third-hand; the alleged plans and concentrations of forces undocumented. The few bits of credible evidence that do exist suggest that, in fact, there was no plan to move against the Pope. Written within a day or two of the events they describe, Goebbels' diary entries are probably more credible than memoirs composed after the war. The diary indicates Hitler's belief that Pius had been involved in the fall of Mussolini, news of which reached the Führer's headquarters on 27 July, and that in a typical fit of rage his reaction was to seize all of Italy including the Vatican. The diary, however, also clearly indicates that once his temper had cooled, Hitler conceded the impracticality of an operation against the Pope and agreed with his advisers that the Vatican be exempted from any measures planned against Rome.[73] As for Martin Bormann, who proved such a useful villain for many post-war memoirists, there can be no doubt of his hostility towards the Catholic Church, but there is no evidence (aside from the recollections of Schellenberg who would also have us believe that Goebbels urged Hitler to kidnap the Pope) that Bormann proposed any operation against the Vatican. The only documentary evidence of the Party Secretary's position on this subject is a directive he circulated to the Party Gauleiters in November 1943 in which he insisted that reports originating with Allied propaganda broadcasts to the effect that Germany would seize Pope Pius were entirely unfounded.[74] Then there is the negative evidence. Throughout the war German intelligence was mystified by reports that the Pope would leave Rome, and on at least two occasions (one following on the German occupation of Rome) the RSHA directed its agents to investigate such reports.[75] In the midst of the rumours and alarms swirling around German-occupied Rome, Herbert Kappler, the Gestapo representative and police chief in the city, assured Ernst von Weizsäcker, the concerned ambassador to the Holy See for whom an invasion of the Vatican would have seemed the height of folly, that he had received no instructions from Berlin to anticipate an operation against Vatican City. After the war Wilhelm Hoettl, who for a time supervised the Vatican desk in the foreign intelligence division of the RSHA, insisted repeatedly that there never was a plan to remove the Pope from Rome, and that if there had been he would have certainly known about it.[76]

Clearly, the evidence concerning an alleged plan to kidnap the Pope is, at best, mixed. The key to resolving the controversy may be found in Bormann's warning to the Gauleiters to be wary of Allied-inspired rumours of such a plan. The Allies had good reason to spread such rumours. An invasion of the Vatican and an assault on the person of the Holy Father would outrage Catholics around the world. The mere suspicion that such actions were in the offing would seriously damage Germany's standing in those neutral countries such as Ireland, Portugal, Spain and Switzerland which had large Catholic populations, and would undermine morale among Catholics within Germany itself. It would also further destabilize the always precarious relations between the Vatican and the Third Reich. The Allies did not shrink from the opportunity. British propaganda may have been responsible for the reports which circulated in France, Germany and Switzerland in the spring of 1940 to the effect that Pius XII was considering abandoning Rome for Lisbon as a gesture of disapproval should Mussolini enter the war alongside Hitler. The Political Warfare Executive (PWE), the wartime department responsible for Britain's 'black' propaganda, was certainly behind stories which appeared in December 1941 indicating that Pius would, for the duration of the war, move the papacy to either Buenos Aires or Rio de Janeiro. Similar stories throughout 1942 and 1943 had the Pontiff moving to Spain, Mexico, North America, and (in a particularly fanciful leap of the imagination) the Belgian Congo.[77] With the German occupation of Rome in September 1943, the propagandists in PWE developed a new slant on what was by now an old story. Within a month of the occupation, the clandestine radio station 'G.9' ('Atlantik Sender'), which purported to be a German station, reported: 'Preparations have been completed for the transfer of the Pope from the territory of Vatican City to the Reich.' Two days later the same radio claimed: 'All preparations have been completed for the reception of the Pope and the cardinals in Lichtenstein Castle [Württemberg], notwithstanding the fact that the Pope has declared his intention to remain in the Vatican.'[78]

These broadcasts apparently set off a surprising echo among German authorities in newly occupied Rome. That autumn the counsellor of the Reich embassy to the Holy See, Ludwig Wemmer, hosted a dinner at his apartments on the Via Gregoriana for several SS officers attached to the city's military administration. Over after-dinner brandies and cigars the conversation turned to the prospect of an eventual evacuation of the Eternal City. When one guest wondered what, if anything, would be done with the Pope, another replied that the Pontiff would probably be removed to Lichtenstein Castle in Württemberg. Subsequently, one of the officers present at the dinner returned to Berlin where he had the opportunity to recount the evening's conversation to Heinrich Himmler. The *Reichsführer* SS was taken aback by the reference to the future of the Pope since he knew of no plans to act against the Vatican. He immediately radioed an inquiry to Herbert Kappler, but the Gestapo representative in Rome knew nothing about an operation against the Vatican. Kappler asked Wemmer for an explanation, but the diplomat (undoubtedly puzzled by the sudden high level interest in his social activities) could only respond that the reference to removing the Pope from Rome had been nothing more than a casual aside made during a convivial social occasion and that, as far as he knew, it had no factual basis.[79] It would appear that the counsellor's voluble guest that night had merely repeated a rumour already set in motion by Allied disinformation services. In fact, the clearest evidentiary trail in the tangle of rumour, memory and fiction that surrounds the purported plot to kidnap the Pope is the one that leads back to London rather than Berlin.

NOTES

1. George C. Browder, *Foundations of the Nazi Police State: The Formation of Sipo and SD* (Lexington: University of Kentucky Press, 1990).
2. Wilhelm Hoettl, *The Secret Front: The Story of Nazi Political Espionage* (New York: Praeger, 1954), p. 38.
3. Günther Deschner, *Heydrich: The Pursuit of Total Power* (London: Orbis, 1981), p. 97.
4. Ibid., p. 107. In the bloodbath surrounding the Röhm Putsch, Adalbert Probst, the charismatic national director of the Catholic sports organization, was also murdered by Heydrich's agents.
5. For the negotiation of the concordat and the conflict surrounding its implementation, see Ernst Helmreich, *The German Churches under Hitler* (Detroit: Wayne State University Press, 1979), pp. 240ff.
6. Ibid., pp. 273, 278; John Conway, *The Nazi Persecution*, pp. 67, 95.

7. J.S. Conway, *The Nazi Persecution*, p. 285; J. Deschner, *Heydrich*, p. 109.
8. NARA. RG 238. Final Interrogation Report (CI-FIR) No. 123: Albert Hartl. Headquarters, 7707 Military Intelligence Service Centre, pp. 3–4. (hereinafter cited as Final Interrogation Report: Albert Hartl).
9. Ibid., pp. 4–5; Nuremberg Tribunal. Case XI. Interrogation 249 1a. Albert Hartl. 12 Dec. 1947.
10. Final Interrogation Report: Albert Hartl, p. 10.
11. Ibid., pp. 17, 20.
12. J.S. Conway, *The Nazi Persecution*, pp. 286–7.
13. John S. Conway, 'Pope Pius XII and the German Church: An Unpublished Gestapo Report', *Canadian Journal of History*, II (March 1967), pp. 72–83.
14. Final Interrogation Report: Albert Hartl, p. 17. Since Hartl did not identify his secret source inside the nunciature it is impossible to determine whether he was the same informant who for many years passed information to the German foreign ministry.
15. Ibid.
16. Ibid., p. 42.
17. Ibid., pp. 36–7.
18. Ibid., p. 11.
19. 'Bericht über die Arbeitstagung der Kirchen-Sachbearbeiter beim Reichssicher-heitshauptamt am 22. und 23. September 1941', Institut für Zeitgeschichte, Munich (Protocol 4920/72. Fa 218). All quotations are from this document.
20. German intelligence was not alone in believing that the Pope controlled a vast intelligence apparatus. The attitude of American diplomatists was indicative of prevailing opinion in supposedly informed circles. Arguing, in 1939, for a separate mission to the Holy See, the American embassy in Rome assured the State Department that the result would be 'a new source of political information of the highest importance'. One senior officer believed that the Vatican had 'the best information service in Europe', while another agreed that 'The detailed and accurate knowledge of the Holy See of conditions in every part of the world, particularly in the countries of Europe, is proverbial', *Foreign Relations of the United States, 1939*, II (Washington: Government Printing Office, 1956), p. 869, n. 4; Hugh Wilson, *Diplomat Between Wars* (New York: Longman's, Green, and Co., 1941), p. 27; Sumner Welles, *Time for Decision* (New York: Harper Brothers, 1944), p. 142.
21. Final Interrogation Report: Albert Hartl, pp. 27–9.
22. H. Stehle, *Eastern Politics*, pp. 27–8, 59–61.
23. O. Chadwick, *Britain and the Vatican*, pp. 201–2. For an appraisal of papal intelligence during the war, see David Alvarez, 'Vatican Intelligence Capabilities in the Second World War', *Intelligence and National Security*, 6 (July 1991), pp. 593–607.
24. Nuremberg Tribunal. Case XI. Interrogation 249 1a. Albert Hartl, 12 Dec. 1947.
25. Final Interrogation Report: Albert Hartl, p. 6. For the 'Black Book' project, see ADSS. Vol. V, p. 84.
26. J.S. Conway, *The Nazi Persecution*, pp. 169–70.
27. O. Chadwick, *Britain and the Vatican*, Ch. 2; François Charles-Roux, *Huit ans au Vatican, 1932–1940* (Paris: Flammarion, 1947), pp. 258ff.
28. Party file for Wilhelm Hoettl, Berlin Document Centre.
29. Final Interrogation Report: Albert Hartl., p. 16.
30. O. Chadwick, *Britain and the Vatican*, pp. 33, 79.
31. Ibid., p. 42.
32. NARA. T-175. Roll 409, 2932612-35.
33. For the implementation of this plan see Ch. 3. One of Heydrich's church specialists recalled that 'Heydrich began by personally selecting a few exceptionally gifted young men from the Hitler Youth. These he intended to send with false names to the various theological colleges and seminaries in Germany and abroad. He elaborated a plan to

penetrate the Protestant Church in a similar manner.' W. Hoettl, *The Secret Front*, p. 39.

34. D. Kahn, *Hitler's Spies*, pp. 253–5.
35. G. Deschner, *Heydrich*, p. 71.
36. J. Weitz, *Hitler's Diplomat*, pp. 217, 268.
37. 'RSHA et Vatican', undated memo from French intelligence, copy in possession of the authors.
38. AA. Staatssekretär. Politisches Archiv. Inland IIg. SD-Meldungen.
39. Ibid.
40. Ibid.
41. Ibid.
42. Ibid.
43. After the war an Italian court would condemn Kappler to life imprisonment for his role in March 1944 in the execution of 335 hostages in the Ardeatine Caves on the outskirts of Rome in reprisal for a bomb attack which killed 32 German soldiers in the city.
44. John V.H. Dippel, *Two Against Hitler: Stealing the Nazis' Best Kept Secrets* (New York: Praeger, 1992), pp. 16, 102. Commenting on the information provided by the erstwhile secretary, the German embassy to the Holy See concluded: 'The extensive material completely substantiates the previous reports of this Embassy on the anti-National Socialist activity of Muckermann.' AA. Politisches Archiv. Botschaft Rom-Vatikan. Emigranten.
45. NARA. T-120. Roll 70, 55947–52.
46. Confidential information.
47. Interrogation Report on *SS-Obersturmbannfuehrer* Kappler, Herbert. NARA. RG 165. CSDIC/SC/15AG/SD18.
48. The Kageneck affair is described in 'RSHA et Vatican'.
49. AA. Inland IIg. 83. Italien. Berichtverzeichnis des Pol. Att. Rom. 1940–1943.
50. 'The SD (Amt VI, RSHA) in Italy'. This is a post-war American intelligence report based on the testimony of Hildegard Beetz, one of Kappler's secretaries whom the Americans considered a reliable witness. Copy in possession of the authors. For Bewley, see John P. Duggan, *Neutral Ireland and the Third* Reich (Totowa: Barnes & Noble, 1985), pp. 28–31.
51. Final Interrogation Report: Albert Hartl, p. 18.
52. Bravo's activities can be traced in AA. Politisches Archiv. Inland IIg. 44. Kirchliche Ang. Bd. 1 and NARA. T-175. Roll 582, 000840–46.
53. Amt. VI tried to convince the foreign ministry to contribute tidbits of information for Bravo's use, but the Wilhelmstrasse flatly refused to cooperate in the operation.
54. At this point in his report to Berlin Bravo modestly commented: 'As I see from the letter [from Noots] a report is always desired and welcomed in Rome.'
55. AA. Politisches Archiv. Inland IIg. Vatikan. Vertrauensleute. SD Berichte. 262341–46.
56. Denk visited Cardinal Bertram three times in the autumn of 1943. The cardinal's appointment book bears the notation 'To Rome' opposite the record of Denk's visit of 28 October, the eve of his departure for Italy. Information from Father Ludwig Volk, SJ.
57. The report, 'Attitude of the Pope on the Contemporary Situation and on National Socialism', can be found in AA. Politisches Archiv. Inland IIg. Vatikan. Vertrauensleute. SD Berichte. Additional information from Fritz Wuchner, a church specialist in the Gestapo's Munich office who had been detailed to accompany Denk to Rome.
58. P. Black, *Ernst Kaltenbrunner*, pp. 148, 222–3.
59. Information from Wilhelm Hoettl. Long after the war Hoettl would admit, 'All these attempts from 1939 to 1941 were an immense over-estimation of our possibilities. We actually thought that Hitler would gladly make peace with the church, and thereby deserve its help, for this fateful struggle of the German people and all of Europe against

Bolshevism. I grant readily that I decidedly deceived myself.'
60. Ibid. Although German intelligence had at least one informant inside the nunciature, there is no independent evidence to confirm Hoettl's account of the incriminating letter. Father Ledochowski died in December 1942 and his papers were destroyed when the Germans occupied Rome, to prevent them from falling into Nazi hands.
61. Walter Schellenberg, *Hitler's Secret Service* (New York: Pyramid Books, 1971), pp. 297–9, 304ff.; P. Black, *Ernst Kaltenbrunner*, pp. 219–20.
62. Information from Wilhelm Hoettl. For Weizsäcker's distortion of papal attitudes, see Ch. 1.
63. NARA. RG 165. Box 707. 'The SD and the RSHA' and 'Amt VI of the RSHA'.
64. David Alvarez, 'The Vatican and Italian Belligerency', pp. 311–13.
65. ADSS. Vol. IV, pp. 483–5.
66. ADSS. Vol. V, pp. 214–15, 396–7.
67. AA. St. Sekretariat. Inland IIg. 330; ADSS. VII, p. 146.
68. Robert A. Graham, SJ, 'Voleva Hitler allontanare da Roma Pio XII?' *Civiltà Cattolica*, 1 (Feb. 1972), pp. 319ff. In fact Cardinal Cerejeira received no such summons and no such instructions from Pope Pius. Information from Cardinal Emanuel Cerejeira.
69. ADSS. Vol. VII, p. 611.
70. PRO. FO 371/37539. The Foreign Office instructed Osborne to destroy the 'W cypher books' and not to worry about the 'ML Tables'.
71. Giorgio Garibaldi, *Il Vaticano nella seconda guerra mondiale* (Milan: Mursia, 1992), p. 180.
72. Walter Schellenberg, *The Labyrinth* (New York: Harper, 1956), p. 370; Louis Lochner (ed.), *The Goebbels Diaries* (Garden City: Doubleday, 1948), p. 409; Richard Lamb, *War in Italy, 1943–1945* (New York: St. Martin's Press, 1993), pp. 45–6.
73. L. Lochner, *The Goebbels Diaries*, p. 416.
74. R.A. Graham, SJ, 'Voleva Hitler allontanare da Roma Pio XII?', p. 109.
75. 'RSHA et Vatican'; AA. Politisches Archiv. Inland IIg. Vatikan. Vertrauensleute. SD Berichte, 262341–46.
76. Information from Wilhelm Hoettl.
77. FO 898/60. Black Propaganda to Italy; FO 898/71. PWE/Sibs. General Index and Correspondence.
78. FO 898/72. German File. G.9 Rumours, 1941–1944. The reference to Lichtenstein Castle in Germany was misunderstood by many who came to believe that the Pope would be relocated to the micro-state of Liechtenstein.
79. R.A. Graham, SJ, 'Voleva Hitler allontanare da Roma Pio XII?', p. 107.

3

A Convent for Cover

Access is, perhaps, the most important element in any effort to cover an intelligence target. The old adage, 'If you want to hunt ducks, go to where the ducks are', is as relevant to those in search of intelligence as it is to those in search of waterfowl. Access was a problem which constantly bedevilled German operations against the Vatican. Unlike secular governments, the Vatican depended little upon walls, locks, guards, or elaborate security procedures to protect its secrets. To be sure, it made modest efforts to improve its physical security during the war. The brick and stone walls surrounding Vatican City were heightened by the addition of steel railings along their tops, an effect local wags immediately dubbed the 'Canali Line' after Cardinal Nicola Canali, the governor of Vatican City who administered the buildings and grounds of the papal enclave in the name of the Pope. Entry controls were tightened at the various gates and Vatican authorities received daily logs of all those entering the papal city. On the military front the Pope's colourful but minuscule 'army' took the field. At the gates to the Vatican and in the corridors of the papal palace the famous Swiss Guards exchanged their picturesque halberds and swords for more practical equipment: pistols, rifles and gas masks. The Pope's Palatine and Noble Guards, part-time, decorative units which assisted at ceremonies in St Peter's Basilica and paraded for visiting dignitaries, recruited additional personnel and went on active service. The Noble Guards were a rather exotic corps even by the exacting standards of the Pope's comic-opera army. The guardsmen were traditionally drawn from the Italian nobility and none held a rank below lieutenant, anything less than officer status being incompatible with their aristocratic background. They affected the sabres, high boots, and plumed helmets of an early nineteenth-century *cuirassier*, but there was not a horse in the troop. During the war the Noble Guards performed the duties of a personal bodyguard, standing in the papal antechamber and following discreetly as the Pontiff took his daily stroll in the Vatican gardens. The Palatine Guards were Roman shopkeepers who enjoyed dressing in military garb and presenting unloaded and antiquated rifles at ceremonial events. Now issued with bullets and bayonets, the Palatines provided armed patrols for papal buildings and basilicas around Rome and for the Pope's country villa at Castelgandolfo in the Alban Hills. Normally responsible for crowd and traffic control inside the papal city, the Vatican police (a professional force whose dress uniforms of fur busbies and white trousers date back to the Napoleonic era) established a small plainclothes 'Special Section' for internal security and surveillance duties.[1]

Despite these measures, the bases of papal security were not so much physical as cultural and social. The milieu of the Vatican was almost exclusively clerical. It was a small world (at the outbreak of the war the staff of the Pope's Secretariat of State numbered 31 including archival and clerical personnel) and those who moved in that world, who understood it and knew its secrets, were priests who were set apart from laypeople by their dress, their education, their language, their rituals, and their lifestyles. It was an exclusive confraternity, one bound by special loyalties and one largely impenetrable to the German intelligence officers who sought to discover its secrets. While the occasional priest, moved by avarice, patriotism or just plain silliness, might be induced to bring bits of news from inside the Vatican, intelligence officers and diplomatic observers remained outsiders, trading gossip and rumours with other outsiders in the salons and cafés of Rome. But what if the intelligence officers could join the confraternity and become part of the ecclesiastical culture? Could priestly garb and a clerical pose provide access to a world normally so resistant to outside scrutiny?

As we have seen, the idea of infiltrating church circles had long attracted Reinhard Heydrich, the chief of the RSHA until his assassination in Prague by the Czech resistance in the summer of 1942. Even before the war, Heydrich had considered introducing trained agents covertly into ecclesiastical institutions in Rome as well as Germany. The plan envisaged recruiting ideologically sound and highly motivated young Nazis to enter Catholic seminaries and complete the course of studies leading to ordination. Hopefully, these 'priests' would eventually rise to positions of responsibility in the Catholic Church from which they would provide intelligence about church affairs and work to undermine church programmes. Heydrich believed that within 20 years his 'moles' would be positioned to begin their work of destruction. Unfortunately, Hitler was cool towards the idea and the plans remained in abeyance. In September 1940 Heydrich again proposed the infiltration of agents into Roman ecclesiastical institutions, but the foreign ministry successfully opposed the project.[2] Unaware of Heydrich's frustration, Allied intelligence agencies periodically warned their governments that German agents posing as clerics were active around the Vatican, and at one point Britain's Foreign Office actually warned its minister to the Holy See that Monsignor Ludwig Kaas, the exiled head of the defunct German Centre Party who was then living quietly in the Vatican as the administrator of St Peter's Basilica, was a Gestapo agent.[3] The charge was preposterous. In fact Berlin made no systematic attempt to infiltrate the Vatican by placing agents in the many ecclesiastical institutions in Rome until the death of a pious old woman provided an unexpected opportunity.

On 26 February 1941, Sofia Goghieli, a wealthy widow who had emigrated with her husband to western Europe from their native Georgia, died in Brussels. A devout woman, sentimental about the culture and the people she had left behind in the Caucasus mountains, Madame Goghieli bequeathed the sum of 360,000 Belgian francs to an obscure Catholic religious order, the Servants of the Immaculate Conception, also known as the Georgian Congregation of Our Lady of Lourdes. Founded in 1881 to minister to the religious needs of the Catholic minority in Georgia and organized according to the monastic rule of St Benedict, this community had been forced by Soviet religious persecution to forsake its homeland and establish its headquarters in a monastery in Istanbul. It was a small order; in addition to the handful of monks in Turkey, there were only three members in all of Europe. One of the latter, Father Michael Tarchnisvili was eventually entrusted by his superior with the responsibility for settling the Goghieli bequest. Father Michael, a studious and unworldly man, was teaching theology at a Benedictine abbey in Bavaria. When repeated requests to the local authorities for permission to visit German-occupied Belgium were denied, he decided to take his case to Berlin. In the capital he met Michael Kedia, a leader in the Georgian emigré movement in Germany. Kedia was well-known in certain governmental circles and he quickly secured the necessary travel papers for his countryman. In Brussels Father Michael completed his task without difficulty, collecting the bequest and liquidating a few pieces of plate and furniture which the good widow had also left to her favoured monks. Soon the priest was back in Berlin with a large sum of money and a dream.[4]

Father Michael had convinced his superiors in distant Istanbul to use the bequest to establish a Georgian College in Rome. Almost every Catholic national group had its own college in the Eternal City so that a tour of ecclesiastical Rome might include the Scots College, the English College, the Spanish College, and over a dozen other national centres. These institutions were really convents or residences for clerical students who would pursue academic programmes in the various universities and institutes in the Italian capital while living with their countrymen in a religious community which reflected their own cultural background. Father Michael had briefly studied in Rome as a seminarian, and he had long dreamed of a student residence in Rome for young Georgians where the national and cultural identity of their homeland would be nurtured and displayed to the Catholic world. Unfortunately, the generous legacy from Madam Goghieli was not large enough to finance such a project. Upon returning to Berlin from Brussels, Father Michael sought the advice of his new friend Michael Kedia. He outlined his plans for a national college in Rome and received from the emigré leader a promise of support. Kedia assured his countryman that he could easily secure additional financing from other sources who would be happy to contribute to such a noble project. He volunteered to approach potential donors and suggested that, in the meantime, Father Michael should go to Rome to search for an appropriate site for the college. Kedia would send word to the German embassy in Rome where Father Michael should contact a certain Herbert Kappler.[5]

Michael Kedia had been captivated by the idea of a Georgian College, and he was well situated to make the idea a reality. An activist in the fiercely nationalistic movement for Georgian

95

independence, Kedia was a leader of the wing of that movement which gravitated to Berlin because it saw in Nazi Germany an instrument for re-establishing the independent national homeland which had been extinguished, first by the Tsars in the early nineteenth century and then, after a brief revival of freedom in the ruins of the Tsarist Empire, by the Bolsheviks who incorporated Georgia as a constituent republic of the Soviet Union. Unfortunately, Kedia's faith in his Nazi patrons was entirely misplaced. In its blueprints for the post-war world, Germany made no provision for an independent state in the strategically important and oil-rich Caucasus, although in their more expansive moods Nazi planners in Alfred Rosenberg's Office for the Occupied Eastern Territories visualized an anti-Russian *cordon sanitaire* of Caucasian vassal states among which the Georgians (because of their allegedly 'Aryan' qualities) would be allowed a certain primacy, albeit under strict German tutelage.[6] In the meantime, the Georgian nationalists could prove useful in the struggle against the Bolsheviks. Even before the invasion of the Soviet Union in June 1941, Amt VI C, the Russian desk in the foreign intelligence division of the RSHA, had developed a close relationship with the more fanatical (and desperate) nationalists around Michael Kedia who had established a small 'research institute' in Berlin and had placed their contacts in the Georgian diaspora and their underground connections with the Caucasus at the service of the Reich. Desperate for reliable information from the Soviet Union, the Russian desk soon came to consider the Georgians one of its most important assets. There were some in Amt VI, however, who grumbled that the Russian specialists were identified too closely with the Georgians and were too susceptible to the fanciful schemes of Michael Kedia.[7]

Some time in the summer of 1943, Kedia told his friends in Amt VI about Father Michael, the Goghieli bequest, and the idea for a Georgian college. The nationalist leader saw in the conjunction of events an opportunity to serve his patrons and advance the cause of Georgian nationalism. Kedia proposed that the RSHA add to the original bequest sufficient money to allow Father Michael to purchase a property in Rome for the college. To disguise the role of the RSHA, the priest and anyone else who might inquire would be told that the additional funds had come from an anonymous benefactor in the Georgian community. For Kedia and his movement the college would be a symbol of Georgian identity and a centre for nurturing nationalist aspirations in the young seminarians who would live there. In return for their covert support, the Germans would be allowed to use the college for certain intelligence and propaganda purposes. Initially, Amt VI reacted coolly to Kedia's proposal; its chief, Walter Schellenberg, was sceptical as was the head of the Italian desk, both of whom dismissed the proposal as another impractical scheme from the tiresome Georgians. By the late summer, however, senior officers, most particularly Ernst Kaltenbrunner, the chief of the RSHA, had warmed to the idea.[8] After all, Kaltenbrunner's predecessor, the late Reinhard Heydrich, had pushed for the use of ecclesiastical fronts to infiltrate the Catholic Church. Now, when in the face of an anticipated Allied offensive in Italy and the effective collapse of Italian support, German intelligence was rushing to establish networks and develop new assets throughout the peninsula but especially in Rome, what would provide a more perfect cover for intelligence operations than a convent of priests and seminarians? Experience seemed to support this conclusion. German intelligence had long suspected that Roman convents and ecclesiastical buildings were used for the clandestine benefit of the Allies. Hundreds of Jews, anti-fascists, and escaped prisoners of war were sheltered by priests and nuns, and many were hiding inside papal properties. The centre of the so-called 'Rome escape line' was actually inside the walls of Vatican City, and several escapees were hidden nearby on the premises of the North American College.[9] Despite this activity, ecclesiastical institutions in Rome had been generally immune from police searches by virtue of being under the informal protection of the Vatican. Kedia's plan provided an opportunity for German intelligence to turn the tables and create its own island of safety in a sea which might soon be teeming with Allied troops and police. The Georgians found their partner.

Given its interest in the Georgian College, it is noteworthy that German intelligence made no effort to utilize the three German-speaking ecclesiastical colleges in Rome: Santa Maria dell'Anima (the 'Anima'), a large establishment near the Piazza Navona, the German-Hungarian College ('Germanicum') on the Via San Nicola da Tolentino, and the Teutonic College and Hospice ('Teutonicum') alongside St Peter's Basilica in Vatican City itself. The failure to utilize the Anima is especially surprising since the rector of this institution, the Austrian bishop Alois Hudal, was already an informant for German intelligence and was sufficiently sympathetic towards the Nazi regime to have been dubbed in Rome the 'Brown Bishop'. In his writings and lectures and through personal diplomacy in Berlin and the Vatican, Bishop Hudal had long sought to reconcile the Catholic Church with National Socialism, whose anti-clerical features he dismissed as the ignorant work of party radicals insensitive (unlike the more conservative and supposedly responsible wing of the movement) to the importance of Catholicism in German culture and society.[10] Although he had a largely honorific appointment as a consultant to the Holy Office (the department responsible for questions of religious doctrine), Hudal had no influence inside the Vatican where his pronounced pro-Nazi views were suspect, especially among the *monsignori* in the Secretariat of State whose direct experience with the regime in Berlin made them much less sanguine than the good bishop about the possibility of reconciling the church with National Socialism. These officials assumed that Hudal was a German informant and treated him with reserve. He had no access to the Pope or to the Cardinal Secretary of State during the war, and no role in policy-making. Notwithstanding his isolated position on the periphery of Vatican affairs, the Brown Bishop was a ubiquitous figure in Roman social and clerical circles and passed items of ecclesiastical rumour and gossip to the German embassy to the Holy See for whom he was a regular source.[11]

In his eagerness to effect a *rapprochement* between the Holy See and the Third Reich, Hudal often exaggerated his influence at the Vatican and encouraged others to believe that he acted unofficially but authoritatively for the Pope. His pretensions were supported by the belief, incorrect but common among poorly informed observers, that any action by a bishop must necessarily have the approval of the Holy Father. Hudal's constant meddling embarrassed the Vatican, further clouded the already murky waters of Vatican–German relations, and misled any number of later historians who have described the Brown Bishop as an *éminence grise* at the Vatican.[12] Towards the end of 1942, for example, he became involved with several personalities, including the Duke of Mecklenburg, Marschall von Biberstein of the German foreign ministry, and Peter Gast and Werner Naumann of the propaganda ministry, who were among those in Germany hoping to use the Vatican to improve Germany's position in any future negotiations with the Western Allies. These officials mistook Hudal's self-promotion for real influence. On their behalf Waldemar Meyer, an SS officer on special assignment to the foreign ministry, travelled secretly to Rome to discuss with the Austrian bishop the bases for an improvement in church–state relations.[13] The conversations (conducted without the knowledge of the Vatican) resulted in a proposal that Hitler make a magnanimous gesture of reconciliation with the Catholic Church by releasing all religious prisoners, honouring the concordat of 1933, and ending the persecution of the Jews. In return, the Vatican would make a clear public statement about the danger of Bolshevism to western civilization, recognizing implicitly the importance of a strong Germany as a bulwark against this threat. When, predictably, this wild scheme came to nought (Hitler had not the slightest interest in reconciling with the Catholic Church, let alone ending the genocidal persecution of the Jews), Meyer returned to Rome, in March 1943, for further consultations with Hudal. This time the indefatigable bishop apparently offered to go to Berlin to negotiate a settlement on behalf of the Pope, and to sweeten the offer he suggested that the Vatican would be willing to replace certain anti-Nazi bishops with more cooperative prelates. This proposal travelled high enough in the Nazi hierarchy that the Propaganda Minister, Josef Goebbels, noted in his diary: 'Through an undercover informant I learn that the Pope intends to enter upon negotiations with us and would even be willing to send incognito to Germany one of the Cardinals [sic] with whom he is intimate.'[14] The 'cardinal' was, of course, Hudal (who held no such rank) and, needless to say, the Pope knew nothing about the initiative which was entirely a product of Hudal's imagination and his quixotic commitment to reconciling the Catholic Church with National Socialism. Indeed, at the very time in March that the Holy See was, according to the Brown Bishop, so eager to accommodate the Reich, German–Vatican relations were at an especially low ebb and the Pope's Secretariat of State was protesting strongly to Berlin about continuing religious persecution. Not surprisingly, Hudal's second initiative also failed, in part because Martin Bormann, the powerful party secretary, would brook no cooperation with the Catholic Church, and in part because the bases for an accommodation quite simply did not exist.

Despite his apparent sympathies, Bishop Hudal was never trusted in Berlin where party stalwarts in particular were sceptical about his allegiance to the Nazi regime. Party ideologues considered his analysis of the relationship between Catholicism and National Socialism mistaken and subversive, and official disapprobation denied his writings general circulation inside Germany. An official in Alfred Rosenberg's office for party doctrine described Hudal as a 'literary terrorist', while an inquiry by the party control commission dismissed one of his publications as 'a theological pamphlet against the National Socialist *Weltanschauung*'. Distrust of Hudal coloured official perceptions of the institution in Rome of which he was rector. In 1940 the ministry for church affairs refused to approve a proposal to transfer funds from Germany to support the German College, Santa Maria dell'Anima. In its arguments against the proposal, the ministry's Catholic desk, noting that the rector's book on Nazism had to be suppressed in the Reich because it misrepresented the movement, concluded, 'The head of the College, Bishop Hudal, is not a reliable personality and is in fact very dangerous for National Socialist Germany.' The bishop, however, was only part of the problem. In Berlin the German and Austrian priests living at the 'Anima' had the reputation of being hostile towards Nazism. The refusal of the College (at the suggestion of the Vatican) to participate in the festivities surrounding Hitler's state visit to Rome in 1938 had made a bad impression on officials who concluded that the students were 'unpleasant spokesmen for the [Vatican] outlook'.[15]

A similar distrust of the students' patriotism and ideological orthodoxy poisoned Berlin's attitude towards the second German College, the Germanicum. Indeed, given the reputation of the Anima and the Germanicum, SS officers were more likely to consider them a target than a base for intelligence operations. As for the third institution, the Teutonicum, its location inside Vatican City, barely a dozen paces from St Peter's, made it unacceptable. The political risks of running an espionage centre under the windows of the Pope were enough to deter even the RSHA. When an effort by the Gestapo early in the war to use a German priest in the Teutonicum as an informant was exposed, the consternation at the Vatican was so great as to require the removal of the priest to Germany.[16] Another episode might be fatal for German–Vatican relations. With their own national institutions disqualified from consideration, German intelligence officers found the proposal for the Georgian College irresistible.

While Michael Kedia sold his plan in Berlin, Father Michael Tarchnisvili established himself in Rome and informed the Vatican that the Georgian expatriate community in Europe wished to establish a national college in the Eternal City. Accompanied by a monsignor from the Vatican's Congregation for the Eastern Churches, Father Michael scouted Rome for a suitable property. After inspecting several likely sites, he settled on a vacant building, once the villa of the fascist publisher Salvatore di Carlo, on the Via Alessandro Brisse in the Monteverde Nuovo district, a sparsely settled, semi-industrial area on the northern outskirts of the city. All that remained was to await the arrival of the funds promised by Michael Kedia. In Berlin Kedia had instructed Father Michael to apply for the funds at the office of Herbert Kappler of the German embassy. If the simple priest thought it odd that the German police attaché should be involved in the affair, he kept his doubts to himself. On 8 September 1943, hardly a week after German troops occupied Rome, he called at Kappler's office and was ushered into the office of Kurt Hass, Kappler's assistant. The embassy had received no money for Father Michael, but Hass knew about the project for a Georgian College and, promising to make inquiries to Berlin, he suggested that Father Michael return in a few weeks.[17]

Meanwhile, in Berlin the officers of Amt VI were refining their plans to use the Georgian College as an espionage base. To maintain a credible cover the college would actually have to be what it purported to be: a convent for Georgian students pursuing clerical studies in Rome. The administration, the rules, and the living arrangements would have to conform to those at similar institutions in the Eternal City. The intelligence component of the project had to fit unobtrusively into this essentially ecclesiastical setting. Amt VI planned to set up a wireless station inside the convent for direct contact with Berlin. It also expected to send to the convent several agents selected from the so-called 'Georgian Legion' which Germany had recruited from Georgians living in European exile or captured while serving in Red Army units.[18] These agents would be trained in espionage, but would pose as clerical students in order to move freely about Rome without arousing suspicion and to ease their penetration of ecclesiastical institutions. Since Father Michael was known to many in Rome and the Vatican as a devout and scholarly priest, his presence as rector of the new college would add the last bit of verisimilitude to the deception.

To finance the project Amt VI decided to divert some of the proceeds from the sale of counterfeit British banknotes. The RSHA had begun to counterfeit British currency in 1942, using the human resources and physical facilities of various concentration camps such as Sachsenhausen. By the middle of 1943 the bogus bills had become a useful tool in German intelligence operations in Italy and the Balkans. Occasionally, the forged notes were used to pay unsuspecting informants as was the case with Elyesa Bazna (CICERO), the valet of the British ambassador in Turkey who photographed his employer's secret papers for Germany. At other times they were used to bribe officials or servants as when certain of the household staff of Prince Colonna were bribed to testify to purported anti-Hitler remarks by the Italian Foreign Minister, Count Galeazzo Ciano. More commonly, however, the counterfeit currency was sold (at a discount, naturally) for local currency on the black market. This game could be very lucrative. In one month Amt VI agents in Italy realized on their sale of forged British pounds more money (in legitimate Italian lire) than the Gestapo office in Rome normally had at its disposal for the entire year. Recalling the financial arrangements for the Georgian convent operation, a former Amt VI officer stated, 'We had lire in abundance, not the least, of course, on account of the sales of counterfeit pounds in Italy.'[19]

In mid-October Father Michael returned to the office of the German police attaché.[20] Kurt Hass now had good news: the long-awaited funds had arrived from Berlin. According to the police official, an anonymous benefactor had contributed generously to the original bequest of Madame Goghieli, and Father Michael would now have the handsome sum of 1,200,000 lire to start his college. The priest was overwhelmed: the amount was more than enough to purchase the building in the Monteverde Nuovo neighbourhood. After congratulating him on his good fortune, Hass asked Michael to remain for a few moments. There were just a few details to settle before the money was transferred, a few questions about future arrangements. The German officer then proceeded to question the priest about his situation in Rome. Did Father Michael have many contacts at the Vatican? Did he know any cardinals? Was he friendly with any of the *monsignori* who worked in the Vatican departments? Did any of these friends speak about their work or their superiors? The elated priest readily admitted that he was on friendly terms with many people at the Vatican, including Cardinal Tisserant, the head of the Congregation for the Eastern Churches. Hass then inquired if Father Michael could pass on any information that he might pick up from his friends inside the Vatican. Somewhat surprised by the direction that the conversation had suddenly taken, the Georgian asked Hass what he meant. Abandoning all pretence, Kappler's assistant bluntly asked the priest if he was willing to collect information on the Vatican for Germany and if he would allow the Germans to set up a radio station in the new Georgian College. Father Michael's surprise now gave way to shock. What Hass had suggested was completely out of the question. He pointed out that such activity would be contrary to his priestly calling and that he could never agree to participate in espionage, especially against the Vatican. In that case, Hass curtly replied, the money for the Georgian College would not be forthcoming, and without further argument he showed the priest to the door.[21]

Confused and dispirited, Father Michael now turned to an old friend. Basilius Sadathieraschvili was two years younger than the priest and from the same town in Georgia. He had been a room-mate of Michael's in a Constantinople seminary where he had briefly tried a religious vocation before returning to his homeland in 1920. Basilius' subsequent movements are unrecorded, but in 1937 he appeared in Italy as a correspondent for Dutch Catholic newspapers as well as certain Scandinavian papers. He also contributed material, especially on Georgia, to the *Corriere Diplomatico-Consolare*, a magazine for the diplomatic community published in Rome by 'Count' Giacinto Cottini-Agostinelli, a spurious aristocrat who was his friend and financial adviser. Basilius told his Italian friends that he had been persecuted in Germany for political reasons, but there were rumours that he had been jailed there briefly for trafficking in counterfeit Russian roubles and that he had also been expelled from France and Switzerland. Politically active in 'White Georgia', the Georgian fascist movement, he had travelled to Berlin with a delegation of his countrymen at the onset of the Russo-German war to plead for the restoration of the Georgian monarchy under Prince Bragatian, an exile then living on the French Riviera. In September 1943, Basilius was making a meagre living in Rome trading in paintings of uncertain provenance and acting as an interpreter for the German military command on the Corso d'Italia and as an occasional informant for the Gestapo on the Via Tasso.[22]

Basilius listened sympathetically to his friend's story and promptly offered to take matters in hand by travelling to Berlin to talk with Michael Kedia and straighten out the 'misunderstanding'. In the meantime, Father Michael should remain patiently in Rome and not abandon hope. At what point Basilius joined the German operation remains unclear, but he had certainly agreed to collaborate in the effort to infiltrate the Georgian College before he left for Berlin in late October. Upon learning of Kurt Hass's bungled attempt to recruit Father Michael, he had probably approached Kappler's office (where he was employed as a low-level informer) with an offer to help them influence or circumvent his old friend who was proving so uncooperative. Kappler paid Basilius 50,000 lire and dispatched him to Berlin for several days of discussions at RSHA headquarters with Kedia, Captain Reissman (the head of Amt VI's Vatican desk), and representatives from Amt VI's Russian section, which handled the Georgian 'account'. Since there was no question of abandoning a project which offered such perfect cover for intelligence operations, the discussions focused on the problem of Father Michael and his refusal to cooperate. Kedia suggested that the priest should be approached again. The emigré leader believed that the priest was a good Georgian, committed to the independence of his homeland and opposed to the atheistic Bolsheviks who oppressed that homeland. If a fellow countryman were to review the situation with Father Michael and explain that he would be helping the Georgian cause by cooperating with the Germans who were, after all, committed to driving the Bolsheviks from the Caucasus, the priest would eventually put aside his scruples for the greater cause of Georgian nationalism. The professionals of Amt VI, however, rejected this approach. In their view Father Michael was not so naïve that he could be led by appeals to nationalism to ignore the fact that he was actually collaborating with the SS; a fact that might well stiffen rather than weaken his scruples. Moreover, they were increasingly convinced that the unworldly priest lacked the temperament and the talent to run a clandestine intelligence centre. They were concerned that even if he agreed to cooperate, at some future date he would lose his nerve and jeopardize the operation.

The professionals wanted to bypass Father Michael, and in the end their approach prevailed. The money at the Rome embassy would be released to the priest to establish the Georgian College. The

Vatican would be told that the funds for the national college came from the bequest of Sofia Goghieli and from a pious Georgian who wished to remain anonymous. Father Michael would become the director of the convent, and the RSHA would not interfere in his administration of the spiritual and educational life of the establishment. He would have to be convinced, however, to accept Basilius as a 'lay administrator' who would oversee the financial and business affairs of the institution on behalf of Michael Kedia and the Georgian emigré community. While Father Michael was presumably preoccupied with the acquisition of devotional books for the college library, the furnishing of the chapel, and the design of an appropriate clerical costume for the students, Basilius would see to the renovation of the building to be purchased in the Monteverde Nuovo district of Rome. The renovation would include the preparation of two rooms which were to be reserved for the exclusive use of Basilius. These rooms (with their own entrance) were to be rebuilt under the supervision of Lieutenant Stephen Untewenger, an SS signals officer attached to Kappler's office in Rome.[23] One of the rooms would house the radio transmitter which Basilius would carry back to Rome, while the other room would serve the needs of the agents who would eventually use the convent for cover or temporary refuge. According to this new plan, Father Michael was to know nothing about the secret transmitter or the clandestine movement of men and material through the rooms reserved for Basilius.[24]

Basilius proceeded to implement this plan upon his return to Rome. He explained to Father Michael that Michael Kedia (to whose fund-raising efforts the good priest now owed the fulfilment of his dream) thought it advisable that a layman familiar with business practices assume responsibility for the financial affairs of the new college. Father Michael readily acceded to this advice and accepted his old friend from seminary days as lay administrator. The next step was to purchase the building on the Via Alessandro Brisse. The controllers in Berlin considered it crucial that the property be registered in the name of the Vatican. They mistakenly believed that under the Lateran Treaty (which the Vatican had concluded with Italy in 1929) all papal properties were considered extraterritorial and, as such, protected by international law and custom from intrusion or seizure by the police of other countries. This impression was reinforced by the fact that throughout the war any building in Rome regarded as having some kind of Vatican character had been generally off-limits to the fascist authorities (always excluding the clandestine activities of the intelligence and security services). In the months immediately following their occupation of Rome in September the Germans had, in the main, continued this practice. This policy of restraint would disappear by the end of the year as the number of Jews, anti-fascists, and escaped prisoners of war finding asylum in ecclesiastical buildings increased, and German police would eventually raid many such buildings including the Pontifical Oriental Institute, the papal palace of San Calisto in Trastevere, and the Basilica of San Paolo.[25] Still, a large notice announcing 'Property of the Holy See' and bearing the signature of the German military commandant or the Reich ambassador to the Vatican was considered a useful shield for any building. In fact, article 15 of the Lateran Treaty granted extraterritorial status only to the Basilicas of San Giovanni, Santa Maria Maggiore and San Paolo, and to a handful of palaces (identified by name) which were used as administrative offices by the Vatican.[26] The dozens of churches, colleges, convents, and hospitals with their official signs proclaiming 'Property of the Holy See' were not, therefore, legally entitled to immunities or special protection. At best the Georgian College would be an uncertain refuge for German agents.

The Vatican's Congregation for the Eastern Churches had been aware of the plans for a Georgian centre since the summer when one of its staff had accompanied Father Michael on his search for a building. In early December Father Michael and Basilius submitted a formal proposal to Pope Pius XII in which they recalled the historical ties that linked Georgian Catholics with the Popes of Rome, revealed the long-standing wish of the Georgian Fathers to establish a centre in the Eternal City, and announced that the generosity of a 'friend and benefactor of the [Fathers]' had now made that fervent wish a reality. They asked the Holy Father to use the funds provided by the anonymous benefactor to purchase a property in the name of the Holy See and to place it under the protection of the Vatican, while entrusting its direction in perpetuity to the Georgian Fathers. On 11 December, Pius discussed the venture with Cardinal Tisserant and indicated his approval. The Vatican always welcomed the establishment of national ecclesiastical centres in Rome, especially those representing areas where Catholics were a religious minority. Tisserant's Congregation for the Eastern Churches, which was administratively responsible for the Georgian Catholics, had a special reason to support Father Michael's proposal. The Georgian Fathers were coming under increasing pressure in Turkey where the government harassed them with charges of espionage and currency violations.[27] Their ability to maintain their headquarters in Istanbul was uncertain, and a centre in Rome would provide a refuge in the event that they were expelled from Turkey.

On 28 December the formalities for the purchase of the property on the Via Alessandro Brisse were completed in the offices of the Vatican's Administration for Ecclesiastical Properties, and the papers were duly signed and witnessed by Monsignor Giulio Guidetti of that office and the Vatican notary, Saverio Urbani. In a formal letter of 5 January 1944 Cardinal Tisserant informed Basilius that the property had been transferred to the Holy See. The cardinal also acknowledged the generosity of the Georgian community, but noted that the funds were sufficient to cover only the purchase price. Fees for the preparation and registration of the contract, as well as various taxes associated with the transfer of property remained to be paid, and left unsaid was the expectation that the Holy See would not be responsible for these additional costs. Still, the temper of the letter was gracious and appreciative. Cardinal Tisserant noted that the Vatican was so pleased at the prospect of a Georgian College in Rome that 'the August Pontiff, after hearing the noble appeal signed by Father Michael Tarchnisvili and your distinguished self, was pleased to grant a special Apostolic blessing to the anonymous benefactor and to all those who intend to work for the fulfilment of the project'.[28] The 'anonymous benefactors' on the Vatican desk at Amt VI were undoubtedly edified by this gracious gesture of papal approbation.

With the formalities completed work could begin on the renovations necessary to convert a family villa into a religious convent and, incidentally, an espionage base. Pursuant to the agreement with Father Michael which designated him lay administrator of the convent, Basilius retained sole control over the renovations, although in the construction of the two rooms earmarked for intelligence functions he consulted quietly with Lieutenant Untewenger, the SS signals officer from the embassy. The lieutenant's presence reveals more than a concern for technical expertise. While prepared temporarily to use Basilius as their man at the convent because of his alleged influence over his old school chum, Father Michael, the Germans did not entirely trust their Georgian agent, who was known in Rome as a venal and unprincipled adventurer. From the outset of the renovations, Berlin warned Herbert Kappler that Basilius was unreliable and inclined to fantastic but unrealistic endeavours. He was to be watched closely to prevent any 'false game' on his part. As soon as the construction work was complete and the secret rooms were ready to receive the radio transmitter, Basilius was to be sent to Berlin on the pretext that his life was in danger in Rome, and a more trustworthy agent was to be installed in the convent in his place.[29]

As for Father Michael, after his encounter with Kurt Hass at the police attaché's office, he was no longer the innocent who had arrived in Rome the previous summer. At the very least he could no longer delude himself as to the existence of the devout but anonymous Georgian benefactor. By now he realized that the funds which were to make his dream a reality had come from the Germans, but he kept silent and revealed nothing about the source to the Vatican. He rationalized this silence and his acceptance of the money by reminding himself that throughout history various governments had financed the Church's educational and cultural programmes, and that the obvious benefits of the convent to the Georgian national cause were such as to allow a certain moral flexibility. Besides, who questions the origins of a windfall gift?[30] If Father Michael wondered why Germany would support a convent for Georgian seminarians, he probably convinced himself that Berlin merely hoped to cultivate the goodwill of the Georgian nation in support of the common effort against the Bolsheviks. If he suspected a more insidious motive, perhaps one related to his unfortunate interview with Kurt Hass, he forced that suspicion to the back of his mind. As the work on his college progressed, he remained unaware of the plan to install a radio in the two rooms he had agreed to reserve for Basilius, and in its directives to its men in the field Berlin reiterated the importance of hiding the operation from the priest.

Berlin's plans for the Georgian convent included more than a covert subsidy and a clandestine radio station. In mid-February, Basilius made a brief visit to the Reich capital, and returned to Rome with six young Georgian men whom he installed in the Hotel Continental. He then surprised Father Michael with the news that while in Germany he had found the first students for the college: good Georgian Catholics who wanted to study theology and philosophy in preparation for the priesthood. Pleased, but rather bewildered by this sudden turn of events, Father Michael hurried to the Hotel Continental to greet his new charges. His reception was rather cool. The young men were surly and uncommunicative, but they assured the priest that they wanted nothing more than to study theology in Rome. Since the renovations at the convent remained unfinished, Michael agreed that they should remain for the present at the hotel, a concession which was received with evident relief by the group. The next day Michael visited Monsignor Arata, Cardinal Tisserant's deputy at the Congregation for the Eastern Churches, and informed him of the latest development. The Vatican official who, before his current assignment had spent 20 years in the papal diplomatic service, found the sudden arrival of six unannounced and untested 'seminarians' suspicious, and he advised the priest to send the young men back to Germany. Father Michael then discussed the matter with Cardinal Tisserant who suggested that the men be examined: those capable of studying for the priesthood could remain, while the others should be sent home.

Accepting the cardinal's suggestion, Father Michael individually interviewed the young Georgians who, to his great consternation, were inordinately fond of talking about women. Brief conversations were enough to reveal that three of the group were most unlikely candidates for the priesthood. Father Michael gave each a small cash gift and advised them to return to their homes. The remaining three appeared to have some potential and they were given temporary lodging at the Russicum, the Jesuit college for the preparation of priests destined for work in Russia, where their expenses were paid by Cardinal Tisserant's department. After a few weeks in this religious community two of the three decided that seminary life was not for them. Sheepishly, they admitted to Father Michael that they had never really wanted to be priests, but had accepted Basilius's invitation to come to Rome because he had promised that they would live in the Vatican and have good food and fine clothes. They too were sent on their way. Only one of the original six remained and by the summer he also decided to forsake the religious life. After the liberation of Rome, he presented himself to the Allied occupation authorities as a Russian soldier who had been captured by the Germans and was duly passed to the Displaced Persons Unit of the Allied Control Commission.[31]

The six 'seminarians' were, of course, imposters. They had been selected from the ranks of the Georgian Legion, an SS auxiliary unit recruited from emigrés and from Georgians in prisoner-of-war camps. After rudimentary training in espionage they were sent to Rome with the intention that they would infiltrate ecclesiastical institutions from the cover of the Georgian College. One of the six was designated to replace the untrustworthy Basilius as lay administrator and covert intelligence controller at the convent. Father Michael was not a party to this deception, and his unanticipated rejection of half of the team threw the plan into confusion.[32] The operation was already in trouble. The renovations at the Via Alessandro Brisse were behind schedule and Basilius's relationship with Father Michael was increasingly acrimonious, in part because he excluded the priest from all matters concerning the renovations and the financial administration of the convent, and also because the priest discovered that his lay administrator had ordered the construction of unnecessary basement rooms, one of which had a hidden entrance from the garden.[33] It was also at this time that Father Michael somehow learned that Basilius intended to install a radio in those mysterious rooms. The priest had recently been distressed to learn from friends that he was being spoken of in Rome as a German spy, so the news about the radio must have been a shock. It precipitated an angry confrontation with Basilius during which Michael categorically refused under any conditions to permit a radio inside the convent or on its grounds. He turned aside Basilius's efforts to placate him with assurances that the transmitter would be used only to broadcast Georgian programmes and to communicate with Michael Kedia in Berlin.[34]

By the end of March, Operation Georgian Convent was in complete disarray. The dispersal of the Georgian agents combined with Father Michael's refusal to cooperate was to deal a mortal blow to Amt VI's plans. Even the principals began to abandon the operation. Basilius (who had probably been skimming money from the accounts) informed Kurt Hass that the convent had run out of money and that the Italian firm engaged to perform the renovations had yet to be paid. The Georgian adventurer clearly believed that the operation had no future because he asked his SS controller if he could have back his old job as translator for the German police. Hass glumly reported to Berlin that it would be a very long time before the convent would be ready for use. Unfortunately, time was something the Germans did not have in the spring of 1944 as Allied forces positioned themselves for the advance on Rome.[35]

When the Allies occupied Rome in early June, counterintelligence officers had Basilius Sadathieraschvili on their 'Personnel Targets, Priority No. 1', a watch list of almost 100 known or suspected enemy agents in Rome who were to be arrested on sight. The wily Georgian, however, had disappeared from the city at the end of May and was never found. Undeterred by the large notice proclaiming 'Property of the Holy See', police raided the building on the Via Alessandro Brisse on 18 June. The only occupant, the Italian caretaker, was removed for questioning, and the unfinished structure was searched. An entrance to the rooms specially constructed for Basilius was discovered behind a heavy wardrobe. The rooms were empty except for pieces of electrical wire, but on the roof the police uncovered a radio antenna inconspicuously strung along the tiles. As for Father Michael, the priest was found bent over his scholarly books in the Centropreti, a centuries-old hospice for poor pilgrim priests on the Lungotevere dei Vallatti to which he had moved when his convent went bankrupt. Since Michael was the only participant in the affair in Allied hands, the hapless priest soon found himself in Regina Coeli prison as the focus of an espionage investigation. Reluctant to implicate the Vatican in the affair, Michael was at first evasive and reticent, but became more cooperative in later interviews. After two months of investigation, counterintelligence officers concluded that 'There is not sufficient evidence to hold subject for trial on espionage charges. It would be difficult to even charge subject as a collaborator of the Germans, for all the telegrams seem to release subject of any knowledge.'[36] The investigators recommended that the Allies release the priest to Vatican authorities with the understanding that for the duration of the war he remain within the confines of a religious establishment. Upon his release from prison, Father Michael entered a papal institution where he remained happily engrossed in his beloved books until his death in the late 1950s.

The Allies passed the final report of their investigation to the Vatican which was chagrined to learn that it had been an unwitting partner in a German intelligence operation aimed, in large part, at itself. Faces must have been especially red in the Congregation for the Eastern Churches when it discovered that it had caused the Pope to bestow an apostolic blessing on the foreign intelligence section of the

Reichsicherheitshauptamt. On 7 November 1944 the Secretariat of State sent a formal protest to the German embassy, which had relocated inside the walls of Vatican City since the arrival of the Allies. After reviewing the incriminating details of the 'mysterious enterprise', the protest concluded: 'The Secretary of State feels it unnecessary to dwell at greater length on the above facts. The German Embassy will have no difficulty in understanding that, if they are true, the Holy See cannot fail to deplore the part taken by the German authorities.'[37] Actually, the Vatican, for all its embarrassment, was the only actor in the affair to emerge with anything to show for its effort. It retained legal title to the villa on the Via Alessandro Brisse. Today, occupied by government offices, the building remains a reminder of an elaborate but futile plan to penetrate the Vatican.

NOTES

1. Carlo Gasbarri, *Quando il Vaticano confinava con il Terzo Reich* (Padua: Edizioni Messaggero, 1984) pp. 90–1, 95, 121–7; Paul Hofmann, *O Vatican!* (New York: Congdon & Weed, 1984) p. 280.
2. AA. Inland IIg. 71. VI. F.3; W. Hoettl, *The Secret Front*, p. 39.
3. O. Chadwick, *Britain and the Vatican*, p. 95. For an example of an intelligence report of German agents in clerical dress, see NARA. RG 226. Box 359. #35770. IDS report of 24 May 1943.
4. 'Interrogation of Father Michael, 29 July 1944, Regina Coeli Prison', Giuseppe Dosi Papers (in the possession of the authors). Giuseppe Dosi, a retired commissioner in the Italian police, was engaged by the Allies as a special investigator to examine the affair of the Georgian convent.
5. Ibid.
6. Alexander Dallin, *German Rule in Russia, 1941–1945: A Study of Occupation Policies*, 2nd edition (Boulder: Westview, 1981), pp. 226–9.
7. Information from Wilhelm Hoettl.
8. Ibid. Kaltenbrunner's support for the Georgian Convent operation suggests that Peter Black is mistaken in his contention that Heydrich's successor rejected any scheme to infiltrate the Catholic Church. P. Black, *Ernst Kaltenbrunner*, p. 148.
9. Sam Derry, *The Rome Escape Line* (London: Norton, 1960), *passim*; Carlo Gasbarri, *Quando il Vaticano*, pp. 92, 117–20.
10. Hudal's attitude towards National Socialism is developed in his book *Die Grundlagen des Nationalsocialismus* (Leipzig–Vienna: J. Gunther, 1937).
11. After the war Hudal achieved further notoriety by helping fugitive Nazis escape to South America. He rationalized his actions by reference to the same charitable imperative which had led him to help fugitive Jews during the war.
12. For a recent exaggeration of Hudal's influence at the Vatican, see Mark Aarons and John Luftus, *Ratlines: How the Vatican's Nazi Networks Betrayed Western Intelligence to the Soviets* (London: William Heinemann, 1991), Ch. 2.
13. The Meyer mission and its outcome are described in Robert A. Graham, SJ, 'Goebbels e il Vaticano nel 1943', *Civiltà Cattolica*, 4 (Oct. 1974), pp. 130–40.
14. L. Lochner, *The Goebbels Diaries*, p. 271.

15. NARA. T-81. Roll 196, 0347308ff.; AA. St.-S. Inland I D. Vatikan. Kirche 3.
16. When the Germans complained that Monsignor Hugh O'Flaherty, an Irish priest attached to the Holy Office, was using his apartment in the Teutonicum to shelter escaped Allied POWs, the Vatican forced the Irish priest to shift his activity to a less compromising locale. S. Derry, *The Rome Escape Line*, p. 200.
17. 'Confession of Fr. Michele', Dosi Papers.
18. Hoping to capitalize on nationalist and anti-Bolshevik sentiments among the Caucasian and Asiatic peoples of the Soviet Union, the German army recruited several national units from these peoples. In December 1941, OKW ordered the creation of an Armenian Legion and a Georgian Legion. The Georgians trained in the western Ukraine and became operational in the autumn of 1942. Despite their early intentions, the Germans neither trusted nor respected the so-called 'Eastern Battalions' and usually relegated them to such tasks as construction, supply and rear-area security.
19. Information from Wilhelm Hoettl.
20. During his interrogation by the Allies, Father Michael recalled that his second meeting with Hass occurred at the end of September. Communications between the Gestapo office in Rome and its headquarters in Berlin, however, indicate that the money for the project was carried to Rome by Amt VI's Vatican specialist, Wilhelm Hoettl, in the second week in October. Kappler to Berlin, 4 Oct. 1943, Dosi Papers.
21. 'Confession of Father Michael', Dosi Papers.
22. 'Attivita politica di Russi-georgiani a favoure dei Nazisti e dei Fascisti in Roma, 1943–1944', Dosi Papers.
23. Untewenger may have surveyed and approved the site of the proposed college as soon as Kappler's office learned about it from Father Michael. 'Memorandum to Sir William Osborne. Subject: Georgian Convent in Rome', 5 Aug. 1944, Dosi Papers. This memorandum is in places mistaken in its account of the origins of the Georgian Convent affair and should be used with caution.
24. Berlin to Kappler, 18 Nov. 1943, Dosi Papers.
25. C. Gasbarri, *Quando il Vaticano*, pp. 170, 212, 216–17.
26. J.F. Pollard, *The Vatican*, p. 201. Formal extraterritorial status did not protect the Basilicas of Santa Maria Maggiore and San Paolo from forcible intrusions by German and fascist police in February and March 1944.
27. ADSS. Vol. IX, pp. 452–7.
28. Tisserant to Basilius Sadathieraschvili, 5 Jan. 1944, Dosi Papers.
29. Berlin to Kappler, 2 Feb. 1944, and Hoettl to Kappler, undated, but apparently early February 1944, Dosi Papers.
30. 'Confession of Father Michele' and 'New declaration written by Father Michele, 13 August 1944', Dosi Papers.
31. Snowden to Sudakov, 16 Aug. 1944, Dosi Papers.
32. For evidence that Father Michael knew nothing about the true identities and assignments of the six Georgians, see Berlin to Kappler, 2 Feb. 1944, Dosi Papers.
33. 'Confession of Father Michele', Dosi Papers.
34. Hass to Reissmann, undated but clearly March 1944, Dosi Papers.
35. Unsigned and undated summary of telegrams exchanged between Berlin and Rome in March 1944, Dosi Papers.
36. CIC Detachment, Rome Area Allied Command, Rome, Italy, 18 Sept. 1944. Subject: Tarchnisvili, Michael, Rev., Georgian Convent, Via Alessandro Brisse 27, Rome. Copy in authors' possession.
37. ADSS. Vol. XI, pp. 609–10.

4

We are from the North

Early one morning in May 1942, Italian military police quietly moved into position around an apartment building in the Via delle Fornaci, a modest street of small shops and simple flats in the shadow of the Vatican wall. A handful of officers climbed to the fifth floor where they forced an entry into the residence of one Holger Tavornen, a Finnish businessman. They were looking for a wireless set. For some time the radio intercept station at Fort Boccea on the outskirts of Rome had been monitoring certain encrypted signals which seemed to originate from the Vatican's radio transmitter, whose tower, on the highest point in Vatican City, rose within sight of the Italian listening post. Italian military intelligence, the *Servizio Informazione Militare* (SIM), had long before penetrated the cryptosystems used by the Holy See, but the mysterious signals were in a code unfamiliar to the cryptanalysts in SIM's communications intelligence section. Initially, Italian intelligence suspected that the papal Secretariat of State was secretly passing military and political information to the Allies in a code much more sophisticated than those normally in service at the Vatican.[1] These suspicions were encouraged by the assumption, common among Axis intelligence services, that the papacy covertly collaborated with London and Washington in diplomatic and intelligence matters. Eventually, the careful application of direction-finding techniques revealed that the transmissions emanated not from the Vatican Hill, but from a building on the nearby Via delle Fornaci. Additional 'reliable information' eventually led the police to the apartment of Holger Tavornen where the elusive transmitter was discovered concealed behind a radiator.[2]

Tavornen was not a Finn, nor was he a businessman, nor was he in fact Holger Tavornen. Under interrogation he revealed that he was really Ernst Hann, a German citizen, and that he was the radio operator for a Soviet intelligence network which had been collecting information on German, Italian and Vatican affairs since 1940. The apartment on the Via delle Fornaci had been deliberately selected as the site for the network's radio because it was only a few steps away from Vatican City. By transmitting on or near the normal wavelength of Vatican Radio, the clandestine Soviet station hoped to 'hide' behind its ecclesiastical neighbour. When questioned about his network's controller, Hann admitted that the leader lived in Rome, but he claimed never to have met this individual since their only contact was by means of a dead-drop in a rock wall in the Borghese Gardens, a large park on the other side of the city. He had met, however, a young Italian woman whom he believed to be the mistress of the chief. From information provided by Hann, counter-intelligence officers were able, within a day or two, to locate and arrest the woman. She immediately gave up her lover who proved to be one Herman Marley, a Soviet intelligence officer living in Rome under the cover identity of Fritz Schneider, a Swiss citizen from Basle. Marley may well have been the 'Schneider' who received a false Swiss passport and, probably, occasional sums of money through the Soviet network in Switzerland directed by the famous Alexander Rado.[3] Information extracted from Marley and Hann soon led the authorities to other members of the network including an official in the Ministry of Agriculture who often worked as a translator and interpreter at the foreign ministry because of his knowledge of Russian, a fascist polemicist who was close to Mussolini's children, and a husband and wife team originally selected by Soviet intelligence for a mission to the United States who had remained in Rome after Italy declared war on America.[4]

Not content with rolling up the Marley network, Italian counterintelligence proceeded to turn Ernst Hann against his distant controllers. Undoubtedly spurred by the promise of his life in exchange for cooperation, the radioman agreed to transmit to Moscow under the control of his captors. When wireless contact was re-established, SIM fed carefully contrived items of information to Moscow and analyzed the return questions and instructions for clues to Russian intelligence priorities and indications of additional Soviet operations in Italy. Most of these items contained misleading intelligence on the equipment, morale and strength of Italian units destined for the eastern front. In an effort to discover if other Russian assets remained at large in Rome, the Italians instructed Hann to signal Moscow that the network needed money. The reply indicated that on a certain day 6,000 lire could be found in an old can in a ditch near the ruins of the Temple of Castor and Pollux in the Roman Forum. SIM hurried to place the site under discreet surveillance in the hope of identifying the individual who brought the money to the drop. From their vantage points around the Forum and the adjoining Palatine Hill, counterintelligence officers eventually observed a man who lingered around the temple and, as dusk fell, carefully surveyed the surrounding area before stepping into the ravine. The officers immediately seized the individual who proved to be a medical officer at the naval ministry. This astonished physician insisted that he had come to the Forum to enjoy the ruins, and that he had entered the ravine only to relieve a personal need. His story was plausible, but upon searching the small ravine the officers discovered a roll of currency in a dirty can. Convinced that they had snared the paymaster or at the very least a courier for a spy ring, the counterintelligence agents transported their prize to headquarters. The naval physician, however, was the close relative of a senior officer in the Italian armed forces, and this personage intervened to force SIM to release their prisoner before he could be properly questioned. Since the suspect remained under the close protection of his highly-placed relative, the mystery of who hid the money in the can remained open.[5]

The frustrated security officers received another break when their doubled radioman received a transmission from Moscow beginning with the phrase 'We are from the north' and directing the radio operator to carry a message to the occupant of a certain apartment on the Via Cheren, a street in a quiet residential neighbourhood in north-east Rome. The message assured this unidentified individual that everything possible was being done for him, and that it was hoped that he would have some interesting information to report. He was to investigate the possibility of obtaining a wireless transmitter, but in the meantime he was to write, in secret ink, to Istanbul in care of the address he already knew. Moscow ended this transmission by warning the radioman that he should not be surprised to find this new contact dressed as a priest and living with a blonde woman of Russian nationality.

Looking over the shoulder of their tame radioman, Italian counterintelligence officers were excited by their good fortune. Was this intriguing resident of the Via Cheren the elusive paymaster who had escaped their trap in the Forum? Could this message lead to the exposure of yet another Soviet spy ring in Rome? SIM moved quickly because it did not know how much longer its radio game with Moscow would continue undetected, or if the news of the arrest of the Marley–Hann group would leak and drive other Russian agents to cover. SIM's effort was temporarily sidetracked by an error in decoding the important transmission from Moscow. The reference to Istanbul had been mistakenly transcribed as 'Strambul' and for a time security authorities fruitlessly arrested and questioned everyone in Rome with a name similar to that reference. Fortunately, surveillance of the apartment on the Via Cheren proved more productive. Officers learned that the flat was shared by a young couple from the Baltic. The blonde woman observed leaving and entering the apartment was Anna Hablitz, a native of Leningrad, who was employed as a singer by the overseas service of Italian state radio. She was arrested. Her husband, Alexander Kurtna, was away on a visit to northern Europe. When he returned on 30 June he was met at Rome's main railway station by two agents of Italian counterintelligence. SIM soon discovered that it had netted an unusual fish.

Alexander Kurtna had been born in 1914 into a middle-class family in Estonia, a part of the Tsarist Empire until it gained independence at the end of the First World War. His father was an official in the office of the Estonian president, and his mother was a schoolteacher. At the age of 19, after two years of service in the Estonian army during which he served in a signals unit and learned wireless transmission, Kurtna entered a Russian Orthodox seminary, but soon abandoned his family's religion and converted to Roman Catholicism. The conversion did not lessen his sense of a priestly vocation and in 1935 he entered the Catholic seminary in Dubno (Poland) which was administered by the Jesuits. The young convert must have impressed his teachers for at the end of his first year in the seminary Kurtna was called to Rome by the Jesuit Superior General, Father Wladimir Ledochowski, and awarded a scholarship to the Pontifical Russian College. Known as the Russicum, this papal college had been founded in 1928 to educate priests for the mission of re-establishing Roman Catholicism in Bolshevik Russia from which, for all practical purposes, it had been driven by relentless persecution. To prepare for this daunting (and dangerous) task, the students spoke only Russian, immersed themselves in Russian culture and history, and often affected the garb and appearance of Orthodox priests right down to the full beards. Kurtna's intelligence and demeanour (describing him, an interrogator would later note, 'an erudite scholar and highly intelligent – very quiet and reserved manner'), as well as his command of Estonian, Russian, Ukrainian, Polish and German made him an attractive candidate for the Russicum's programme. Despite his academic commitments, Kurtna was able to return to his homeland and to visit Latvia and Poland during a leave of absence in the summer and early autumn of 1938. In 1939 he visited Estonia again and received from the government a grant for research in the Vatican Archives on the subject of medieval relations between the Baltic and the papacy.[6]

Whatever hopes the young seminarian had for a clerical life were cut short in 1940 when the Jesuits concluded that, despite his intellectual talents, the Estonian lacked an authentic vocation for the priesthood. Kurtna left the Russicum but maintained his academic standing by enrolling as a lay student in the Vatican's School of Paleography and by continuing his researches in the Vatican Archives. Since he was no longer a dependent of the Jesuits, his financial status was now precarious. Seeking an extension of his research stipend, Kurtna returned to Tallinn, the Estonian capital, in September 1940. Of course by this time Tallinn was a Soviet city, the Red army having occupied Estonia (as well as Latvia and Lithuania) the previous June as a prelude to incorporating the Baltic republics into the Soviet Union. Kurtna later claimed that the local authorities could do nothing about his scholarship and referred him to the Academy of Sciences in Moscow where, in fact, he was able to receive approval for the continuation of his research at the Vatican and a larger monthly stipend. By the end of November 1940 he was back in Rome.[7]

Although security officers would later wonder why Russia's strict travel controls were inexplicably relaxed to allow an unemployed, military age Estonian (who was now a *de facto* Soviet citizen) not only to move freely within Russian territory, but actually to leave the country, Kurtna's reappearance in the Eternal City apparently caused no comment in the Vatican where by now the former seminarian was a familiar face in the archives as well as the cafés patronized by papal functionaries outside the Vatican walls. Shortly after his return Kurtna began to supplement his research stipend by translating letters and documents for the Congregation for the Eastern Churches, the Vatican department concerned with ecclesiastical affairs in the Soviet Union. Upon their occupation of the Baltic States, the Soviets had closed all diplomatic missions, including the papal nunciatures formerly accredited to those republics. For news from the region the Vatican now depended upon the occasional letter from a bishop or priest which slipped through Russian and German controls and survived the long journey to Rome. Even less frequently, similar channels might bring some news from other parts of the Soviet Union. This meagre and dismal correspondence with its reports of arrests, deportations and executions found its way to desks in the Vatican's Secretariat of State and the Congregation for the Eastern Churches.[8] As a translator for the latter department, Kurtna was gradually introduced into the small circle of priests, some in the papal administration, some in religious orders, who tried to follow church affairs in Russia. In this way he became acquainted with Monsignor Antonio Arata, the former nuncio to Latvia and Estonia, who was the executive secretary of the Congregation for the Eastern Churches, and Monsignor Mario Brini, the Russian specialist in the small Secretariat of State who was also the personal assistant to Monsignor Giovanni Montini, the deputy Secretary of State (and future Pope Paul VI) who saw the Pope on a daily basis.[9]

Kurtna gradually extended his contacts into the large German community in Rome. In the spring of 1941 he appeared at the German Historical Institute, one of the several national facilities in the Eternal City devoted to supporting historical and archeological research. Ostensibly, he was seeking additional financial support. Although the Director of the Institute, Dr Ferdinand Bock, must have wondered why an Estonian was soliciting assistance from a German organization, he was sufficiently interested in the struggling scholar to agree to provide a monthly stipend from the Institute's research funds.[10] It is unlikely that Bock's interest was aroused solely by Kurtna's research project. During the war the German Historical Institute was an informal arm of German intelligence in Rome and its director maintained close connections with Major Herbert Kappler, the police attaché and Gestapo representative at the Reich embassy.

Meanwhile, Kurtna did not neglect his Russian contacts. He visited the Russian embassy at least twice that spring. On the first occasion he was invited for an interview with the cultural attaché who had noticed an article which Kurtna had recently published on the historical collections of the Hermitage, the famous state museum in Leningrad. Cardinal Eugène Tisserant, the prefect (director) of the Congregation for the Eastern Churches, had provided some assistance in the preparation of this article, and the Russian diplomat was apparently interested in Kurtna's contacts with this prelate who was rumoured to be preparing priests to infiltrate secretly the Soviet Union. The second visit occurred shortly before Germany's attack on the Soviet Union. Disturbed by reports of German–Soviet tensions, the Estonian scholar called at the embassy to clarify his status in the event of war between Italy and the Soviet Union. An embassy official advised him to try to stay in Rome as a researcher, and asked him to report on events in the Vatican and the fascist capital. Kurtna agreed.[11]

Kurtna had almost certainly been 'spotted' by Soviet intelligence during his visit to Estonia the previous autumn. His freedom to travel unmolested in Soviet territory at a time when thousands of middle-class Estonians of the governing class like himself were being deported to the east, and his ability to secure from Moscow's Academy of Sciences a travelling scholarship to the Vatican to study the papacy even as the Soviet occupiers of Estonia were prohibiting the study of ecclesiastical subjects and destroying theological libraries suggests a certain degree of official interest in the former seminarian.[12] It is perhaps more than coincidence that Kurtna returned from his rather remarkable visit to Soviet territory during the same year, 1940, that the Marley–Hann network had been activated in Rome by its Soviet controllers. If Kurtna was not actually recruited during this trip, his status as an intelligence source was clear by the outbreak of the Russo-German conflict on 22 June 1941. Unfortunately, details concerning his activities in the months immediately following his last visit to the Soviet embassy remain elusive.[13] Since his name did not figure among those revealed by Herman Marley and Ernst Hann during their interrogations, it is unlikely that Kurtna was a Vatican source for the Marley network. He may have reported to a different controller (despite rolling up the Marley network, Italian counter-intelligence suspected that additional Soviet agents remained at large in Rome) or he may have been a 'sleeper' and Moscow's instructions to the radioman Hann to contact the inhabitant of the Via Cheren may have been an effort to activate the Estonian. Whatever the nature of his connections with Moscow, Kurtna maintained his residence in Rome and continued his studies in the Vatican Archives protected for the moment from the close scrutiny of the Italian police by his quiet lifestyle and his uncertain citizenship (as an Estonian was he an enemy, an ally or a neutral?). He did not, however, escape the notice of the Gestapo.

In early 1942 Kurtna learned from Dr Ferdinand Bock that in accordance with new instructions from the Reich embassy in Rome prohibiting employment of non-Germans by the German Historical Institute his monthly research stipend had been cancelled. Expressing great chagrin at this unfortunate development, Dr Bock assured his Estonian colleague that he would do everything to help him through this difficult time. He arranged for Kurtna to meet his good friend Herbert Kappler, the police attaché at the German embassy. As luck would have it, Major Kappler needed someone to prepare monthly summaries of press coverage of German–Vatican relations, the officer normally responsible for this task having just been reassigned to North Africa. Kurtna was hired on the spot.[14]

At first glance, Kurtna's attachment to Kappler's office seemed to provide Soviet intelligence with an ideal opportunity to penetrate the German police apparatus in Rome. It was a significant target since the office of the police attaché supervised all police and security cooperation with Mussolini's regime and informally collected information on political affairs in Italy and the Vatican. A penetration of that office would not only tap a potentially rich vein of intelligence, but with judicious control might also serve as a channel for disinformation to mislead the Germans. There is strong evidence, however, that the Gestapo officer knew from the start that the Estonian was a Soviet agent. In February 1942 he informed Berlin that he had opened a connection with the Russian intelligence service, and a report in April referred to a Soviet intelligence officer from the Baltic. In a post-war interrogation the police attaché would acknowledge recruiting Kurtna, whom he described as 'an ex-Soviet agent'.[15] Although Kappler's intentions in recruiting Kurtna remain obscure, the Gestapo officer seems to have prepared a complicated game. He would use Kurtna as a source of information on Vatican affairs, knowing full well that the same information might also make its way to Moscow, but he could also carefully feed the Estonian false information deliberately contrived to mislead his Soviet controllers.

Although Kurtna later claimed that his work for Kappler in the first six months of 1942 was strictly limited to the preparation of monthly press summaries, the evidence indicates that he actively collected information on Vatican affairs for his new employer. Kappler would later confirm that the Estonian had worked as his agent during this period. During these months the police attaché's reports concerning the Vatican were suddenly rich in East European topics, the very area most familiar to Kurtna given his background, his work for the Congregation for the Eastern Churches, and his circle of acquaintances.[16] On 14 February Kappler passed to Berlin a report on the Vatican's Russian policy, another on a 'Jesuit information bureau for Slovak and Czech affairs', and a third on alleged clandestine radio contact between the Vatican and the Ukraine. The following week he informed Berlin that two priests close to the Pope had been ordered by the Pontiff to begin studying Russian. In March there were separate reports on the role of the Jesuits in the Vatican's 'Ostpolitik', the arrival of letters from Lithuania at the Vatican Information Office (an agency organized to trace prisoners of war but suspected by Germany as well as other belligerents of covert intelligence functions), the identities of important Catholic personalities in eastern Europe, and the clandestine channels by which the Vatican received information from German-occupied territories in Poland and the Baltic States.

There can be little doubt that Alexander Kurtna was the source of these reports. In 1942 Kappler's penetration of the Vatican was rather shallow. In addition to his Estonian scholar, the police attaché's network consisted only of a librarian at the Pontifical Gregorian University, across town from the Vatican, and a researcher who worked at times in the Vatican Archives.[17] It is unlikely that the latter two sources would have had access to much of the information Kappler passed to Berlin. Kurtna was far better placed to report such confidential information as a result of his work as a translator in the Congregation for the Eastern Churches and his contacts in the ecclesiastical circles concerned with eastern Europe. Though careful never to reveal his source, Kappler once had an occasion to describe the individual. The German foreign ministry had asked its ambassador to the Holy See, Diego von Bergen, to confirm Kappler's report that two officials in the papal Secretariat of State had taken up Russian. The Secretariat was a small organization. If two of its staff of scarcely a score of officials had suddenly been ordered to learn Russian, then the papal foreign ministry was anticipating greater involvement in Soviet affairs. This was a matter that clearly required clarification. After inquiries Ambassador Bergen had replied that the Secretariat denied the report. The police attaché was outraged that the foreign ministry would challenge his information, but he was even more upset that the ambassador's inquiries might have compromised his important source. The Gestapo officer assured his superior in Berlin, Heinrich Müller, that the report was accurate. The papal officials were receiving instruction from Bishop Alexander Evreinoff, a former Tsarist army officer who was one of the directors of the Vatican Information Office, and one received special tutoring from Monsignor Mario Brini of the Secretariat of State. In a separate letter to his friend Werner Picot, the head of the Vatican desk at the foreign ministry and a former official in the German embassy to the Holy See, Kappler objected to his intelligence reports being submitted to the embassy for verification. Such a practice might inadvertently expose his informant whom the police attaché described as 'a regular collaborator of Evreinoff, a personal friend of Brini and a good acquaintance of Rossi and de Costa. The reliability of my informant has been proved many times.'[18] Among Kappler's informants only Kurtna fits this description.

The contents of Kappler's reports also point to the Estonian as the source. Often they contain a richness of detail that suggests the observations of a participant or a witness. The long report of 24 March 1942, for example, describes the handling of clandestine mail reaching the Vatican's Congregation for the Eastern Churches from German-occupied areas of Eastern Europe. According to the informant, the messages are translated into Italian from Estonian, Lithuanian, Polish, Russian or Latin, and then given to Cardinal Tisserant, the head of the Congregation, who passes the more interesting items to the Pope. From remarks dropped by Monsignor Salvatore Pappalardo, an official in the Congregation, the informant suspects that these letters are often entrusted to Catholic soldiers returning home to Germany or Italy on leave from the eastern front. Among the items recently received from Estonia was a letter from the

Jesuit Father Charles Bourgeois who described the arrival of the Germans in that country. At first the Germans had been welcomed as liberators, but the Estonians soon discovered that they had merely exchanged one master for another. According to Father Bourgeois (as related by Kappler's source) some Estonians had freely transferred their support to the Russians. Within a month of Kappler's report to Berlin Father Bourgeois was arrested by the Gestapo and transported to a concentration camp on the charge of illegally corresponding with foreigners. Kappler's source inside the Vatican also reported the arrival of letters from Jesuits in Poland, as well as a letter from a Jesuit in Lithuania, who described the German occupation as no better than the Russian occupation. Kappler's intelligence report also noted that Monsignor Arata, Tisserant's deputy in the Congregation for the Eastern Churches, was considering the dispatch into the German-occupied territories of 'special emissaries' to verify the disturbing reports of religious persecution which were reaching the Vatican.[19]

The information passed on by Kurtna must have been seized upon eagerly by the Russian and Vatican desks at RSHA headquarters. As we have seen (Chapter 1), Reinhard Heydrich and his senior officers believed that the Vatican hoped to use Germany's drive to the east to infiltrate priests into the Soviet Union as part of a long-term project (the 'Tisserant Plan') to convert Russia and encircle Germany with Catholic states. Of course the Vatican had no such plan, but the RSHA saw disguised Jesuits behind every bush in the Ukraine and Belorussia. In this fanciful scenario Cardinal Tisserant was responsible for implementing the plan to which end he directed a vast clandestine apparatus of disciplined priests and pliant laypeople. To thwart this dangerous threat to the Reich, the RSHA needed intelligence on the activities of this apparatus. With his source in the Congregation for the Eastern Churches Kappler seemed to have penetrated the very heart of the conspiracy.

In June 1942 Kurtna made another visit to Estonia, ostensibly to seek a further renewal of his research grant from whatever responsible authorities might be found in Tallinn. There are several puzzling aspects to this trip, not the least of which is its short duration. Kurtna left Rome on 23 June (having married his fiancée, Anna Hablitz, five days earlier) and returned on 30 June only to be arrested by Italian counterintelligence officers as he stepped from the train. Even today, a one-way rail journey from Rome to Tallinn would require the better part of three days. In the wartime conditions of 1942 the trip might easily have taken even longer. In seven days Kurtna would hardly have had time to complete the travel portion of his journey, yet he subsequently claimed to have secured from the Estonian authorities a small research grant, learned from friends that one of his brothers (a volunteer in the Soviet army) had been executed by the Germans, and interrupted his return to Rome with a visit to the papal nunciature in Berlin.[20] The alleged reason for the trip seems equally implausible. Although Kurtna's application for travel permits was warmly endorsed by the directors of the German Historical Institute and German Library in Rome, it is unlikely that police and military authorities would have permitted a 28-year-old Estonian to travel across the Reich to Tallinn for *any* reason, let alone one so irrelevant to the war effort as the renewal of a small research grant. Such a trip could only have occurred with the support of the Gestapo representative in Rome. In the absence of documentary evidence, only speculation is possible, but it is not unreasonable to suppose that Kappler hoped to collect intelligence on ecclesiastical affairs in Poland and the Baltic States by sending to those areas an individual who was sufficiently trusted in the Congregation for the Eastern Churches that he might be asked by the Vatican (when plans for his journey became known) to carry messages or make clandestine contact with bishops and priests in the occupied territories. It is also possible that the trip to Estonia might have been a cover story to explain his absence from Rome while on some other mission for Kappler.

June 1942 was a bad month for Herbert Kappler. As the senior security officer in the German embassy he was embarrassed early that month when Italian counterintelligence revealed that Kurt Sauer, a cultural attaché at the embassy and a popular figure in Roman diplomatic circles, had been passing information to the Swiss military attaché in Rome and also to Ernst Hann, the radio operator of the rolled-up Soviet spy ring. Sauer had been exposed when Italian agents covertly entered the Swiss embassy one night, burgled the safe of the military attaché, and discovered documents which incriminated the German diplomat.[21] More seriously, with Alexander Kurtna's arrest by Italian counterintelligence at the end of the month Kappler lost his most important source inside the Vatican. For their part, the Italians suspected that they had netted another Soviet agent. Their suspicions increased when they intercepted a letter addressed to the Estonian from a Russian woman in Istanbul who inquired about the latest news. This letter appeared to connect with the earlier radio transmission from Moscow which instructed Kurtna to write to an address in Istanbul. During 14 months of incarceration and 20 interrogations by the Italians Kurtna persistently denied that he was a Soviet agent, although he apparently acknowledged his connection with the German police attaché. He claimed that he was the helpless victim of a Russian ploy to involve him in espionage, that he knew nothing about radio transmissions from Moscow or the expression 'We are from the north', and that the letter from Istanbul was exactly what it appeared to be – an innocent contact from a friend. The Italians remained unconvinced. They knew enough about Kurtna's connection with Kappler that, for a time, some counterintelligence officers wondered whether their man's allegiance was to Berlin or Moscow. On the strength of his casual connection with Cardinal Tisserant, a former cavalry captain in the French army who was suspected by both German and Italian security services of passing information to French intelligence, some officers even suspected the Estonian of working for France. The capable officer directing the investigation, Lieutenant Colonel of *Carabiniere* Manfredi Talamo, eventually concluded that Kurtna was a Soviet agent who had been used by Moscow to penetrate Kappler's operations and to collect intelligence on the Vatican.[22]

Kurtna's trial for espionage, eventually scheduled for August 1943, was delayed in the aftermath of Mussolini's fall from power in July. When the Germans occupied Rome in September, Herbert Kappler, effectively now the police chief in the city, intervened to save his erstwhile agent. Kurtna and his wife were released from Regina Coeli prison, and all files relating to the investigation were removed to the Gestapo's offices on the Via Tasso.[23] The Kurtnas found a flat a few blocks from the Vatican on the Via Cola di Rienzo, and Alexander returned to his work as a part-time translator for the Congregation for the Eastern Churches. Apparently the Vatican, which always exhibited a rather cavalier approach to security, remained unimpressed by the charges swirling about the head of their Estonian employee.[24] Kappler, however, did not intend to allow his former agent to retreat into quiet domesticity. Within a few weeks of his release Kurtna was summoned to the Via Tasso for a meeting with his saviour. He learned that he and his wife were to have been deported to Germany to meet an uncertain fate, but that Kappler had countermanded the order and they would now be allowed to remain in Rome. The Gestapo chief explained that the reversal was due entirely to the kindly intercession of Dr Ferdinand Bock, Kurtna's old patron at the German Historical Institute, but Kappler obviously had his own plans for the young translator. He had Kurtna sign a document which stipulated that the Estonian would do nothing prejudicial to Germany and its war effort on pain of execution without a trial.[25]

Not surprisingly, Kappler's plans for Kurtna included a resumption of his espionage at the Vatican. With Allied armies in southern Italy and the Pope suspected by Berlin of collaborating in Mussolini's overthrow and abetting Italy's subsequent abandonment of the Axis cause, intelligence from the Vatican was more important than ever. Kurtna began again to visit the Gestapo offices on a regular basis. Although he would later explain to Allied interrogators that he was merely seeking news of his mother in Estonia, he usually met two of Kappler's aides, Kurt Hass and Norbert Meyer, who questioned him about personalities and events at the Vatican. During these visits Kurtna ingratiated himself with Kappler's secretary, a Fraulein Schwarzer, to whom he had been introduced by another employee of the German embassy who confided that despite her sensitive position Kappler's secretary secretly nurtured communist sympathies. Kurtna apparently made quite an impression on Schwarzer for at his urging the secretary removed certain compromising documents from the files of his arrest and interrogation which Kappler had confiscated from the Italians. She also shared with the charming young Estonian all the office gossip. In December 1943, for instance, Schwarzer mentioned a rumour that Berlin was preparing to send to Rome an important SD officer to reorganize the intelligence effort against the Vatican. The next month she reported the arrival from Germany of an 'interesting man', an historian named Elling, who might be able to help Kurtna with his 'research'. Kurtna correctly guessed that the new intelligence officer had reached Rome.[26]

Georg Elling was a very special historian. After military service in the First World War, he had entered a Benedictine monastery and been ordained a priest, but had abandoned both his vocation and his

Catholic faith by 1931. Casting about for a means of livelihood, he began desultory studies in medicine and worked at various jobs while satisfying his residual spiritual appetite by preaching occasionally before a number of 'free' religious communities which had splintered off from mainstream German Protestantism. Perceiving, like so many others, an avenue for preferment in the electoral victory of the National Socialists in March 1933, Elling joined the Nazi party in May of that year and entered the SS in November. He found employment in the SD, the party intelligence organization, and followed the path of other apostate and renegade priests who had drifted into the intelligence and security services by specializing in the surveillance of religious organizations. In 1935 he was the section chief for 'Churches and Sects' in the SD regional office in Stuttgart and was selected to lecture the service's religious affairs specialists on the recruitment of informants inside the churches. By 1939 he was in Berlin, and after the consolidation of state and party security services into the *Reichssicherheitshauptamt* (RSHA) he assumed duties on the 'Religious Life' desk of the new organization's domestic intelligence department. After a temporary assignment to the RSHA office in Metz and a brief tour of active duty with a headquarters unit on the eastern front in 1941, Elling was posted, as an instructor, to an RSHA academy and was tipped for a teaching position at a new *Führerschule* for party officials.[27]

Georg Elling's transfer to Rome marked the end of another skirmish in the RSHA's long-running battle to wrest control of all intelligence activities in the Reich. In this particular encounter the opponent was the foreign ministry while the battleground was the German embassy to the Holy See. As we have seen, Reinhard Heydrich had sought to attach an SD officer to that embassy as early as January 1941, but his plan collapsed in the face of stiff opposition from Ribbentrop. The plan resurfaced in the spring of 1943 when Walter Schellenberg, the director of Amt VI (foreign intelligence) in the RSHA, approached the foreign ministry with a proposal to improve the collection of intelligence at the Vatican by the assignment of an officer of his department to the Reich embassy.[28] Schellenberg had just the man for the job, an experienced intelligence officer and 'an outstanding expert on Vatican affairs'. He was referring to Georg Elling. The foreign ministry received this proposal in silence, hoping perhaps to deflect the unwanted intervention by inattention. The RSHA tried again in August, but this time there was a certain urgency in their formal application to attach Elling to the Vatican mission. Since the first approach in the spring, Mussolini had fallen, the Allies had taken Sicily, and German intelligence had begun to prepare for the expected invasion of the Italian mainland. Amt VI believed that in preparation for the battle for Italy the Allies would increase their political and intelligence operations in the Vatican. Only an experienced intelligence officer could monitor such operations and 'get behind the intrigues of the English and American citizens who even now are coming and going', but it was difficult for an SD officer to gain entry to Vatican City. Embassy cover, however, would allow an officer access to papal territory and provide an opportunity to mix with papal officials at official receptions and dinners. To assuage any suspicion that their officer would usurp the responsibilities of the diplomats at the embassy, Amt VI assured the foreign ministry that the proposal envisaged 'less the observation of the Vatican itself, though this is naturally also in question, but more the primary surveillance of enemy agents and other circles unfriendly to the Reich'.

The Wilhelmstrasse remained unconvinced. The new ambassador at the Vatican, Ernst von Weizsäcker, strongly resisted the assignment of an SD officer to his mission. He argued that the officer's cover would be transparent, remarking that 'the Vatican is a village as far as personnel is concerned'. The diplomatic missions to the Vatican, including Germany's, were small, and the assignment of an additional attaché, especially at that particular time, would cause much comment and speculation. Weizsäcker also scoffed at the idea that embassy cover would provide an intelligence officer with opportunities to encounter papal officials at diplomatic receptions. According to the ambassador, Vatican personnel rarely socialized; the principal diplomatic contacts, Cardinal Secretary of State Luigi Maglione and his two deputies in the Secretariat of State, Monsignors Domenico Tardini and Giovanni Montini, had left the precincts of the Vatican to attend a diplomatic function only twice in the past six months. Finally, Weizsäcker suggested that even the most experienced officer would have little success in discovering the real secrets of the Vatican.

> In the Vatican and in circles around the Vatican, there are always a lot of reports, assertions and rumours in circulation. Our informers overwhelm us with their information. There is

no shortage in this respect. But what is needed, instead of this deluge of unreliable reports, is to get the few bits of information that are really important. But in the Vatican only a very small circle of persons are informed about any political facts worth knowing. This small circle keeps the secret of office, to which they are held by a special religious obligation, with the utmost strictness.

In the end, such arguments were of no avail. Heinrich Himmler, the *Reichführer SS*, let it be known that he was personally committed to the assignment of an SD officer to the Vatican embassy, and as had been demonstrated in the past, Ribbentrop was unable to resist for long the will of this powerful figure. The foreign minister's resistance was also seriously weakened by his department's lacklustre record in the area of intelligence collection and by the fact that (as a result of his agreement with Heydrich in 1941) he had already accepted RSHA intelligence and security officers in over a dozen embassies.[29] In early December the foreign ministry informed the RSHA that it would accept Georg Elling at the Vatican embassy and for purposes of cover would designate him a cultural attaché.

Anticipating the Wilhelmstrasse's agreement, Amt VI had already sent Elling to Rome in November. Posing as a freelance historian investigating the life of St Francis of Assisi, Elling was informally attached to Herbert Kappler's office where Hass and Meyer provided a general orientation concerning current intelligence efforts against the Vatican and began the process of turning over to him the handful of informants currently working against that target. Among the latter was Alexander Kurtna. Elling first met Kurtna in January 1944 when the Estonian called at his rooms in the Hotel Maestoso. Later, Kurtna would try to convince Allied interrogators that this visit was nothing more than an innocent effort to find scholarly work to supplement his modest earnings as a part-time translator at the Vatican. According to his story, Fraulein Schwarzer had told him that the new arrival from Berlin was an historian who needed a research assistant familiar with the Vatican and comfortable in German, Italian and Latin. During this visit Kurtna offered his services and was engaged by 'Professor' Elling to summarize several Italian books relevant to the latter's research into the history of German–Vatican relations.[30] Kurtna maintained that when he was hired by the 'professor' he did not know that Elling was on the staff of the German embassy to the Holy See. He also claimed that it was only six months later that he discovered, through Schwarzer, that his employer was using the radio of the Rome Gestapo office to send reports to Amt VI in Berlin.[31]

While Elling may have adopted the persona of an amateur historian in order to protect his diplomatic cover of cultural attaché, it is unlikely that Kurtna (who by then had accumulated more than a little clandestine experience himself) could have been misled as to his real work in Rome. In fact, Fraulein Schwarzer had earlier told him specifically that Elling was an SD officer, and since Elling had been temporarily assigned to Kappler's office until he could join the embassy, the police chief's confidential secretary would have known about his mission and passed the information to her Estonian friend as she seemed to pass everything else of interest. Indeed, her trust and generosity would soon place an intelligence windfall in Kurtna's hands.

Originally, Amt VI had wanted to place an officer in the Vatican embassy in part to monitor more closely the activities of enemy diplomats accredited to the Holy See, most of whom had been forced to take up residence inside Vatican City when Italy entered the war in June of 1940. Berlin suspected that these diplomats, particularly Francis d'Arcy Osborne of Britain and Harold Tittmann of the United States, were engaged in various political intrigues aimed at securing the sympathy of Pope Pius XII and undermining the Axis position in Italy. By January 1944, however, the intelligence focus had expanded. The Allies had captured Naples and were pushing north, and while fierce German resistance had slowed their progress, the threat to Rome was serious. In Berlin, Amt VI's Italian desk had decided to concentrate on preparing stay-behind networks in anticipation of further Allied advances. In January, Elling had been summoned to Berlin to receive a new mission from Schellenberg: the organization of a network of agents in Rome who would maintain the intelligence flow to Berlin should Germany have to abandon the city. The intelligence chief believed that Elling would be ideally placed to control such a network since, in the event of a German withdrawal, the Reich embassy to the Holy See would repeat the experience of its Allied counterparts by moving into the sanctuary of Vatican City.[32] Schellenberg probably foresaw another purpose for the Elling mission. As we have seen, the intelligence chief had long been deeply pessimistic about the course of the war and convinced that Germany should seek a negotiated settlement, Schellenberg may have wanted to have a loyal and competent officer inside the Vatican in the event that it became necessary to use the Pope as a channel for peace overtures to Britain and the United States.[33]

Elling returned to Rome and proceeded dutifully to fulfil his dual mission of reporting on Vatican affairs and recruiting a stay-behind network to cover all of Rome. There was, however, a certain lack of enthusiasm in his labours. In its efforts to convince the foreign ministry to attach Elling to the Vatican embassy, Amt VI had exaggerated his skills as a Vatican specialist. In reality the SD officer knew little and cared hardly more about the Vatican, his previous experience being limited to penetrating religious organizations inside Germany. He was also rather sceptical about the potential intelligence benefits of his mission and believed that the real reason for his assignment was a desire by Heinrich Himmler to counter the suspected intrigues of Martin Bormann, the powerful head of the Party Chancellery, who had succeeded in securing a place in the Vatican embassy for one of his protégés, Ludwig Wemmer. Apparently Bormann planted Wemmer in the embassy because he distrusted Ambassador Weizsäcker and wanted his own window on the Vatican. Finally, Elling's relationship with Herbert Kappler was marked by tension growing into outright hostility as the intelligence officer became aware of the notorious reputation of the Nazi police chief in Rome whose offices on the Via Tasso were the scene of countless 'radical' interrogations.[34]

Whatever his misgivings about his mission or his associates, Elling gradually began to build his networks. An 'ecclesiastical' group generated information on the Vatican and church circles in Rome. Alexander Kurtna (codename 'Ulrich') was probably the star of this network which also included a monsignor in the Vatican Information Office (the office concerned with tracing prisoners of war), another monsignor who worked in the Congregation for the Concistory (the Vatican department concerned with the creation of new dioceses and the appointment of bishops), two Jesuit priests, one assigned to the Russicum and the other (a former student at the Russicum) to the historical office and archives at the Jesuit headquarters near the Vatican, and three Benedictine monks at their order's headquarters on the Aventine Hill across the Tiber. Except for Kurtna, the members of this group were all Germans or Italians. A so-called 'diplomatic' group probably represented Elling's effort to put together a network to cover Rome after the arrival of the Allies. This group included a Finnish journalist, a Swedish journalist and a former Yugoslavian diplomat.[35]

From his ecclesiastical group and his personal observations as a member of the embassy, Elling conscientiously collected information on Vatican events and personalities for his monthly reports which were well received in Berlin. These reports were shown to Ambassador Weizsäcker before their consignment to the embassy pouch.[36] Additional reports were apparently transmitted directly to Amt VI by means of the radio facilities at the Via Tasso, but it is unlikely that these were first submitted to the ambassador. Elling's coverage of the Vatican was sufficient to satisfy his superiors in Berlin, but his efforts to build a stay-behind network for operations in Allied-occupied Rome lagged.

Throughout this period Alexander Kurtna continued to work as an informant for Elling and probably also his old friend Herbert Kappler.[37] Indeed, the Estonian had become so valuable a source that German intelligence officers were competing for his services. Early in 1944 he was approached by Norbert Meyer, one of Kappler's aides who was organizing his own stay-behind network, and asked if he intended to remain in Rome if the city fell to the Allies. When Kurtna replied that he did indeed intend to stay, Meyer arranged for him to meet a woman of Yugoslavian background who had been serving as a mail drop for German intelligence in Rome and who, in the event of an Allied occupation, would also stay in the city to maintain covert postal and radio communications with the retreating Germans. When informed of this encounter, Elling warned Kurtna to stay away from Kappler's organization and to deflect any future approaches by stating his intention to leave Rome.[38] Clearly, the embassy attaché intended to be Kurtna's sole controller, and he feared that any further association with the notorious operation on the Via Tasso would only draw attention to his prize agent when the Allies arrived.

Whatever plans Elling had for future operations began to collapse in the hectic final days of the German presence in Rome. Although Amt VI had been anticipating the loss of the city since January, arrangements for shifting and protecting intelligence assets and resources remained incomplete. Elling discovered that the funds necessary to develop and maintain his networks during the Allied occupation, though long-promised, would not be forthcoming. The day before the Germans withdrew from the city, Kappler's office sent Kurtna to Elling with a sealed packet containing 100,000 fast-depreciating lire and a few gold coins. The sum was woefully inadequate for the indefinite maintenance of intelligence networks, and Elling disdainfully sent Kurtna back to inquire as to how Kappler expected the money to be used. Then, on the eve of the Allies' arrival, the operator assigned to maintain Elling's covert radio link with Berlin turned in his radio set and codebooks to the embassy and simply disappeared into the streets of Rome. It was probably that same day that the by now disillusioned intelligence officer learned that Weizsäcker had exacted a measure of revenge on the RSHA for forcing him to accept one of its officers into his mission. Elling's name did not appear on the short list of embassy personnel who would accompany the ambassador into Vatican City. The superfluous 'cultural attaché' could only await the arrival of the Allies who would take him to an internment camp in Sicily where he would await the end of the war.

Elling was probably unaware of the final disaster to befall German intelligence during the rush to leave Rome. On 1 June Fraulein Schwarzer informed Alexander Kurtna that a new codebook had arrived from Berlin for Elling. From the surviving evidence it is impossible to determine with any certainty if Kurtna had re-established contact with Soviet intelligence after his release from Italian custody. His response to Schwarzer's latest news suggests, however, that despite his recent incarnation as a German agent the Estonian had never abandoned his allegiance to the Soviet Union, or perhaps he merely hoped to ingratiate himself with his former masters in order to counter any suspicions that might arise when word leaked out of his release from prison under the auspices of the Gestapo. Whatever his motive, he easily persuaded Kappler's secretary to copy as much of the codebook as she could and to extract from Kappler's files as many documents as possible. The last hours of the Gestapo's Rome centre were hectic. In the rush to evacuate the offices on the Via Tasso, the Germans grabbed whatever files were readily at hand and threw them into hastily collected vehicles. Confidential files were strewn about the offices and hallways, and many would be left behind.[39] In the confusion Kappler's secretary (motivated perhaps as much by her communist sympathies as by her affection for the young Estonian) managed to secure for Kurtna a copy of the codebook as well as a list of agents and radio operators in various networks including Georg Elling's. The list indicated that Kappler was running a certain 'Alfredo', an engineer whose contact site was a beer-garden, the *Birreria Fiorelli*. Alfredo was the head of two groups of informants, each consisting of six members. Another group of eight informants was directed by one 'Attilio' from his apartment on the Via Donatello. The purloined list also identified three radio operators who would service the stay-behind networks when the Germans withdrew from Rome.[40] On 5 June (the day Allied forces began to consolidate their control over the city), Kurtna deposited the documents from the Via Tasso with his friend Monsignor Mario Brini of the papal Secretariat of State with the request that the Vatican pass the material to Soviet representatives in Italy at the first opportunity, a commission that Brini eventually fulfilled. The next day, while walking in the Parco Virgiliano, Kurtna was arrested by the same SIM officers who had seized him at the Rome railway station in 1942. He was held again in Regina Coeli prison and interrogated by American and British counterintelligence officers, but the Allies had little time for, and even less interest in, a case of apparent espionage against the Vatican. At the request of Russian authorities, Alexander Kurtna was released into Soviet custody and removed to Moscow.[41]

In the winter of 1948, Father Walter Ciszek, an American Jesuit who had been arrested in the Soviet Union in 1940 for practising his ministry and condemned to 15 years' hard labour, visited the medical clinic of his Arctic labour camp in the hope of securing a medical release from that day's backbreaking work. As he waited in the anteroom of the small infirmary, an inmate bearing a sheaf of papers came out of the registry office. To his surprise, Ciszek recognized a former classmate of his at the pre-war Russicum, the Jesuit College of Russian Studies in Rome. This individual surveyed the crowded room, checked his papers, and was about to return to the office when the astonished priest blurted out 'Sasha?' (Alex). The man turned and stared at Ciszek for a moment, then whispered in Italian, 'Zitto!' (Hush) and stepped into the office. Later, when the crowd in the anteroom had thinned, the man reappeared, a file in his hand, and, approaching the Jesuit, asked in a loud and official manner, 'You are Ciszek?' When the priest nodded, he turned towards the registry, adding in the same manner, 'Come into my office. We have to straighten out this file.' When the door was closed, the clerk dropped his official pose. It was a reunion of sorts, for 'Sasha' was none other than Alexander Kurtna. For a few minutes the two reminisced about the pre-war days in Rome when both were students at the Russicum, and commiserated about life in the isolated camp where Kurtna had one of the coveted assignments in the administrative offices. While the Estonian was genuinely glad to see Ciszek and arranged with his contacts in the infirmary to have his old classmate transferred temporarily to inside work for reasons of health, Kurtna would say nothing about the path that had brought him as a prisoner to an Arctic labour camp. Like so many before him, he had reaped a twisted reward for his service to Stalin's intelligence organizations.[42]

NOTES

1. As early as November 1941, the Vatican's Secretariat of State had been warned by a source in the Italian foreign ministry that SIM believed that Vatican Radio was transmitting intelligence to the Allies. ADSS. Vol. V, p. 299.
2. Memorandum by General (ret.) Eugenio Piccardo (copy in the possession of the authors). Piccardo was a wartime counterintelligence officer in SIM.
3. (CIA), *The Rote Kapelle: The CIA's History of Soviet Intelligence and Espionage Networks in Western Europe, 1936–1945* (Washington: University Publications of America, 1979), p. 232.
4. Memorandum by Eugenio Piccardo.
5. Ibid. A second appeal to Moscow for funds led Italian counterintelligence to the Swiss border where an Italian officer, posing as a courier for the Rome network, received money from a Swiss train conductor working on the Switzerland–Italy railway line. This further suggests a connection between Marley's network in Rome and the organization of Alexander Rado in Switzerland.
6. 'Interrogation Report on Kurtna, Aleksander.' Document provided to the authors by a former American counterintelligence officer.
7. Ibid.
8. Clandestine communication between the Vatican and German- and Russian-occupied territories in the east was so tenuous that a letter from the Pope to the surviving bishops in Lithuania took a full year to reach its destination. David Alvarez, 'Vatican Intelligence Capabilities in the Second World War', p. 601.
9. For Monsignor Brini, see NARA. RG 59. Records of the Personal Representative of the President to Pope Pius XII, Box 11, Tittmann to Taylor, 25 Oct. 1944.
10. 'Interrogation Report on Kurtna, Aleksander.'
11. Memorandum by Eugenio Piccardo; 'German Espionage Organization'. Counter-Intelligence Corps. Detachment 6750th Hq. Co., Rome Allied Command, 11 July 1944. Case No. 242. (Copy in authors' possession.)
12. Toivo Raun, *Estonia and the Estonians* (Stanford: Hoover Institution Press, 1987), pp. 154–5.
13. The documents relating to Kurtna's arrest as a Soviet agent by the Italians were seized by the Germans in September 1943 and sent to Berlin where they disappeared. Allied

investigators were only concerned with Kurtna's work for German intelligence and they passed over his connections with the Russians.

14. 'Interrogation Report of Kurtna, Aleksander.' In 1944 Kurtna told Allied interrogators that his first meeting with Kappler occurred in March of 1942. Kappler's reports to Berlin, however, suggest that he was already working with Kurtna in February of that year.

15. NARA. RG 165. Interrogation Report on SS Obersturmbannfuehrer Herbert Kappler. CSDIC/SC/15AG/SD18.

16. An index of Kappler's reports is in AA. Politisches Archiv. Berichtverzeichnisse des Pol. Att. in Rom, 1940–1943, Inland IIg. Italien (83-60E).

17. Interrogation Report on SS Obersturmbannfuehrer Herbert Kappler. Kappler mistakenly reported that his librarian worked at the Russicum, but this individual, a native-born German named Engelfried, was employed only at the Gregorian University.

18. Monsignor Rossi was an official in the Vatican Information Office. The wartime editions of the Annuario Pontificio contain no listing for a 'de Costa', although a Paolo Costa is listed as an archivist in the Secretariat of State.

19. ADSS. Vol. III, p. 827; Vincent Lapomarda, The Jesuits and the Third Reich (Lewiston: E. Mellen, 1989), p. 159.

20. 'Interrogation Report on Kurtna, Aleksander.' Kurtna's return date is definitely fixed by his arrest. He may have confused the date of his departure for the north, although his marriage on 18 June would have provided a good reference point for his memory.

21. Information from General (ret.) Giulio Fettarappa-Sandri who was a senior officer in Italian counterintelligence during the war. The CIA's history of wartime Soviet networks in Europe is apparently mistaken in suggesting that an officer in the German embassy in Rome (whom it does not identify, but who must be Sauer) was exposed as a Russian agent during interrogations of the Schulze-Boysen Soviet network in Germany. Kurt Sauer was arrested in June 1942, but Harro Schulze-Boysen was not seized until 30 August 1942.

22. Memorandum by Eugenio Piccardo. Kurtna may not have been the first Soviet spy to penetrate the Vatican. In the 1930s documents were reported missing from the files of the Pontifical Commission for Russia, an office attached to the Secretariat of State. In private notes made public only after his death in 1957, Father Michel d'Herbigny, the former director of the Commission, accused a particular archivist in the Secretariat of passing documents to the Soviets. This archivist was not dismissed from papal service until after the war, and then only because of his alleged involvement in a financial scandal. H. Stehle, Eastern Politics, p. 411.

The cases of a certain Soviet agent (Kurtna) and an alleged agent (the archivist) may reopen the question of the elusive 'Lilly' who was purportedly the Vatican connection of Alexander Rado's Swiss branch of the Rote Kapelle. Historians have speculated about the existence of 'Lilly', although an official American report concluded that such a source probably did not exist. (CIA), Rote Kapelle, p. 211.

23. Lieutenant Colonel Talamo, the Italian officer responsible for Kurtna's case, was among those executed under Kappler's authority at the Ardeatine Caves outside Rome on 24 March 1944.

24. Owen Chadwick maintains that papal authorities knew that the Gestapo had had an agent inside the Secretariat of State since 1939. This individual allegedly was responsible for matters concerning the German bishops, but his effectiveness as an informant, according to Chadwick, was undermined by the fact that his superiors in the Secretariat were aware of his treachery. Chadwick believes this agent was Alexander Kurtna. O. Chadwick, Britain and the Vatican, p. 176.

As we have seen, Kurtna worked for the Congregation for the Eastern Churches. While it is possible that he did the odd translation for the Secretariat of State, he certainly was never responsible for the affairs of the German bishops. Furthermore, Kurtna was not recruited by Kappler until 1942. According to a former papal diplomat, a particular official in the wartime Secretariat was strongly suspected of being a German informant. This individual was a priest and after the war rose to more responsible posts in the papal service. Clearly this could not have been Alexander Kurtna, who left the seminary before he could be ordained and whose employment by the Vatican ended in 1944. Information provided by a confidential Vatican source. Since the authors have found no trace of this informant in the available records, the suspicions may have been unfounded.

25. 'Interrogation Report on Kurtna, Aleksander.'
26. Ibid.
27. Career details drawn from Elling's party file in the Berlin Documents Centre.
28. The background to Elling's assignment to the Vatican embassy can be traced in NARA. T-120. Roll 713, 330647-68. All quotations are from this source.
29. By October 1943 there were 73 SD officers serving in 19 embassies or legations. D. Kahn, *Hitler's Spies*, p. 62.
30. 'Interrogation Report on Kurtna, Aleksander.' On another occasion, Kurtna testified that he agreed to undertake for Elling research into the administrative regulations of the papal bureaucracy. Affidavit by Alexander Kurtna, 31 July 1944, Regina Coeli Prison (copy in the possession of the authors).
31. Affidavit by Alexander Kurtna, 31 July 1944.
32. Apparently Schellenberg was not aware that the *Abwehr* was also arranging to insert an agent into the safety of Vatican territory in anticipation of an Allied occupation of Rome. See above, pp. 41–2.
33. Elling's projected mission inside Vatican City is outlined in a memorandum of 7 Feb. 1946 from Francis d'Arcy Osborne to the papal Secretariat of State. Information from this memorandum was provided by a confidential source.

   During his interrogations by Allied officers, Kurtna suggested that Elling had been instructed by Schellenberg to improve Germany's image in Vatican circles and to investigate the possibility of a separate peace (under papal auspices) with the Western Allies.
34. Information from Wilhelm Hoettl. Elling's attitude towards Kappler is described in a memorandum of 10 Nov. 1945 from Weizsäcker to Monsignor Montini of the Secretariat of State. Information from this memorandum was provided by a confidential source.
35. The informants are identified in a handwritten list taken from the files of Herbert Kappler shortly before the German withdrawal from Rome. (Copy in the possession of the authors.)

   With the exception of Kurtna, it is impossible to determine from the available information whether these informants were conscious agents or merely acquaintances of Elling who innocently passed on information at social events. A former Amt VI officer recalled that RSHA headquarters liked to see evidence (such as lists of informants recruited) to justify budgetary allocations. Information from Wilhelm Hoettl.
36. Osborne Memorandum of 7 Feb. 1946.
37. Kurtna may also have occasionally slipped information about the Germans to his contacts in the Vatican. He was probably the source which warned Monsignor Arata that the Gestapo knew that escaped Americans and Britons were hiding inside Vatican City. C. Gasbarri, *Quando il Vaticano*, p. 94.
38. 'Interrogation report on Kurtna, Aleksander.'
39. When curious Romans examined the abandoned headquarters building they found documents stamped 'Reich Secret' scattered along the street. Information from Giuseppe Dosi.
40. A copy of this list is in the possession of the authors.
41. Memorandum by Eugenio Piccardo. Another version of the story maintains that upon his release by the occupation authorities Kurtna returned to his apartment on the Via

Cola di Rienzo. Several days later he was snatched from the street by Russian agents and taken to a Soviet vessel in Naples for transport to the Soviet Union. Information from Walter Ciszek, SJ.

42. Walter Ciszek, SJ, *With God in Russia* (New York: McGraw-Hill, 1964), pp. 207–8. Information from Walter Ciszek. In his memoirs, Father Ciszek refers to Kurtna by the pseudonym 'Misha'.

5

Eavesdroppers

Among the various elements of the intelligence history of the Second
World War, probably none has captured the attention of historians
more than communications intelligence. Quite naturally this interest
has focused on the efforts of the principal belligerents to penetrate
the signals secrets of their opponents. Still, in the fascination with
ENIGMA, PURPLE, and their various relations it is easy to forget that
wartime signals intelligence encompassed an array of operations
against a range of diverse targets, and that minor belligerents and
neutrals were also participants in the signals war, either as aggressor
or victim. To its great frustration the Vatican found itself throughout
the war in the latter category.

The Vatican communicated with the world on several levels. On the
public level its daily newspaper, the Italian language *L'Osservatore
Romano*, published papal addresses and encyclicals, reported the
actions of curial offices, announced ecclesiastical appointments and
promotions, and commented on important international events.
Vatican Radio, broadcasting in a variety of languages including English,
French, German, Italian, Latin and Spanish, offered programmes of
news, religious ceremonial and spiritual direction. In 1940 the station
began transmitting the names of prisoners of war and interned civilians
collected by the Vatican Information Office, a special agency organized
to trace the missing. On the private level the various departments of the
Vatican corresponded with bishops, priests, nuns, and lay Catholics in
matters concerning ecclesiastical administration and discipline, church
ritual, religious education, and personal conscience. Finally, in the areas
of diplomacy and church–state relations the Holy See communicated
confidentially with its nuncios and delegates around the world.

Throughout the war, Germany and its Axis partner, Italy, closely monitored the communications of the Vatican. As the only information outlets in Italy free from fascist censorship, Vatican Radio and *L'Osservatore Romano* could challenge official versions of the causes and conduct of the conflict. Moreover, careful scrutiny of their contents could reveal shifts in papal sympathies which might support or undercut the position of one belligerent side or the other. For those convinced that the Vatican was a nest of spies or the centre of a conspiratorial web which stretched around the globe and along whose strands moved information assiduously collected by millions of faithful Catholics, the close surveillance of the mail flowing into the Vatican promised to reveal a treasure trove of secrets inaccessible to other governments. Finally, the interception of papal diplomatic correspondence would provide a window on the attitudes and policies of an influential neutral and expose efforts by the enemy to cultivate the support of the papacy.

Comprehensive surveillance of Vatican communications required varying degrees of effort and guile. The press and broadcast services were relatively easy to monitor. Readily available by subscription or from kiosks in Vatican City and around Rome, *L'Osservatore Romano* was required reading at the German embassy which would extract articles and commentaries for inclusion in its reports to Berlin. German and Italian authorities considered the papal daily newspaper hostile to their cause and scrutiny of the paper increased as its circulation rose from 80,000 copies in the first months of the war to 150,000 copies by May 1940.[1] Surveillance of Vatican Radio required somewhat greater effort. Established in 1931 when Guglielmo Marconi set up a 10-kilowatt transmitter on the highest point in Vatican City, and refurbished in 1937 with a 25-kilowatt German transmitter and an omnidirectional antenna, Vatican Radio broadcast on four short-wave bands. Although its signal was weak (reception was usually best in Italy and southern France), the station received the special attention of the *Sonderdienst Seehaus* (Lake House Special Service), Germany's main agency for monitoring foreign news broadcasts. Named after its headquarters in a shoreline villa on the Wannsee, a bay of the Havel River in south-west Berlin, the *Seehaus* was jointly administered by the propaganda and foreign ministries. Over the course of the war, this unit monitored broadcasts from more than 45 countries in 37 languages. Each day the recorded transcripts were printed and bound into thick volumes for distribution to various government departments.[2]

Because Vatican Radio's signal to Germany was often faint and subject to unpredictable meteorological conditions, the *Seehaus* utilized a special monitoring post in the Reich embassy to Italy to record all German-language broadcasts from the Vatican hill. The transcripts were then sent by air to headquarters in Berlin for evaluation. Vatican broadcasts in other languages (especially English and French) were also monitored for anti-German remarks. Throughout the war German authorities worried that the papacy harboured pro-Allied sentiments, and they scrutinized the transmissions of Vatican Radio for evidence of this bias. After all, the station's director, the Jesuit Father Filippo Soccorsi, was known to believe that Nazism and Fascism were the enemies of the Catholic Church, and Mussolini's secret police were sufficiently suspicious of the station's orientation that they had two informants among the small staff of lay technicians.[3]

Events seemingly confirmed the worst suspicions. Soon after the fall of Poland the Polish-language service of Vatican Radio began broadcasting information concerning German atrocities in that country, and on 28 September 1939 it transmitted a fiery speech by Cardinal August Hlond, the Primate of Poland, then a refugee in Rome, who condemned the aggression against his country and proclaimed, 'Martyred Poland, you have fallen to violence while you fought for the sacred cause of freedom . . . On these radio waves, which run across the world, carrying truth from the hill of the Vatican, I cry to you. Poland, you are not beaten!'[4] Such broadcasts, which were often picked up and reported by the news services of other countries, could have a powerful impact on international opinion.[5] They could also encourage captive or threatened peoples and undermine German efforts to pacify occupied territories. In unoccupied France, for example, the French-language broadcasts from the Vatican of Father Emmanuel Mistiaen, a Belgian Jesuit, who made little effort to disguise his pro-Allied sentiments, were transcribed by Dominican friars in Marseilles (where the Vatican signal was especially strong), duplicated, and circulated as the 'Voice of the Vatican' (*la Voix du Vatican*) among the young activists of the Catholic Action organization. In a broadcast in January 1941 Father Mistiaen reminded his listeners that 'Men must be free. Therefore the

Church will never submit to the claim that might is right', while on another occasion he warned, 'There is an order of slavery and death, quite unsuitable for the whole of humanity. Is that what those who talk about *new orders* mean?' Listeners could have little doubt that the scarcely veiled criticisms were aimed at Germany. By calling the radio audience to their moral duty, such broadcasts fostered a Christian resistance to Nazi totalitarianism.[6]

The nuncio in Berlin warned the Secretariat of State that the Vatican's broadcasts were closely monitored and that transcripts were distributed to various agencies of the Nazi regime.[7] This came as no surprise at the Vatican where the Secretariat received numerous protests from the German embassy against the content of Vatican Radio's transmissions. Indeed, a veritable 'radio war' ensued in the autumn of 1940 and the winter of 1941 as Germany pressured the Vatican to curtail or censor these transmissions, while the Secretariat of State defended the editorial independence and integrity of the radio station. Berlin maintained that the station, in a most unneutral manner, had insulted Germany through numerous broadcasts which, among other provocations, denied that National Socialism could be reconciled with Christianity and criticized the military bishop of the German army for saying that his country was not responsible for the war.[8] In October 1940 the German embassy delivered an especially strong protest to the Secretariat of State after an English-language transmission described the German occupation of Alsace-Lorraine as 'tragic and inhuman' and referred to the 'immoral principles of Nazism'. Concerned that such comments were compromising the Vatican's neutrality, Pope Pius instructed the Jesuit-run station to reduce the number of its broadcasts and avoid political commentary. The Pope, however, withdrew these instructions after a personal appeal from Father Wladimir Ledochowski, the Superior General of the Jesuits, who believed that the United States needed to know about the persecution of the Church in German-controlled areas. Broadcasts resumed, although they were frequently jammed by an unknown, presumably German, source. In the spring of 1941 the *Sonderdienst Seehaus* monitored several broadcasts that described anti-Catholic policies in the Reich. Berlin was outraged and grim German diplomats again called at the Secretariat of State. Fearing that Vatican Radio might provoke the Nazis to escalate their attacks on the Church, Pius ordered the station to refrain from any further mention of religious persecution in Germany. This time there was no appeal and the critical voice of Vatican Radio fell silent.[9]

While preparing responses to these protests, the Secretariat became aware that, in reporting the broadcasts of Vatican Radio, some foreign news agencies could not resist the temptation to embellish or distort by paraphrasing the contents of such broadcasts. Not surprisingly, this temptation was especially strong among Allied propaganda services which were eager to 'improve' the comments concerning German policies. The Vatican also suspected that certain clandestine radio stations under Allied control were broadcasting violent attacks against the Axis under the pretence of speaking for the Holy See. The suspicions were well-founded since the British propaganda effort included the so-called 'Radio Christ the King' which broadcast into the Greater Reich. Each transmission of this station began with a selection of classical and religious music and a brief prayer by the announcer, a refugee Austrian priest, who then spoke at length about the Nazis' contempt for law and morality, citing such examples as the regime's persecution of Jews, its attacks against religious institutions, and its policies in the areas of euthanasia and eugenics. British agents assiduously spread the story in neutral capitals that 'Radio Christ the King' was a Catholic station operated secretly by Vatican Radio, a rumour that had special effect in Switzerland and Austria. Because of such propaganda operations by the Allies, the German-language service of Vatican Radio repeatedly warned its listeners to beware of fraudulent 'Vatican' broadcasts.[10]

Close surveillance of the press and radio of the Vatican may have turned up the occasional item of special information, but for the intelligence services of Germany and Italy the real prize remained the diplomatic communications of the papacy. The timely interception of a telegram from the apostolic delegate in Washington or instructions for the nuncio in Berlin could be more valuable than a year's worth of press commentaries, news broadcasts and personal letters to the Pope. It was a precious prize, but one difficult to win because the Holy See, like other governments, jealously guarded its secret communications.

The Vatican communicated with its diplomatic missions by telegram and diplomatic pouch. For most of the war the Secretariat of State, understaffed and underfinanced, had no courier service of its own, but depended upon the services of friendly powers. The Secretariat routinely entrusted its diplomatic bag to the couriers of the Italian foreign ministry until 1941 when, in the face of evidence that the bags were being tampered with, it switched to the messengers of Switzerland and, less frequently, Spain. Official mail from the British Empire or areas under British influence, such as Iraq or Iran, sometimes moved in the Foreign Office bag, and by the end of the war even American couriers occasionally carried packets closed with the seal of St Peter.[11] Despite the availability of foreign couriers, the pouch service remained irregular. At times over a month's worth of mail might accumulate at a particular nunciature awaiting clearance or transport. Since some nunciatures (Madrid, for example) were reception centres for papal diplomatic mail from North and South America and Asia, irregular service was a serious irritant. A dispatch from the papal chargé in Slovakia containing early reports on the Auschwitz death camp took almost five months to reach Rome. A letter from the papal representative in Tokyo dated 29 November 1941 arrived at the Secretariat of State on 24 March 1942. In the last year of the war the pouch from the Berlin nunciature took up to 38 days to reach the Vatican.[12] In 1945 the Secretariat of State temporarily established a rudimentary courier service of its own by selecting several young priests to carry official mail, although this service seems to have been limited to western Europe and North Africa.[13]

By entrusting its mail to foreign powers, the Vatican risked the security of its communications. Under international law the diplomatic pouch was immune from search or seizure, but few belligerents, Allied or Axis, could resist the temptation to peek at the secrets of an important neutral like the Holy See. In Washington, for example, American intelligence (which was concerned that the Vatican pouch might be used by Axis agents to send intelligence to Europe) considered it prudent to establish discreet surveillance over the diplomatic mail and the telephones of the papal delegation.[14] In British-controlled Cairo there were occasionally inexplicable delays in delivering the Vatican pouch to the local papal mission, and on at least one occasion Allied authorities in the Middle East temporarily confiscated some pouches in transit to Rome from the papal delegations in Iraq and Lebanon. In Iran (nominally independent, but effectively under London's influence), the papal delegation was prohibited by the British from using its cipher and required to consign its dispatches to His Majesty's embassy in Teheran for transmittal to the Vatican.[15] For the Axis the temptation to divert the papal pouch was all the greater after Italy entered the war and Allied diplomats accredited to the Holy See were compelled to forsake their chancelleries and accommodations in Rome and take up residence inside Vatican City. Although the Lateran Treaty of 1929 guaranteed to diplomats accredited to the Holy See the right to communicate freely with their governments, the fascist regime chose to interpret this right narrowly after Italy entered the war. The Vatican protested against this restricted interpretation, but was forced to acquiesce in its application. Under the restrictions, the Allied diplomats who crowded into Vatican City could neither send nor receive cipher telegrams, nor could they use their own couriers to carry dispatches to their governments. They were free to consign their reports to the Italian postal service, but fascist censorship of all mail made this option unacceptable. As a courtesy to its involuntary guests, the Vatican allowed them to use its diplomatic pouch but only for material directly related to their official mission to the Holy See. Under no circumstances, however, could the diplomats use the telegraphic service of Vatican Radio to transmit or receive enciphered messages.[16] As a result, the missions confined to papal territory could communicate with their capitals only through a cumbersome and roundabout channel. The British minister, Francis d'Arcy Osborne, for example, would give his dispatches, including enciphered telegrams, to the papal Secretariat of State for inclusion in the papal pouch which departed, via Swiss courier, twice a week for the nunciature in Berne. There the nuncio would transfer Osborne's packet to the British legation in the Swiss capital which would add the dispatches to its own bag for London and cable the enciphered telegrams directly to the Foreign Office from Berne. London's responses and instructions reached Osborne by the reverse procedure.[17] Despite the suspicions of German and Italian authorities that the British mission harboured a wireless set, Osborne was never in direct radio contact with London during his sojourn in Vatican City.[18]

Since Allied representatives could effectively communicate with their governments only by means of the papal diplomatic bag, that bag became a doubly attractive target for Axis intelligence. The Italian secret service managed to intercept and covertly open the papal pouch on at least an occasional basis.[19] For its part, German intelligence was always keenly interested in the Vatican's procedures for handling its confidential mail, and it is safe to assume that there were efforts to intercept such mail. In February 1942, for instance, a German priest employed at the Berlin nunciature was summoned by the police and, under the pretext of confirming his labour status, questioned about his work inside the papal embassy, in particular his knowledge of the procedures for sending mail to the Vatican. German security was especially interested in these procedures since the nunciature collected and forwarded to Rome information on events and conditions in Poland and other occupied territories. On another occasion an agent of the RSHA, who had insinuated himself into the circle of the papal chargé d'affaires in Slovakia, almost blew his cover by inquiring persistently into the channels by which the diplomat's dispatches were carried to Rome. The diplomat, Monsignor Giuseppe Burzio, had taken a special interest in the fate of Slovakian and Russian Jews and had revealed his concerns in his reports to the Vatican. In Lisbon the nuncio learned from the Portuguese police that the German security service believed that the Polish government-in-exile used the Vatican bag to transmit intelligence collected by Polish sources around the world. On at least one occasion a courier carrying the papal bag was detained by German police.[20] The Vatican knew, of course, that its ordinary mail was screened by the fascist postal authorities, and it suspected (correctly) that its diplomatic pouches were opened when in the custody of Italian couriers. The security of bags entrusted to the couriers of other countries also could not be taken for granted. In February 1941, the British minister to the Holy See warned his government.

> I dare not either write or telegraph... for I have not entire faith in my communications by either Bag or cypher telegram. The Bags I send by Vatican [sic] courier go a long way round via Berne and thence Barcelona, Madrid and Lisbon. I have entire faith in the Vatican authorities here and elsewhere, but I cannot entirely exclude the possibility on so long and complicated a journey of misfortune or carelessness. And the Germans are diabolically ingenious and would be pleased to get anything against the Vatican or the diplomats in the Vatican City.[21]

The following month Osborne repeated his suspicions in a warning to London: 'I won't discuss the war because I am never quite sure of the courier service.'[22] Of course such suspicions were well-founded. As late as January 1943, a personal letter from Pope Pius to President Franklin Roosevelt disappeared from a Vatican diplomatic pouch while *en route* to Switzerland. In such circumstances it was prudent to assume that the correspondence of the Secretariat of State was not secure. Until the creation of its own small courier service in 1945, the Secretariat would often hold especially sensitive dispatches until a secure channel of communication could be arranged.[23] It could sometimes spare one of its officials for temporary courier duties, as when, in December 1942, it alerted its missions in Bucharest and Sofia that Monsignor Luigi Arrigoni was departing for the Balkans to deliver and collect official mail. Papal diplomats travelling to or from their posts would also carry dispatches. Particularly confidential material was entrusted to special messengers. Instructions concerning the role of Carlo Sforza in a post-fascist Italian government, addressed to the apostolic delegate in Washington and marked 'Destroy this letter and keep nothing concerning this matter in the records' were secretly carried to the United States by a lay employee of the Vatican.[24]

Sometimes communication of any sort, secure or otherwise, was difficult or impossible. This problem was especially serious in Poland and the Baltic States. Official communication with these areas being prohibited by the Germans, the Secretariat of State turned to informal and clandestine channels. Catholic chaplains and soldiers in the armies of Germany and its allies would sometimes accept a message or carry a small packet. Priests and lay people might pass on a letter. In this way messages from the occupied areas would slowly make their way to the nunciatures in Berlin, Bratislava and Bucharest. It was at best a makeshift system. A letter from the Pope to the bishops of Lithuania, for example, took a full year to reach its destination.[25]

Like other foreign ministries, the Secretariat of State enciphered its confidential communications to enhance their security. Papal cryptography had a long and illustrious tradition dating back to the fourteenth century when a papal cipher clerk compiled a set of cryptographic keys which remain the oldest extant and which included the first nomenclature, that hybrid cryptographic system which combines a cipher table of substitutes for individual letters with a code list of substitutes for entire words. Two hundred years later, the papacy dominated the cryptography of the late Renaissance, in large part because of the brilliance of Giovanni and Matteo Argenti (uncle and nephew), cipher secretaries to six Popes, whose accomplishments included the first use of a mnemonic key to mix a cipher alphabet, an early solution of a polyalphabetic cipher, and the compilation of a treatise on cryptography which represented the state of the art at the time.[26] By the modern period, however, the lustre had faded. Through a combination of complacency, lassitude and inattention, the cryptography which had once been the envy of Europe slipped into mediocrity. In 1829 a senior official in the Secretariat of State complained that 'our ciphers are known by everyone', and occasional efforts at reform could not reverse the decline. By the end of the nineteenth century the papacy still relied on nomenclatures to hide its secret messages even though other European governments had abandoned that antiquated system in favour of full-fledged codebooks. The Vatican waited until 1913 to experiment (and then only briefly) with enciphered codes, a technique which by then had been common among foreign chancelleries for over 30 years. During the First World War (which witnessed the first systematic application of signals intelligence on a large scale), the Vatican tried to modernize its cryptographic procedures. By 1918 the basic system in service at the Secretariat of State was a two-part code of several thousand four-digit numerical groups. For especially sensitive messages this code was superenciphered by means of short cipher tables which replaced each pair of numbers in the encoded version of the message with a pair (digraph) from the table to form the enciphered version. Despite such efforts, several countries, including Germany and Italy, successfully attacked papal cryptosystems through to the end of the war.[27]

From the available evidence it is possible to trace only the general outlines of papal cryptography in the period 1939–45.[28] Over the course of the war, the Secretariat of State used several different codes, each designated by a colour. The RED code had been in service at all papal diplomatic missions since the early 1930s. By 1939 the Secretariat of State considered it insecure and throughout the war used it only for routine administrative matters and messages of no particular sensitivity. It was a one-part code of approximately 12,000 groups printed 25 lines to a page in the codebook.[29] For an extra layer of security the code groups were enciphered (numbers to letters) by a process that replaced the page number with a digraph from a pair of tables which were used, in turn, on odd and even days. The line number was enciphered on odd days with a direct standard English alphabet (1=A, 2=B . . .), minus E which was used as a null, and on even days with that alphabet reversed (1=Z, 2=Y . . .). For more secret communications the Secretariat depended upon systems such as the YELLOW code (1941) and the GREEN code (1942). The former, which was distributed to all posts except a handful in the Middle East, the Far East, and Central America, was a one-part code of approximately 13,000 groups enciphered by digraphic tables (for page numbers) and random mixed alphabets (for line numbers). Tables and alphabets varied on each circuit (Vatican–Berlin, Vatican–Madrid, and so on) and for each day of the month. The characteristics of the GREEN code remain shrouded in secrecy as do the characteristics (and designations) of the other systems used by the wartime Secretariat of State.[30] One of the remaining systems seems to have been a numerical code of five-digit groups which were enciphered through the use of short additive tables, each of which contained only 100 five-digit additive groups.[31] There is some evidence that the more important papal diplomatic missions may have had special cryptosystems. In the summer of 1943, for example, the Secretariat of State compiled a new system for the exclusive use of the papal delegation in Washington. It was delivered to the United States by a special courier. The London delegation also possessed a system which was used by no other papal mission.[32] At no point in the war did the Vatican possess machine ciphers. This is evident from instructions telegraphed on 9 September 1939 to the nuncio in Poland who was about to follow the Polish government as it abandoned Warsaw for a place less immediately threatened by the advancing German armies. The Secretariat authorized the nuncio to destroy confidential papers in the nunciature's archive and urged him to 'look after safety of code' (the use of the singular noun suggests that the nuncio had only one codebook), but it made no reference to securing or destroying cipher machines. Similarly, instructions telegraphed to the nuncio in Budapest in the autumn of 1944 referred specifically to the destruction (in the event of an emergency) of codebooks without any mention of cipher machines.[33]

Throughout the war papal cryptosystems provided uncertain security against surveillance by the Axis alliance. Hungary, a junior member of the alliance, had an excellent cryptanalysis unit that read some part of the diplomatic traffic of a dozen European governments including the Vatican. The Hungarians solved at least one papal cryptosystem (probably the RED code), and in 1942 they shared this solution with Finland which was fighting alongside Germany against the Soviet Union. In return the Finns routinely passed to the Hungarians any Vatican traffic intercepted by Finnish listening posts.[34] Among the Axis powers, however, Italy was the most immediate threat. Italian military intelligence, the *Servizio Informazione Militare* (SIM), entered the conflict with a highly developed signals intelligence capability. In an average month SIM's radio interception unit (with its main listening post at Fort Boccea near the Vatican) would snare from the atmosphere about 8,000 radiograms. Its cryptanalytic unit would scrutinize around 6,000 of these and eventually decode more than half. This effort was greatly assisted by a special department, the *Sezione Prelevamento* (Removal Section), which specialized in clandestine incursions into foreign embassies and legations for the purpose of photographing secret documents. By suborning servants, doorkeepers and watchmen, the nocturnal burglars of *Sezione P* had the run of almost every diplomatic mission in Rome. The British embassy, for instance, was regularly penetrated, and its ciphers had been photographed as early as 1935. A moonlight incursion into the American embassy in August 1941 resulted in the acquisition of the so-called BLACK code then in service among American military attachés. The last incursion into the French embassy in the Palazzo Farnese immediately preceded Italy's declaration of war on 10 June 1940, but SIM's agents had long been accustomed to entering the palazzo to photograph documents in the office of the naval attaché.[35] Before the war only the Russian and German embassies remained impenetrable, although a thwarted attempt against the latter in the 1920s resulted in the arrest of one of the burglars who was duly tried and sentenced before being quietly released.[36] The Italian operatives were able to adapt quickly to changing circumstances. Just before the armistice by which Italy abandoned its Axis partners, Germany and Japan, *Sezione P* began photographing the dispatches of the Japanese military attaché in Rome.[37] The haul from such operations was significant. In 1941 alone

Sezione P surreptitiously acquired for SIM approximately 3,000 secret documents, including some 50 items of cryptographic interest such as enciphered cables, codebooks, and cipher tables.[38]

Naturally, the Vatican did not escape the attention of SIM. During the First World War the surveillance of papal diplomatic communications had been one of the great achievements of Italian signals intelligence. Encoded telegrams passing between the Secretariat of State and papal diplomatic missions around the world had been intercepted, decrypted and delivered to the Italian foreign ministry within hours of their transmission.[39] This achievement would be repeated during the Second World War. SIM certainly read the Vatican's RED and YELLOW codes and may have read other papal systems as well.[40] Interception of Vatican radiograms was never a problem. SIM's principal intercept station, Fort Boccea, was practically in the Pope's back yard; moreover, the official in Vatican Radio responsible for processing the enciphered radiograms of the Secretariat of State was an agent of the Italian police.[41] The successes against papal cryptosystems depended in large part upon the ubiquitous *Sezione P* which before 1943 managed at least once to enter covertly the offices of the Secretariat of State to steal or photograph secret documents including cryptographic materials.[42] Access to restricted areas of the Vatican was undoubtedly facilitated by penetration of the papal gendarmerie which patrolled the precincts and buildings of Vatican City. Most officers of this force were recruited from the Italian police, and relations between the Vatican and Italian services were close. Not surprisingly, the papal police were easily penetrated by agents of the Italian intelligence and security services, who monitored events and personalities in the Vatican, paying special attention to the activities of Allied diplomats living inside the papal territory. When the commander of the papal police retired early in the war, Cardinal Nicola Canali, the Governor of Vatican City and a prelate suspected by some of certain fascist sympathies, appointed as a replacement an officer who happened to be an agent of OVRA, Mussolini's secret police. The chief of the gendarmerie's 'special section', a small unit which provided a modest internal security and surveillance capability, had been, before his entry into papal service, an early member of the fascist party who had led strong-arm squads against opponents of *Il Duce*.[43] Even if Vatican security guards could be neutralized or circumvented, the covert incursions into the Secretariat of State were not without their special risks. On one occasion a Catholic agent was shaken to discover that the cover of the codebook he was about to purloin carried a warning that anyone possessing that document without authorization would automatically incur religious excommunication.[44]

It is unlikely that, before the war, the diplomatic missions accredited to the Holy See escaped the predations of *Sezione P* any more than did the embassies accredited to the Italian government. With Italian belligerency and the withdrawal of Allied embassies from Rome, these missions became even more tempting targets as isolated outposts of Allied diplomacy and intelligence in the heart of hostile territory. Of course, the relocation of most of these embassies and legations to Vatican City provided little more than theoretical protection. With its characteristic disregard of papal sovereignty and diplomatic immunities, SIM periodically launched successful incursions into these missions inside papal territory.[45] As always, cryptographic materials were a high priority for these operations. Perhaps the most successful raid netted the codebook of the British legation. Security at the British mission to the Holy See had long been a problem. Before the war the tiny mission had been housed in a building owned and occupied by the Italian armed forces. A security survey by the Foreign Office in 1937 concluded that the premises 'are quite unsuitable for their purpose and afford no protection whatever for the documents they house'. The investigating officer, who one night entered the unguarded legation without challenge or trouble and easily found the keys which provided access to the files, recommended the mission's 'early removal to other, less blatantly insecure, premises'. The minister, Sir Francis d'Arcy Osborne, who believed that the location of his office in a building occupied by the Italian army was a guarantee against burglary, dismissed the security threat, but his superiors in London were less sanguine. The Permanent Under-secretary, Robert Vansittart, angrily concluded, 'That Italian authorities themselves would take, or suborn others to take, our papers did not seem to occur to him [Osborne]. The Vatican mission is a scandal.'[46] Given such lax security and the ubiquity and skills of *Sezione P*, it is highly probable that the cryptographic systems of the British legation had been purloined before the war. During the conflict London correctly surmised that its encrypted communications with Osborne, now installed in cramped quarters in Vatican City, were insecure. In May 1941 a Foreign Office functionary warned 'I am afraid our cypher to Osborne is not sufficiently secure to make this telegram in complete safety', and the next year London decided not to pass to their minister at the Vatican certain information from Moscow because of the 'doubtful security' of his cipher.[47] On at least one occasion during the diplomat's Vatican sojourn, SIM again gained access to his code. Under the terms of the Lateran Treaty, the Italian government could not refuse diplomats accredited to the Holy See an opportunity to take home leave. Accordingly, in April 1943, Osborne departed from Rome for a two-month visit to London. When he returned on 18 June (little more than a month before the fall of Mussolini), his baggage included a new cryptosystem for secure communications with the Foreign Office. Unfortunately, this system had hardly been unpacked before it was compromised. When the British minister left his apartment for a daily stroll in the papal gardens, his footman, whom the Italian authorities had suborned by a combination of threats and bribes, passed the new codebook and cipher tables to a waiting agent of SIM, who photographed them. The bulkiness of the documents and the fact that Osborne was only briefly absent forced the conspirators to extend the operation over three days.[48]

Despite such misadventures, London's representative to the Holy See was not the complete *naïf*; indeed, with Italy's declaration of war Osborne had abandoned his rather insouciant approach to communications security. The advice of Alexander Kirk, the American chargé d'affaires in Berlin, had done much to alert the British minister to the threat. Kirk, whom Osborne considered 'the most able American diplomat I know', had warned his colleague that no cipher was safe from the skilful German cryptanalysts and that Berlin had probably broken all the British and American cryptographic systems.[49] Osborne accepted this exaggerated estimate of German capabilities and changed his behaviour accordingly. For fear of compromising the Vatican should his messages be read by the enemy, he was now reticent in reporting evidence of Vatican sympathy for the Allies. In February 1941 he wrote to the Foreign Secretary, Anthony Eden:

> . . . I am careful not to say anything of sentiments or expressions of opinion here that might be incriminating. And my style is

consequently somewhat cramped in representing the Vatican attitude.

I hope that you will bear this in mind if you are inclined to condemn me for lack of precision or the Vatican for lack of understanding of what is at stake in the war.[50]

Osborne decided to turn the threat to his communications into an opportunity for some discreet disinformation. He began to prepare his reports with the prying eyes of German and Italian intelligence in mind. At times he would deliberately misrepresent Vatican attitudes and policies in order to assuage Axis fears concerning the papacy's sympathies in the war. In order to protect the Vatican from Axis pressure or retribution, the British representative was especially concerned to play down anything that might suggest papal support for the Allied cause. It was a risky game since the same reports might very well mislead his own foreign ministry as to the real situation at the Vatican. On at least one occasion, he sent a telegram containing a calculated falsehood. In August 1943, at a time when the post-Mussolini Italian government was sending out feelers about an armistice with the Allies, Osborne informed London that, despite reports to the contrary, no emissaries of the Badoglio regime had approached him. In fact, he had provided one such emissary with a letter of introduction to the British ambassador in Lisbon. Osborne managed to send a general warning to London in 1941 of his intentions to dissemble and trusted that the Foreign Office thereafter would read between the lines of his reports.[51]

Perhaps the only Allied diplomat inside the Vatican to escape the depredations of *Sezione P* was the American chargé d'affaires, Harold Tittmann, for the simple reason that he had no code. The policy of the American State Department was to issue cryptographic systems only to duly constituted diplomatic missions. Despite his diplomatic title and the fact that he was an officer of the State Department, Tittmann was at the Vatican in the capacity of resident assistant to Myron Taylor, who bore the rather anomalous title of 'Personal Representative of the President to His Holiness Pope Pius XII'. For domestic political reasons the Roosevelt Administration chose not to establish formal relations with the Holy See, but used Taylor (who resided in the United States and made occasional visits to the Vatican) as a channel of communication. The State Department did not consider a 'personal representative' the equivalent of a formal diplomatic mission, and so refused the use of its cryptosystems. Indeed, Department officials considered Taylor's position so irregular that at first they refused him Department stationery. Tittmann was reduced to sending his messages (*en clair*, but sealed in the Vatican pouch) to the American legation in Berne where they would be enciphered for transmission to Washington. On a few occasions in the days immediately following America's entry into the war, the Secretariat of State (in an exception to its standard practice) allowed the American chargé to use its facilities for urgent communications with Washington. Tittmann would hand his message to the Secretariat where it would be enciphered in a Vatican cryptosystem and transmitted to the apostolic delegation in Washington where, after deciphering, it would be delivered to the Department of State.[52] Of course, the Secretariat's courtesy to the American diplomat involved a potentially serious breach of security. Should American intelligence have been monitoring Vatican diplomatic transmissions, it would have been able to break into papal cryptosystems by comparing the plaintext of Tittmann's messages as delivered to the State Department with the intercepted cipher text. American codebreakers did not turn their attention to Vatican cryptosystems until September 1943. They succeeded in solving the RED code, but they did not use Tittmann's messages as 'cribs'.[53]

Italy, Finland and Hungary did not necessarily share their knowledge of Vatican codes with Germany. In matters of cryptology, cooperation, even among allies, is constrained by a reluctance to forsake an intelligence advantage. The Axis partners certainly exchanged cryptologic information. German and Finnish codebreakers, for example, collaborated closely in attacking Russian military and American diplomatic ciphers. Cooperation, however, was limited. The Finns seem not to have shared their knowledge of Vatican codes with their German partners.[54] The limited partnership among the Axis powers is especially evident in German–Italian cryptologic cooperation. As early as September 1939, nine months before Italy entered the war alongside Germany, Mussolini's cryptanalysts were passing to their German counterparts intercepted French diplomatic cables.[55] Cryptanalytic results were also shared. In the summer of 1941 General Vittorio Gamba, the chief of SIM's signals intelligence unit, sent to his German counterpart, Colonel Siegfried Kempf, a

Swiss diplomatic code with its attendant cipher keys, and followed that gift with the contribution, in the autumn of the same year, of a new Turkish military attaché code and an American diplomatic code. Colonel Kempf reciprocated by providing a Turkish diplomatic code and suggesting collaboration on Russian cryptographic systems.[56] In 1942 an Italian officer briefly visited Berlin to observe German codebreaking efforts and to negotiate the delivery of German tabulating machinery to SIM's cryptanalytic section.[57] Collaboration, however, was never unconditional. The Germans revealed few of their cryptanalytical methods because they distrusted Italian security and feared that the information would leak to their enemies. They were also not prepared to share methods which enabled them to crack Rome's own diplomatic codes. For its part, Italy was selective in the information it chose to reveal to its partner. Rome, for example, did not share with Berlin its knowledge of British diplomatic ciphers acquired through the efforts of *Sezione P*, nor did it pass along details of the BLACK code purloined from the office of the American military attaché.[58] In such a climate SIM may well have held back information on Vatican codes.

If papal codes were among the items withheld by SIM from its Axis partner, it is unlikely that Italian reticence did much to constrain German surveillance of the Vatican's diplomatic communications. Germany had its own highly developed (though fragmented) communications intelligence capability. Among the many competing agencies in the world of German signals intelligence, three were particularly active in attacking papal cryptosystems. The cryptanalysis unit of the foreign ministry, known as 'Pers Z' since it sheltered under the innocuous cover of the Z section of the ministry's administrative and personnel division, read all or part of the encrypted diplomatic traffic of 34 countries including Britain, France, Italy, Japan, Spain, Switzerland and the United States. Its successes included the solution of Vatican codes. During the war the papal nunciature in Berlin used at least four different cryptosystems: RED, YELLOW, GREEN, and a system whose Vatican designation remains unknown, but which was known to Allied codebreakers as KIF. The latter code was distributed to the Vatican's more important missions (Berlin, Berne, Madrid, Washington) in 1942 and was reserved for highly confidential messages. When Germany invaded Poland, the foreign ministry's cryptanalysts were already reading one papal system, but this success was undercut when the Secretariat of State soon recalled this pre-war code from service at most of its missions. By 1940 they had reconstructed the RED system, although many of the plaintext values had been provided by the *Forschungsamt* (Research Office), a cryptanalytic agency reporting to *Reichmarschall* Herman Göring from the cover of the Reich air ministry. Papal codes were never a priority for Pers Z and it is unclear how many of these systems were successfully attacked. The effort, at least early in the war, must have been significant because by the end of 1940 the foreign ministry was reading 50 per cent of Vatican traffic.[59]

The cryptanalysts of Pers Z were helped in their attack against papal systems by a stream of intercepts. Since the papal nunciature in Berlin (like all nunciatures) lacked a radio transmitter/receiver, all encrypted messages between that nunciature and the Vatican would pass through the telegraph bureau of the German post office, which routinely forwarded to the foreign ministry copies of all incoming and outgoing diplomatic telegrams. Occasionally, espionage generated additional materials. In February 1942, for instance, Rudolf Likus, Ribbentrop's special assistant for intelligence matters, sent Curt Selchow, the director of Pers Z, six encoded telegrams with the request that Selchow's office provide cleartext versions of each.[60] One telegram was addressed to the Cardinal Secretary of State, Luigi Maglione, from the apostolic delegate in Tokyo, Monsignor Paolo Marella. Three others were from Cardinal Maglione to the delegate in Istanbul, Monsignor Angelo Roncalli (the future Pope John XXIII). The last two were from the Irish ambassador to the Holy See to his foreign ministry in Dublin. Likus's claim that he obtained these documents from the 'papal chancellory' seems unlikely. It is difficult to imagine how the Secretariat of State would come to have two telegrams of the Irish ambassador who, as the representative to the Vatican of a neutral power, continued to live and work in Rome unlike his colleagues from Allied states who were confined to Vatican City.[61] Furthermore, if Likus's source inside the Secretariat had access to cable traffic, then why did he not provide the cleartext of the messages concerning Tokyo and Istanbul? It is more likely that the source was an employee of the Rome telegraph office or the Italian intercept service.[62]

Pers Z also received Vatican intercepts from the radio monitoring stations of the Cipher Branch (*Chiffrierabteilung*) of the Armed

Forces High Command (OKW), although this unit, commonly known as 'Chi', independently attacked the diplomatic cryptograms of foreign governments. From its main listening posts at Treuenbrietzen outside Berlin and Lauf-an-der-Pegnitz near Nuremberg, as well as from a network of secondary posts throughout Europe including (after the Italian armistice) a post on Monte Cavo in the Alban Hills barely 25 miles from Vatican City, Chi searched the ether for diplomatic and military transmissions. Coverage was comprehensive. By 1944, major targets like the Soviet Union received round-the-clock attention from as many as 46 radio monitoring desks, while even minor targets like Haiti, Costa Rica and the Portuguese colonies in Asia warranted individual intercept desks. Before the war Chi's codebreakers had not targeted the Vatican, but after the attack on Poland a separate desk had been established to monitor Vatican traffic and attack papal cryptosystems, and the military cryptanalysts were successful against at least one of these systems.[63] In numerical terms Chi's Vatican intake was probably never large. In each of two months, December 1939 and January 1940, it intercepted only 14 papal cryptograms, although in the latter month alone it captured 796 British, 460 French, 209 Turkish and 143 American messages. In February 1940 the number of papal intercepts increased to 38 and in March rose again to 40, but comparatively the totals remained low. The March total still placed the Vatican only fifteenth among the 27 states whose diplomatic cryptograms had been intercepted that month by Chi stations. In the March returns the papacy was clustered in a group that included Spain (49 intercepts), Poland (43) and Portugal (39), far behind more important intelligence targets like the Soviet Union (1,649), Britain (838) and France (676).[64] Chi's coverage of Vatican diplomatic transmissions, however, was probably more complete than these relatively modest totals suggest. Papal diplomatic missions (especially in the first year of the war) were more likely to communicate with the Secretariat of State by pouch than by telegraph. On one occasion in the months of crisis leading up to the outbreak of the war, the Secretariat actually had to order the nuncio in Warsaw to use the telegraph for important news.[65] In the first four months of 1940, the nunciature in Brussels sent only six telegrams to the Vatican, while that year the nunciature in The Hague sent one telegram in January and none at all in February and March. Even the more important posts generated relatively little cable or radio traffic.

Between 31 August 1939 and 15 May 1940 the nunciature in Paris telegraphed 45 cryptograms, an average of one roughly every six days.[66] In such circumstances, the interception of only a few dozen messages could very well represent a significant majority of the total transmitted each month.

The *Forschungsamt* (Research Office), tucked away in the recesses of the air ministry under the personal control of Herman Göring, was another agency which took a special interest in papal communications. The *Forschungsamt* engaged in the full spectrum of communications intelligence: wiretaps, mail interception, radio and cable surveillance, and cryptanalysis. Collection was enormous. The evaluators in the foreign politics section of the agency might receive in any given month as many as 2,400 cryptanalysed messages, 42,000 cleartext radio and cable messages, and 11,000 transcripts of radio broadcasts, while their colleagues in the economics section received some 20,000 items a day. The specialists in the cryptanalysis bureau solved three-quarters of the diplomatic codes it attacked, including American, British, French, Polish and Russian systems. Turkish diplomatic traffic proved an especially valuable source of information on developments in London, Moscow and Washington. The diplomatic codes of Germany's friends received as much scrutiny as those of its enemies. At least one Japanese system was broken, while new Italian keys, which went into service every three months on the Berlin–Rome circuit, were solved within hours of their introduction. Even minor powers did not escape the attentions of Göring's codebreakers: a new Mexican code was cracked in 1942 by the niece of the *Reichmarschall*'s sister-in-law.[67]

The *Forschungsamt*'s interest in the papacy extended back to the 1930s when the Catholic Church had ranked third, behind the German armed forces and the leadership of the Nazi party, in the surveillance priorities of the agency, which was particularly concerned to monitor the communications between the Vatican and various bishops and Catholic organizations inside Germany.[68] During the war the agency focused its attention on the papal nunciature in Berlin. The nunciature's telephones were tapped as were those of such anti-Nazi prelates as Cardinal Michael von Faulhauber of Munich, and Bishops Konrad von Preysing of Berlin and Clemens August von Galen of Münster. Additionally, the nuncio's telegraphic traffic with the Secretariat of State was closely monitored by Göring's cryptanalysts who had broken at least some of the codes in service on the Berlin–Vatican circuit.[69] The nuncio, Archbishop Cesare Orsenigo, sometimes tried to circumvent audio surveillance by using Latin with his staff and in his telephone conversations with German bishops and priests, but this rather feeble effort proved futile since the *Forschungsamt* merely hired a Latinist to translate such conversations.[70] Such surveillance provided insights into the always problematic state of German–Vatican relations. It also generated collateral intelligence on events, personalities, and public opinion in German-occupied territories. With the closure (at German insistence) of the nunciatures in Brussels, The Hague, Warsaw and Riga, the Berlin nunciature became a collection centre for appeals, complaints and reports from priests and lay people living in these territories. By the end of 1940, Archbishop Orsenigo's mission had become the Vatican's most important source of information on ecclesiastical and political conditions in occupied Europe. By monitoring the nunciature's mail, phones and telegrams, the *Forschungsamt* was able to tap this important source of information. Göring himself testified to the value of the intelligence concerning the Vatican acquired by his eavesdroppers.[71]

Other members of the German intelligence community occasionally attended to papal communications. In the summer of 1940, for instance, the *Abwehr*, the military intelligence service, passed to the German foreign ministry the plaintext of an encrypted telegram from the Secretariat of State to the apostolic delegate in London concerning the chances for a negotiated settlement of the war. Since the *Abwehr* had no independent intercept or cryptanalysis capability, but as part of the armed forces depended upon the *Chiffrierabteilung* of the high command for any signals intelligence, it probably obtained this telegram from Chi's cryptanalysts.[72] In 1942 and 1943 the *Abwehr* obtained summaries of a series of reports addressed to the Spanish government by its ambassador to the Holy See. These reports, which included information about the Vatican's possible participation in the surrender of Italy, were almost certainly obtained by the *Abwehr* from a source in the Spanish diplomatic service.[73]

Before the war, the SD (the Nazi party security and intelligence organization which considered the Catholic Church a major ideological threat to the New Order) had sought to trace the clandestine channels by which the Vatican allegedly communicated with Catholic organizations and personalities in Germany. The security service expected to discover evidence of a conspiracy by the Catholic Church to undermine the National Socialist state. Such evidence would be collected into a 'Black Book' for use against the Church on the 'day of reckoning'. This effort intensified after Palm Sunday 1937 when parish priests across Germany stepped into their pulpits to read to their astonished congregations an encyclical, *Mit brennender Sorge*, in which Pope Pius XI denounced the anti-clerical actions of the Nazi regime, and condemned racialism and the elevation of anti-Christian doctrines and values by the state. This document had been printed in Italy, secretly carried into Germany by special couriers and distributed to bishops and then to parish priests, all without raising the slightest suspicion in the security services which were supposed to protect the regime against such subversive outrages.[74] This obsession with uncovering the papacy's clandestine communications channels continued after the outbreak of the war and the amalgamation of the SD into the Reich Security Administration (RSHA). A list of intelligence requirements concerning the Catholic Church which Reinhard Heydrich, the Chief of the RSHA, circulated among his intelligence officers in April 1940 identified the following priorities: '1. All material suggesting that the bishops are using the Nuncio's courier service to maintain contact with the Vatican is to be carefully collected and sent to headquarters. 2. Trustworthy contact men are to be found who can determine the identity of the episcopal and Vatican couriers.'[75] In 1942 the reports forwarded to Berlin by Herbert Kappler, the RSHA representative in Rome, routinely included such topics as 'Vatican radio contact with Lvov', 'Transmittal of correspondence of the Vatican Secretariat of State', and 'Swiss river barges as courier channels for the Catholic intelligence service'.[76] In one notable success the Gestapo turned an individual in Munich who served the Vatican as a mail drop for clandestine messages from German-occupied territories in the east. This individual gave the Gestapo access to all papal messages passing through his hands.[77] The effort against Vatican communications, however, involved traditional espionage more than cryptanalysis. Although the RSHA set up a so-called 'Radio Observation Post' in its foreign intelligence section to collect signals intelligence, this unit managed to penetrate the cryptographic systems of only a few of the smaller powers and it was disbanded in 1943. It is uncertain whether, during its brief existence, the Radio Observation Post had any success against papal codes. The RSHA probably acquired details about Vatican codes from the Hungarians who had cracked one or two papal cryptosystems. Wilhelm Hoettl, the director for south-east European affairs in Amt VI (foreign intelligence), had established a productive liaison relationship with the Hungarian cryptanalysts, who quickly became an important source of signals intelligence for the foreign intelligence department.[78] Given his special interest in the papacy and the fact that the Vatican fell under his section of Amt VI, it is unlikely that Hoettl passed up an opportunity to gain access to papal diplomatic communications. The RSHA may also have acquired at least one Vatican code from a disgruntled Italian nobleman who had been dismissed from the Pope's service and sought revenge (and money) from the Germans. It may also have purchased Vatican codes (as well as Brazilian, Portuguese, Turkish and Yugoslavian systems) from the chief of Japanese intelligence in Europe.[79]

The Vatican was not unaware that its cryptosystems had been compromised on a major scale by German and Italian intelligence. For Germany, the first warning had come from an unimpeachable source: German military intelligence. Shortly after their first contacts with Pope Pius in the early months of the war, the anti-Hitler resistance cell in the *Abwehr* to their dismay heard rumours that Himmler's security service had acquired at least one papal code. This posed a serious threat not only to the Vatican but also to the conspirators in Germany. Should the SD intercept a telegram in the compromised code which made even the vaguest reference to the Pope's contacts with opposition circles in the period November 1939–March 1940 when Pius had served as a channel between the opposition and the British, there would be an immediate investigation by the secret police. Someone in the *Abwehr*, perhaps Admiral Canaris himself, decided to warn the Pope.[80] Josef Müller, the original intermediary between the conspirators and His Holiness, was dispatched again to Rome to inform Father Robert Leiber, the Pope's personal assistant and confidant, of the danger. To Müller's chagrin, Leiber refused to credit the information, explaining in detail (in what was itself a major security lapse) why the papal cryptographic systems were unbreakable. When they learned of this disappointing reaction, the *Abwehr* group decided that the only way to convince the Vatican was to produce the plaintext of an intercepted telegram in one of the supposedly unbreakable codes. Müller memorized the text of an intercepted message to the nuncio in Lisbon and, returning to Rome, dictated it word for word to an astonished Leiber. This was enough to convince the Pope, who until then had been inclined to consider his cryptosystems 'perfect [and] beyond attack'.[81]

Confirmation of the vulnerability of its codes reached the Vatican at about the same time from another German source. A young Catholic soldier in the section of the *Forschungsamt* responsible for monitoring diplomatic traffic experienced a crisis of conscience. At the time (shortly after the fall of Poland), the nunciature in Berlin was in frequent contact with the Secretariat of State about several sensitive issues: the dismal condition of church–state relations in the Reich, the harsh occupation policies in Poland, and the increasingly desperate plight of Jews for some of whom the Holy See was seeking protection. The soldier knew that the *Forschungsamt* had broken at least some of the cryptographic systems in use at the nunciature and was reading much of its traffic with the Vatican. Decrypts were often passed to the Gestapo. The conscience-stricken young man cast about for a way to alert the nuncio without danger to himself. From his own experience he knew that the mail and telephones of the nunciature were monitored, and he was also aware that the papal diplomatic mission was under physical surveillance by police agents who routinely stopped and questioned visitors. A caller in uniform could not expect to escape their attention. In the end, the soldier chose an indirect contact. Separately he approached three priests of his acquaintance, told them the secret, and asked them to carry the warning to the nuncio. The news, while sobering, was probably not a complete surprise to the staff of the nunciature which had long accustomed itself to the special attentions of the Reich security services.[82]

Evidence of Italian success with papal codes had begun to accumulate by the spring of 1940. During the first winter of the war, a junior officer in the nunciature to Italy was summoned to the foreign ministry by the *chef de cabinet* of Foreign Minister Galeazzo Ciano to review some matter of ecclesiastical property. To the young monsignor's surprise, the aide furtively took him aside and whispered that Vatican ciphers were in the hands of the Italian government and that someone had to warn the Pope. The Secretariat of State received this news with some scepticism, but its attitude changed when the officer secured from his source in Ciano's private office the cleartexts of enciphered radiograms sent and received by the Secretariat.[83] At the end of March the Secretariat received a similar warning from the mouth of the Foreign Minister himself. Monsignor Francesco Borgongini Duca, the nuncio to the Italian government, had a long meeting with Count Galeazzo Ciano, which turned into something more than a routine exchange of views. Ciano had revealed to the nuncio his efforts to dampen Mussolini's enthusiasm for joining Hitler's war. When the papal representative warned Ciano against excessive risks, the Foreign Minister (with characteristic indiscretion) responded with a bombshell:

> Do not trust the diplomats accredited to the Holy See who in their telegrams and reports give information about Italy as heard in the Vatican and also mention my name. *We read everything, and Mussolini also reads everything.* You must consider my position, otherwise I shall be obliged not to tell you anything more.[84] (emphasis added)

The Vatican did not have to wait long for confirmation of Ciano's boast. On 3 May 1940 the Secretariat of State sent telegrams ('To be decoded only by the Nuncio') to the papal representatives in Brussels and The Hague warning that 'an attack on the Western front is imminent, striking also at Holland and Belgium and possibly Switzerland'. The telegrams, which reflected information passed to the Vatican by opposition elements in the *Abwehr*, ended with the instruction, 'destroy this coded message'. Somehow, the Secretariat of State learned that these sensitive communications had been immediately intercepted and decrypted by Italian intelligence and brought to Mussolini's attention.[85] Additional evidence (if any was needed) of the security problem confronting the Vatican came at the end of May when Monsignor Borgongini Duca learned from a source in the Italian government that a circular telegram to papal representatives in various capitals, including London, Paris, Berne, Madrid and Washington, had been intercepted and decoded. Borgongini Duca reported that the source knew the exact contents of the message and 'He [the source] added that all telegrams in code are read.'[86]

To deal with the serious threat to the security of its diplomatic communications, the Secretariat of State introduced more sophisticated cryptographic systems. One such system was distributed to the papal representatives in Berlin, Berne, Lisbon, Madrid, Vichy and Washington in mid-1942. The codebook contained approximately 15,000 groups which were enciphered with 25 distinct keys each consisting of a digraphic table (for page numbers) and a random mixed alphabet (for line numbers). Each key used a different null. Each post received a different set of 16 of these 25 keys. Finally, there was a provision for switching the keys (as many as eight times) within a single message. From the evidence presently available it is impossible to determine whether German cryptanalysts had any success against this system, although American codebreakers tried without success to solve it.[87]

The Vatican would have been hampered in its effort to improve the security of its cryptographic systems by the complete absence of professional cryptologists in the Secretariat of State. In the seriously understaffed office, responsibility for codes and ciphers was assigned to a single priest who had no particular training for the task save what he picked up on the job. Though American intelligence concluded that this individual (whose identity remains unknown) was 'a cryptographer of no mean ability', there was a limit to what one man could produce.[88] The lack of an independent courier system to distribute new codes as frequently and securely as might have been desirable was also an impediment. Distributing new cryptosystems by means of the diplomatic pouches of Spain and Switzerland was an insecure expedient since even friendly neutrals might be tempted by the communication secrets of the Vatican. Furthermore, despite their theoretical immunity from search, neutral pouches in transit across the territory of belligerents were often opened and their contents examined.[89] Distant posts, like the apostolic delegation in Tokyo, were all but isolated, and distributing new codes to these posts was especially difficult. Most of the European nunciatures had the full repertory of cryptosystems (RED, YELLOW, GREEN, and so on), but as late as the autumn of 1944, many papal missions (including the delegation in Tokyo and all the missions in the Middle East) had only the RED code for communicating with the Vatican.[90] Unfortunately, this system was so hopelessly compromised that an internal memorandum of the Secretariat freely acknowledged that 'all governments are able to decipher [it] with great facility'.

The Secretariat introduced new codes during the war, but remained uncertain about the security of the new systems. It knew that foreign governments, particularly Germany and Italy, possessed Vatican codes, but it did not know which systems were compromised. Security was further undermined by occasional lapses in communications procedures. The Secretariat restricted access to its cipher office and periodically reminded its diplomatic missions of the importance of security. It issued strict orders about keeping cryptographic material under lock and key, maintaining absolute secrecy concerning the nature and use of such material, and avoiding the repetition of the literal text of enciphered messages (including the number and subject of the message) in open dispatches, but personnel were sometimes careless. The papal delegate in Tokyo received a reprimand after his secretary, in an open dispatch, repeated the text of an enciphered message the delegation had recently received from the Secretariat of State. The delegate in Washington was admonished for using a code 'not at all secure' for a telegram reporting the possible date of the Allied invasion of France. When the papal representative in Australia reported the name of the priest in Dutch New Guinea who was the secret source of information about Japanese atrocities on that island, the Secretariat's cipher office recommended that the diplomat be warned that 'his cipher is not entirely secure'.[91] Unfortunately, the cipher office itself was not immune from the occasional mishap. The RED code may have been first compromised when the cipher office used it to transmit to the various nunciatures and delegations the text of a papal address which, subsequently, was published *verbatim* in the press. A more serious lapse occurred on 3 May 1940 when the Secretariat of State sent identical messages to the nuncios in Brussels and The Hague warning of the imminent German attack against the Low Countries. Through a misunderstanding, the cipher office sent one of the warnings in the RED code, which was known to be insecure, and the other message in a more secure system, thereby facilitating entry into the latter by any cryptanalytic service, such as the Italian and the German, which had already broken the RED code.[92]

There was little confidence in the Secretariat of State that *any* measures would be effective. The conclusion by a *minutante* (senior clerk) in the department that 'They read everything' suggests a certain fatalism, as does a bitter joke then current in the Vatican that if the Secretariat could not decipher one of its incoming telegrams, it had only to apply to SIM for the cleartext. Monsignor Domenico Tardini, the second-ranking officer in the Secretariat of State, eventually concluded that no cryptographic system (at least none that the Vatican might contrive) could withstand systematic study or avoid deliberate or accidental betrayal. Once, when the British representative, Francis d'Arcy Osborne, assured him that his legation's reports to London concerning Vatican–Japanese relations were protected by the Foreign Office cipher, Tardini dismissed the assurances as 'simpleminded'.[93] For pragmatists like Tardini the Vatican might tinker with its cryptosystems, obscure the meaning of a message by means of vague or indirect phrasing, and entrust its most sensitive messages to special couriers, but such measures were, at best, weak expedients. In the end the Vatican accepted the fact that many of its diplomatic communications were open to German and Italian (and probably other) eyes. Obviously, this placed a severe constraint upon the conduct of papal foreign relations since the Secretariat of State could not always communicate freely and frankly with its representatives and often had to delay action or response until a secure channel became available. This vulnerability in the face of Axis signals intelligence was probably the greatest weakness of wartime papal diplomacy. It was certainly the greatest success of Axis intelligence against the Vatican.

NOTES

1. ADSS. Vol. I, p. 456, n. 1. The Fascist regime was especially obsessed with the Vatican newspaper and actively sought to discredit it and intimidate its readership. See O. Chadwick, *Britain and the Vatican*, pp. 107ff.
2. D. Kahn, *Hitler's Spies*, pp. 162–6.
3. O. Chadwick, *Britain and the Vatican*, p. 141.
4. Quoted in ibid., p. 81.
5. On 24 January 1940 the *New York Times* reported, 'Today the radio station of Vatican City has put on the air two broadcasts which add many details concerning the atrocities allegedly committed in German-occupied Poland.' Quoted in Robert A. Graham, SJ, 'La Radio Vaticana tra Londra e Berlino', *Civiltà Cattolica*, 1 (Jan. 1976), p. 139.
6. Ibid., p. 137. Mistiaen quoted in O. Chadwick, *Britain and the Vatican*, p. 145.
7. ADSS. Vo. IV, p. 192.
8. Ibid., pp. 189–90, 216–17, 250–1.
9. O. Chadwick, *Britain and the Vatican*, pp. 146–8.
10. R.A. Graham, 'La Radio Vaticana tra Londra e Berlino', p. 146; Sefton Delmer, *Black Boomerang* (New York: Viking Press, 1962), pp. 139–41.
11. PRO. FO 371/30190 and 371/5104; NARA. RG 59 (State Department Records),

Records of the Personal Representative of the President to Pope Pius XII, Communications File, Box 11, Montini to Taylor, 15 March 1945.

12. ADSS. Vol. II, p. 25; Vol. V, p. 320; Vol. X, p. 5.

13. NARA. RG 59. Records of the Personal Representative of the President to Pope Pius XII, Communications File, Box 11, Neuburg to Tittmann, 6 Oct. 1945.

14. The Federal Bureau of Investigation recently released documents which, though heavily sanitized, suggest that the surveillance was sufficient to enable the FBI to receive a breakdown of the mail sent and received by the delegation. Federal Bureau of Investigation, Memorandum for the Director from Edward Tamm, 28 Sept. 1942, and 'Allegations of the Misuse of the Washington Papal Embassy Diplomatic Pouch' (internal memorandum, date and attribution deleted). Documents released to the authors under the provisions of the Freedom of Information Act.

15. ADSS. Vol. V, p. 624. Information from Cardinal Silvio Oddi. Cardinal Oddi, who as a young monsignor served in various papal diplomatic missions in the Middle East during the war, recalled, 'The bags were apparently not opened, but I say "apparently", because it was easy to suspect that the police had ways of opening and closing a bag without leaving any traces.'

16. Vatican Radio had a telegraphic service with scheduled short-wave appointments with stations in various countries. For its use by the Secretariat of State, see ADSS. Vol. I, p. 250.

17. O. Chadwick, *Britain and the Vatican*, pp. 152, 181; ADSS. Vol. V, p. 413.

18. In 1940 Osborne had turned down a suggestion from the Foreign Office that he take a radio set with him into the Vatican. When Axis diplomats exchanged places with their Allied counterparts after the liberation of Rome, the German ambassador, Ernst von Weizsäcker, carried a wireless set (disguised as a record player) into his new quarters. O. Chadwick, *Britain and the Vatican*, p. 106; NARA. RG 59. Records of the Personal Representative of the President to Pope Pius XII, Box 35, Tittmann to Department of State, 29 June 1945.

19. NARA. RG 226 (Records of the Office of Strategic Services), Box 359, No. 35770.

20. NARA. T-175. Roll 582, 000840-46; ADSS. Vol. V, p. 406, n. 2; private information.

21. Quoted in O. Chadwick, *Britain and the Vatican*, p. 182.

22. Ibid., p. 183.

23. ADSS. Vol. VII, pp. 181, n. 5, 309. The Vatican's definition of sensitive material may have disappointed foreign intelligence services. A former employee of the Secretariat of State recalled an occasion towards the end of the war when he was detailed to collect official mail from the nunciatures in Lisbon and Madrid. The accumulated mail filled an entire train compartment which the young courier was reluctant to leave for even a moment on the long train journey for fear of leaving the Vatican's diplomatic pouches unprotected. After his arrival in Rome, he learned that the documents for which he was prepared to risk his life were mainly testimonials supporting the proposed sainthood of an obscure Portuguese monk. Information from Brother Edward Clancy.

24. ADSS. Vol. VII, pp. 131, 167.

25. ADSS. Vol. III, pp. 14–15, 437, 897.

26. David Kahn, *The Codebreakers: The Story of Secret Writing* (New York: Macmillan, 1967), pp. 106–7, 113; Aloys Meister, *Die Geheimschrift im Dienst der Päpstlichen Kurie* (Paderborn: Ferdinand Schöningh, 1896), *passim*.

27. David Alvarez, 'Faded Lustre: Vatican Cryptography, 1815–1920', *Cryptologia*, XX, 2 (April, 1996), pp. 97–131.

28. The Vatican is no more forthcoming about its cryptographic practices than other governments. The Vatican Archives are open only to 1922, and even for the open period most cryptographic materials have been removed from the files of the Secretariat of State available to researchers. Unless otherwise noted, all information about papal codes and ciphers during the Second World War was provided by a confidential source.

29. In a one-part code the plaintext elements (letters, words and phrases) are listed in alphabetical order with their corresponding code groups in straight numerical order (a=0001, ab=0002 . . .). In a two-part code, the code groups are in mixed numerical form (a=1784, ab=3011 . . .). The latter requires separate codebooks for encoding and decoding.

30. NARA. RG 457, Historic Cryptographic Collection, Pre-World War I through World War II, Item 3823, 'Cryptographic Codes and Ciphers: Vatican Code Systems', pp. 53–4.

31. Information provided by Ottfried Deubner. During the war, Dr Deubner was deputy chief of the Italian-language desk in Pers Z and directly responsible for the study of Vatican codes. By 1940 this five-figure system was in service only at minor papal missions in the Far East (Bangalore and Hue).

The additive system of superencipherment was commonly used by foreign ministries at the outbreak of the war. In this process a number is added to each numerical group in the encoded version of a message to produce a new numerical group which is the enciphered version. The Vatican's table of a hundred additive groups seems puny when compared to a contemporary British system which used a book of 40,000 additive groups. D. Kahn, *The Codebreakers*, pp. 252, 444.

32. NARA. RG 457, 'Cryptographic Codes and Ciphers: Vatican Code Systems', p. 47. American codebreakers were never able to solve the special Washington system, although their British counterparts were able to read the simpler code reserved for London.

33. ADSS. Vol. I, p. 293. Private information.

34. Information from Pentti Aalto. During the war Professor Aalto was a cryptanalyst in the diplomatic section of Finnish signals intelligence. For Hungarian codebreaking see Army Security Agency (ASA), *European Axis Signal Intelligence in World War II*, Vol. 8 (Washington: Army Security Agency, 1946), pp. 17–21 (hereinafter cited as EASI with volume and page number). This document was released to the authors under the Freedom of Information Act. For Finnish codebreaking see David Kahn, 'Finland's Codebreaking in World War II', in Hayden Peake and Samuel Halpern (eds), *In the Name of Intelligence: Essays in Honor of Walter Pforzheimer* (Washington: NIBC Press, 1994), pp. 329–47. Kahn implies that the Finns actually cracked papal codes, but Aalto recalled that his section 'did not actually solve [Vatican codes], just used the tools sent by the Hungarians'.

35. F.H. Hinsley *et al.*, *British Intelligence in the Second World War*, Vol. 2 (New York: Cambridge University Press, 1981), p. 642; D. Kahn, *The Codebreakers*, pp. 472–3; Paul Paillole, *Service Spécial, 1935–1945* (Paris: R. Laffont, 1965), pp. 132–5. The Italians probably made occasional incursions into the British embassy as early as 1924. These operations may explain the disappearance in 1925 of two copies of the embassy's R CODE, an unenciphered bookcode used by the Foreign Office for low-level messages. Christopher Andrew, *Her Majesty's Secret Service: The Making of the British Intelligence Community* (New York: Penguin Books, 1987), p. 404.

36. Information from General (ret.) Giulio Fettarappa-Sandori.

37. NARA. RG 226, Entry 108A, Box 205.

38. Cesare Amè, *Guerra segreta in Italia, 1940–1943* (Rome: G. Casini, 1954), pp. 47, 51; General Mario Roatta, the director of SIM between 1934 and 1937, claimed that in one outstanding year his agency acquired over 16,000 documents including 70 foreign ciphers. NARA. RG 226, Entry 108A, Box 205.

39. David Alvarez, 'Vatican Communications Security, 1914–1918', *Intelligence and National Security*, 7, 4 (Oct. 1992), p. 447. Italian efforts faltered only in the last year of the war when the Vatican began to superencipher its codes.

40. NARA. RG 457, Historic Cryptologic Collection, Pre-World War I through World War II, item 1974, 'First Detailed Interrogation of Augusto Bigi'. Bigi was an officer in SIM's cryptanalytic section.

41. Information provided by a former director of Vatican Radio.
42. In a post-war interrogation, the wartime director of SIM, General Cesare Amè, revealed the incursions into the Vatican palace. NARA. RG 226. Entry 108A, Box 205.
43. O. Chadwick, *Britain and the Vatican*, pp. 168–70.
44. Robert A. Graham, SJ, 'L occhio del SIM sulla Città del Vaticano', *Civiltà Cattolica*, 4 (Oct. 1978), p. 50.
45. Carlo De Risio, *Generali, servizi segreti e fascismo* (Milan: Mondadori, 1978), p. 183.
46. Quotes in C. Andrew, *Her Majesty's Secret Service*, p. 405.
47. PRO. FO 371/33419; O. Chadwick, *Britain and the Vatican*, p. 184. After the war the British concluded that the Italians 'had fairly regular access to the cyphers at the Mission to the Holy See during the war, so that they might have read . . . telegrams to and from the Mission to the Holy See from the outbreak of war to the autumn of 1943'. F.H. Hinsley, *British Intelligence*, p. 642.
48. O. Chadwick, *Britain and the Vatican*, p. 167. Chadwick doubts that such an operation ever took place, but the facts were confirmed by Osborne's American and Yugoslavian colleagues. Letter to Robert Graham from Costa Zoukitch, 16 Sept. 1975, and Robert Graham interview with Harold Tittmann, 19 March 1972. In a series of articles in its issues of 8, 11 and 12 Aug. 1958, the Rome daily paper, *Il Messagero*, published the texts of several telegrams intercepted and decrypted by SIM during the war. The collection included telegrams sent by Osborne to London between 18 June and 25 Aug. 1943. When the Public Record Office opened the relevant files to scholars, the official texts in the Foreign Office files were found to match the newspaper versions.
49. PRO. FO 371/24382.
50. Quoted in O. Chadwick, *Britain and the Vatican*, pp. 182–3.
51. Ibid., p. 185.
52. Information from Harold Tittmann. For an example of Tittmann's use of the Secretariat's facilities, see ADSS. Vol. V, p. 334.
53. Although the Americans solved the RED code, they had no success against other papal cryptosystems. For the American effort, see David Alvarez, 'No Immunity: SIGINT and the European Neutrals, 1939–45', *Intelligence and National Security* (forthcoming, 1997).
54. Information from Pentti Aalto.
55. NARA. RG 457, SRH-373, p. 41.
56. NARA. RG 457, SRH-375.
57. ASA, EASI, Vol. 3, p. 106.
58. D. Kahn, *Hitler's Spies*, p. 193.
59. ASA, EASI, Vol. 6, p. 33. For a description of Pers Z see D. Kahn, *The Codebreakers*, pp. 436ff.
60. NARA. T-120. Roll 34, 31050-31052.
61. Since Vatican Radio refused to handle any encoded messages but those of the papal Secretariat of State, the Irish telegrams could not have been acquired from a source in the station.
62. The last possibility is supported by the fact that the codetexts are introduced by brief comments typed in Italian. These comments ('The date of transmission . . . could be the key to identify the code which, perhaps, varies from day to day.') suggest that the source had a certain knowledge of cryptology.
63. ASA, EASI, Vol. 3, p. 69. For Chi's coverage of signals intelligence targets, see NARA. T-77. Roll 1456, pp. 207–33.
64. NARA. RG 457, SRH-373, pp. 51–2, 58, 73. Apparently the figures for the Vatican represent only incoming telegrams.
65. ADSS. Vol. I, p. 104.
66. Figures determined from the registry numbers of telegrams in ADSS. Vol. I.
67. D. Kahn, *Hitler's Spies*, p. 181; Günther W. Gellermann, *Und lauschten für Hitler. Geheime Reichssache: Die Abhörzentralen des Dritten Reiches* (Bonn: Bernard & Graefe,

1991), p. 43.
68. Wilhelm Flicke, *War Secrets in the Ether*, Vol. 1 (Laguna Hills: Aegean Park Press, 1977), p. 106.
69. ASA, EASI, Vol. 7, p. 88.
70. Information from Ernst Nienhaus, a wartime employee of the *Forschungsamt*; additional information from the unpublished memoirs of a former *Forschungsamt* officer in the possession of Richard Bauer.
71. PRO. WO/898/425.
72. NARA. T-120. Roll 315, 239532. The *Abwehr* told the Wilhelmstrasse that it obtained the telegram in Madrid. It seems odd that a cable from the Vatican to London would be intercepted in Madrid. Out of solidarity with his friend Mussolini, Hitler had prohibited intelligence operations in Italy. German services circumvented this prohibition by claiming that information collected in Italy had actually been collected in another country. Alternatively, if the telegram was relayed to London via Spanish radio or cable facilities, then a codetext may have been acquired from a Spanish source and decrypted by Chi. Since Vatican Radio's signal was too weak to reach many areas, the Secretariat of State routinely relayed its messages through Swiss telegraphic facilities. Perhaps Spanish facilities were also used.
73. NARA. T-77. Roll 1135, 244.
74. O. Chadwick, *Britain and the Vatican*, p. 20. For examples of efforts to identify clandestine couriers and their routes, see NARA. T-175. Roll 511, 9377696-731.
75. J. Conway, *The Nazi Persecution*, pp. 243–4.
76. AA. Inland IIg. 83. Italien. Berichtverzeichnis des Pol. Att. Rome, 1940–1943 (83-60 E).
77. Final Interrogation Report: Albert Hartl, p. 18.
78. D. Kahn, *The Codebreakers*, p. 452.
79. Walter Schellenberg, the head of foreign intelligence in the RSHA, purportedly recounted the story of the Italian nobleman to Arthur Nebe, the chief of the criminal police division of the security services. Hans Gisevius, *Wo ist Nebe?* (Zurich: Droemer, 1966), p. 228. For the purchase of codes, see D. Kahn, *The Codebreakers*, p. 450. During the war there were rumours in the papal diplomatic service that a codebook had been stolen and sold to one of the belligerents. Information from Cardinal Silvio Oddi.
80. In February 1943 Canaris arranged for Allen Dulles, the OSS representative in Switzerland, to be informed that one of the codes of the American legation in Berne had been broken by the Germans. Canaris acted to protect members of the German Resistance whose activities in Switzerland might have been mentioned in the cable traffic of the legation. K. von Klemperer, *German Resistance*, p. 399, n. 38.
81. Information from Josef Müller.
82. Information from Ernst Nienhaus, who was the *Forschungsamt* officer in question. In July 1943 when Italian emissaries, hoping to extricate their country from the war, tried to enlist the Vatican as an intermediary with the Allies, they explicitly warned the Secretariat of State not to trust its codes: 'The Germans intercept everything and they know all the codes.' ADSS. Vol. VII, p. 522.
83. Private information.
84. ADSS. Vol. I, pp. 412–13.
85. Ibid., p. 436, n. 2.
86. Ibid., pp. 473–4.
87. NARA. RG 457, 'Vatican Code Systems', pp. 39–44.
88. Ibid., p. 57.
89. For the seizure of Spanish diplomatic bags by American and British intelligence see, NARA. RG 457, 'Magic Diplomatic Summaries', 21 Oct. 1942 and 19 Nov. 1942.
90. Direct evidence of Japanese success against Vatican communications is lacking, but it is likely that the Secretariat of State's encrypted exchanges with its delegate in Tokyo were compromised. The Secretariat could communicate with the delegate only in the

RED code, a system known to be insecure. Furthermore, the Vatican was not allowed by Japanese authorities to communicate directly or in code with its representatives in China (Peking), Indochina (Hue) and the Philippines (Manila). All correspondence with these representatives had to be sent through the delegate in Tokyo, who could forward dispatches and telegrams to his colleagues only if the messages were in clear and in Japanese. ADSS. Vol. XI, pp. 240, 631.

91. ADSS. Vol. X, pp. 131–3; private information.
92. Information from Federico Alessandrini; private information.
93. ADSS. Vol. V, p. 460.

6

Conclusion

During the Second World War Nazi Germany considered the Catholic Church in general and the papacy in particular to be a potentially serious threat to its domestic security and international ambitions. As a result, the Vatican became the object of a significant intelligence offensive as the Nazi regime sought to uncover its secrets and anticipate its initiatives. Against this covert attack the Vatican could find protection in neither its neutrality nor its religious character. At its height this offensive attracted the attention and consumed the resources of agencies from throughout Germany's large and disparate intelligence community: codebreakers at the foreign ministry, the Armed Forces High Command and the *Forschungsamt*; news analysts at the *Sonderdienst Seehaus*; diplomats at the Reich embassy to the Holy See and on the Vatican desk at the Wilhelmstrasse; church specialists in the RSHA; and an assortment of spies and informants reporting to the *Abwehr*, the Gestapo and the SD. It was a significant effort. For its small size, the Vatican was perhaps covered more densely than any other intelligence target in the war. The results for Germany were, at best, mixed.

As was so often the case with both sides in the war, communications intelligence proved the most successful tool. Early in the war German cryptanalysts broke some of the Vatican's codes and ciphers and thereafter maintained close coverage of papal diplomatic signals with the result that, throughout the conflict, Berlin was often able to eavesdrop on the papacy's secret communications, most notably on the Berlin–Vatican circuit. This achievement was qualified, however, by the fact that by 1942 the Vatican had adopted more secure cryptosystems and was careful to commit nothing truly secret to the airwaves or telegraphic cables. The successes registered by the cryptanalysts stand, nevertheless, in stark contrast to the mediocre record of their compatriots in other German agencies who sought to penetrate the Catholic Church with agents and informants. To be sure, the results of human intelligence were uneven. Inside Germany, where the security services more easily wielded economic, legal, and psychological sanctions and rewards, the Gestapo and the SD successfully recruited informants at all levels of the German Catholic Church, with the result that the two agencies remained relatively well-informed about the organization, operations and finances of the German Church and the political sympathies of the German bishops. Efforts to penetrate the Vatican, which had become a priority target by the second year of the war, were far less successful.

During the First World War, German intelligence planted an agent at the highest levels of the papacy. A Bavarian priest, who served as Pope Benedict XV's private chamberlain and confidential aide, passed information on papal diplomatic plans and initiatives to his German controllers in Switzerland until his exposure in late 1916.[1] Berlin would never duplicate that success in the next war. There was no high-level German agent at the Vatican during the Second World War. The Pope's personal entourage remained immune to penetration even though Pius surrounded himself with Germans such as Father Leiber, his confidential assistant, Monsignor Kaas, an adviser on German affairs, and Mother Pasqualina, the head of the Pope's household staff of German nuns. German intelligence was no more successful in gaining direct access to the Secretariat of State, the nerve centre of papal administration and diplomacy, or other important targets such as Vatican Radio and the *Reparto Segreto* (Secret Department) of the Vatican printing office which printed confidential documents. To be sure, it had had at least one informant inside the Berlin nunciature since before the war, but his usefulness once the conflict began was limited. Pope Pius, who had served as nuncio in Germany for seven years and as Cardinal Secretary of State for eight, was an experienced and self-confident diplomatist, and at the onset of his pontificate he decided to keep German affairs under his direct control. Important matters were handled through the German embassy to the Holy See. Consequently, the Berlin nuncio, Archbishop Cesare Orsenigo (whose stock was never very high in Rome), became little more than a messenger, passing official notes and memoranda between the two governments. As the war progressed the Secretariat of State became less inclined to solicit Orsenigo's opinions. His influence over policy, never very great, declined further, and he was not informed of Vatican initiatives and policies in areas beyond Germany. Moreover, by 1942, German–Vatican relations had chilled to such a degree that official contacts were reduced to scarcely more than the exchange of protests. In such a situation the Germans would have learned little from their inside contact(s) that they did not already know from their surveillance of the nunciature's communications. Alexander Kurtna, the part-time translator at the Congregation for the Eastern Churches, was the Reich's best penetration at the Vatican and he provided useful information concerning ecclesiastical affairs and public opinion in eastern Europe and the occupied territories in Russia. However, 'Eastern Churches' was a minor department on the periphery of papal diplomacy, and Kurtna's value to Germany was compromised by his work as a double agent for Soviet intelligence. As for Germany's other human sources, they were either crypto-Nazi clerics, such as Bishop Alois Hudal, who were kept at arm's length by papal officials because of their known sympathies, or professional tipsters and hangers-on whose access to Vatican affairs was limited to the reading room of the Vatican Archives, the bars patronized by the Swiss Guards, or the cocktail parties of Catholic aristocrats.

Several factors may explain Germany's lacklustre record against the Vatican. Any explanation must include an appraisal of the resistance of the target. In many ways the Vatican was an easy target: some of its codes were weak, its security procedures minimal, its communications channels vulnerable, its territory minuscule, its population rife with German nationals. Such weaknesses, however, were offset by several factors which made the Vatican resistant to intelligence attack. The predominantly ecclesiastical character of the papal administration has already been noted. Aside from labourers, gardeners, guards, a few technicians in the museums and library, and a scattering of junior clerks in a few departments, all posts in the Vatican were filled by priests or members of religious orders. The ecclesiastical flavour of Vatican City was so intense that even the small pharmacy, the telephone exchange and the papal kitchen were staffed entirely by nuns or religious brothers. This community of priests, nuns and brothers represented a largely closed society which consciously recognized boundaries between itself and secular society, and which encouraged only limited interaction across those boundaries. Distinguished by dress, education, lifestyle and discipline from their counterparts in the secular world, the ecclesiastical citizens of the Vatican were also products of an administrative tradition and culture which emphasized prudence, secrecy and, above all, allegiance to the Church and its Pontiff.[2] In curial departments, such as the Secretariat of State, which supervised especially sensitive areas of church affairs, this administrative culture was reinforced among the personnel by oaths of office which explicitly committed the staff to secrecy and loyalty. Such oaths with their administrative and religious sanctions were not taken lightly.[3] In post-war evaluations of the Secretariat of State and its personnel the American mission to the Pope recorded the consensus of the diplomatic corps in Rome that perhaps only the Soviet Union had a diplomatic service as disciplined and secretive as the Vatican. The American and British representatives agreed that it was impossible to extract, even from their own nationals in papal service, any information about affairs inside the Secretariat.[4] While never completely impervious to attack, the secretive ecclesiastical society of the Vatican was, as the Germans discovered, a formidable obstacle to any intelligence service.

German efforts were additionally hindered by long-standing administrative practices in the Curia which tended to reserve important and confidential affairs to only a few officials. It is axiomatic that the security of a secret is in inverse proportion to the number of people who know that secret. In the Vatican secrets were very closely held. Throughout the war Pope Pius reserved all major and many minor diplomatic matters to himself, and he frequently kept his own counsel. When requiring advice or information he turned to a handful of trusted priests: his confidential aide, Father Robert Leiber, the Cardinal Secretary of State, Luigi Maglione, or the latter's two under-secretaries, Domenico Tardini and Giovanni Montini. Even the members of this inner circle were often ignorant of important policy initiatives. For example, in the autumn of 1939 when Pope Pius decided to act as a link between London and the anti-Nazi resistance in Germany, neither Maglione nor his two deputies were aware of the Pope's decision. The small size of the Secretariat of State further limited the number of people who were privy to diplomatic secrets.[5] In the crucial area of German–Vatican relations probably no more than seven individuals worked with the files: Pius, Leiber, Maglione, Tardini, Montini, Monsignor Antonio Samoré, the *minutante* (senior clerk) responsible for German affairs in the Secretariat, and, perhaps, a junior assistant (*addetto*). If one includes the nuncio and his officers in Berlin, as well as archivists and cipher clerks in the Secretariat, the number of papal officials with any access to material on German–Vatican relations would still scarcely exceed a dozen. To place the issue in perspective it is instructive to recall that in 1943 over 700 individuals had access to the minutes of the daily conferences of the British Chiefs of Staff.[6] For German intelligence officers seeking information about Vatican attitudes and intentions towards the Reich the pool of potential informants was disconcertingly small.

Within Germany, organizational weaknesses contributed to the disappointing record against the Vatican. Students of wartime espionage have noted that the Reich's intelligence effort in general was undermined by a proliferation of agencies which duplicated each other's work and competed for influence and resources. This wasteful situation was reflected in operations against the Vatican. At any given moment three cryptanalytic services were monitoring papal diplomatic communications and attacking papal codes, while in Rome four organizations (*Abwehr*, Gestapo, Amt VI of the RSHA, and the embassy to the Holy See) were competing to cover a target whose total area was less than the Washington Mall. Operations were further compromised by the tendency of some of these organizations, such as the embassy during the ambassadorship of Ernst von Weizsäcker and the *Abwehr* throughout the war, to slant the information they were reporting to Berlin in order to advance particular agendas. There was never agreement within the Nazi intelligence community on the goals of intelligence coverage of the Vatican and never any effort to coordinate resources and operations. The lack of coordination reflected not only the shifting needs and interests of the various agencies, but all too often the personal interests of the agents acting for those agencies.

Intelligence efforts were also undermined by an organizational mind-set (especially prevalent in the RSHA, the circle around the Führer, and certain desks in the foreign ministry) which projected a distorted image of the target. This image reflected the religious prejudice, historical ignorance and ideological paranoia of many

German intelligence officers and Nazi party hierarchs, but it also grew out of the real tensions in church–state relations and the accurate perception that the goals of the Catholic Church and those of the Nazi regime were fundamentally incompatible. The mind-set, which exaggerated the power of the Vatican and imagined all manner of papal conspiracies against the Reich, often distracted German intelligence from a realistic appraisal of their target and encouraged officers to waste time and resources on the pursuit of such phantasms as the 'Tisserant Plan' for the evangelization of Russia, Jesuit plots to overthrow the regime, or the Vatican's supposed intelligence collaboration with the Allies. Their inability to give substance to such phantasms with hard intelligence from such sources as signals intelligence merely confirmed officers in their suspicions of Vatican subtlety and duplicity and made them more susceptible to the 'intelligence' fabricated by confidence men only too happy to fuel their fantasies.

In the Byzantine world of Nazi politics, where the possession of information provided courtiers like Bormann, Göring, Heydrich, Himmler and Ribbentrop with status and influence, intelligence became an end in itself. Questions of utility, relevance and accuracy were subordinated to the relentless accumulation of information which, by creating the appearance of knowledgeability, could be used to attract the attention and favour of the Führer and to assert and defend a personal position while undercutting that of a competitor.[7] This approach encouraged the proliferation of agencies and the duplication of collection efforts as each Nazi hierarch sought his own intelligence sources. At times the intelligence coverage of the Vatican seemed a caricature of this internecine competition. For example, rather than depend on the hateful Ribbentrop for information on the papacy, Martin Bormann and Walter Schellenberg each succeeded in placing his own protégé on the staff of the Reich's small embassy to the Holy See. Ostensibly working for the foreign ministry, these agents reported separately (and secretly) to their real masters in Berlin. Sometimes the duplication of effort was ludicrous, as when cryptanalysts working for Ribbentrop, Göring and the Armed Forces High Command separately intercepted and decoded the two or three telegrams the Secretariat of State exchanged each day with its nunciatures.

The Nazi approach to intelligence also discouraged analysis and evaluation of incoming information. After all, evaluation might discredit the information, thereby disarming the Nazi courtier in his battle for influence in Hitler's court. Nothing was allowed to challenge the courtier's control over the information and its meaning. Above all, nothing was allowed to challenge the dominant political and military paradigm as articulated by the Führer. Intelligence suggesting a reality at odds with that paradigm was simply dismissed, as was the official so misguided as to persist in reporting such intelligence. On the other hand, intelligence confirming that paradigm was embraced along with its source. For Ribbentrop or Heydrich or Göring the question was not whether his information was accurate, but whether it was acceptable. In an environment where accuracy was sacrificed to expediency and sycophancy, falsehood flourished. This may further explain why the German intelligence effort against the Vatican was so often victimized by fabricators and confidence tricksters. Not only was a lie as good as the truth, it was sometimes better than the truth. That could well stand as the epitaph of Germany's intelligence effort against the Vatican during the Second World War.

NOTES

1. David Alvarez, 'A German Agent at the Vatican: The Gerlach Affair', *Intelligence and National Security*, 11, 2 (April, 1996), pp. 345–56.
2. Only a small proportion of the individuals working in the Vatican were actually citizens of Vatican City. Under Vatican law, citizenship is restricted to 1) cardinals resident in Vatican City or Rome, 2) nuncios and delegates on foreign service, 3) all who permanently reside in Vatican City by virtue of their office or employment, and 4) the immediate relatives of a Vatican citizen, on condition that they reside with that citizen in Vatican City. Given the very limited accommodations in the tiny city-state, few employees of the Vatican could claim citizenship. H. E. Cardinale, *The Holy See and the International Order* (Toronto: Macmillan, 1976), pp. 108–10, 353.
3. Half a century after the war the commitment to secrecy remains strong. In the preparation of this volume the authors asked 20 surviving members of the wartime papal diplomatic service to respond to five questions concerning administrative and security procedures in the Secretariat of State during the war. Nineteen of these elderly priests declined to respond, often adding that even after the passage of 50 years they did not feel at liberty to discuss any aspect of their service in the Secretariat of State. The remaining priest was willing only to confirm in one or two cases the accuracy of information received from other sources.
4. NARA. RG 59. Records of the Personal Representative of the President to Pope Pius XII, Political-General, Box 17, Memorandum by McFadden, 5 Dec. 1947; ibid., Memoranda-Confidential, Box 19, Memorandum by Parsons, 22 May 1948.
5. Even in comparison to the foreign ministries of minor powers the Secretariat of State

180

was an exceptionally small organization. In the first year of the war the Secretariat employed 31 individuals including archivists and typists. The foreign ministries of Norway and the Netherlands had staffs of 119 and 80 respectively.

6. George C. Constantinides, 'Security Slip-Ups: Ultra, Magic, Bigot and Other Secrets' in H. Peake and S. Halpern (eds), *In the Name of Intelligence: Essays in Honor of Walter Pforzheimer* (Washington: NIBC Press, 1994), p. 175.

7. Michael Geyer, 'National Socialist Germany: The Politics of Information' in E.R. May (ed.), *Knowing One's Enemies: Intelligence Assessment Before the Two World Wars* (Princeton: Princeton University Press, 1984), pp. 310–46.

Bibliography

Alvarez, David, 'Vatican Intelligence Capabilities in the Second World War', *Intelligence and National Security*, Vol. 6, No. 3 (1991) pp. 593–607.

—, 'The Vatican and Italian Belligerency' in D.W. Pike (ed.), *The Opening of the Second World War* (New York, 1991), pp. 311–14.

—, 'Vatican Communications Security, 1914–18', *Intelligence and National Security*, Vol. 7, No. 4 (1992), pp. 443–53.

Amè, Cesare, *Guerra segreta in Italia, 1940–1943* (Rome, 1954).

Andrew, Christopher, *Her Majesty's Secret Service: The Making of the British Intelligence Community* (New York, 1987).

Army Security Agency, *European Axis Signal Intelligence in World War II*, 9 vols. (Washington, DC, 1946).

Barros, James and Gregor, Richard, *Double Deception: Stalin, Hitler and the Invasion of Russia* (DeKalb, 1995).

Bernabei, Domenico, *Orchestra Nera* (Turin, 1991).

Black, Peter, *Ernst Kaltenbrunner: Ideological Soldier of the Third Reich* (Princeton,1984).

Blet, Pierre, Graham, Robert A., Martini, Angelo and Schneider, Burkhart (eds), *Actes et Documents du Saint Siège relatifs à la seconde guerre mondiale*, 11 vols. (Vatican City, 1968–81).

Boberach, Heinz, *Berichte des SD und der Gestapo uber Kirchen und Kirchenvolk in Deutschland* (Mainz, 1971).

Browder, George, *Foundations of the Nazi Police State: The Formation of Sipo and SD* (Lexington, 1990).

Chadwick, Owen, *Britain and the Vatican during the Second World War* (Cambridge, 1986).

Charles-Roux, François, *Huit ans au Vatican, 1932–1940* (Paris, 1947).

Central Intelligence Agency, *The Rote Kapelle: The CIA's History of Soviet Intelligence and Espionage Networks in Western Europe, 1936–1945* (Washington DC, 1979).

Conway, John, *The Nazi Persecution of the Churches, 1933–45* (New York, 1968).

Dallek, Robert, *Franklin D. Roosevelt and American Foreign Policy, 1932–1945* (New York, 1979).

Delmer, Sefton, *Black Boomerang* (New York, 1962).

De Risio, Carlo, *Generali, servizi segreti e fascismo* (Milan, 1978).

Derry, Sam. *The Rome Escape Line* (New York, 1960).

Deschner, Gunther, *Heydrich: The Pursuit of Total Power* (London, 1981).

Deutsch, Harold, *The Conspiracy against Hitler in the Twilight War* (Minneapolis, 1968).

Doeschner, Hans-Jurgen, *Das Auswärtige Amt im Dritten Reich* (Berlin, 1987).

Fogarty, Gerald, *The Vatican and the American Hierarchy* (Stuttgart, 1982).

Gariboldi, Giorgio, *Il Vaticano nella Seconda Guerra Mondiale* (Milan, 1992).

Gasbarri, Carlo, *Quando il Vaticano confinava con il Terzo Reich* (Padua, 1984).

Gellermann, Gunther, *Und lauschten für Hitler* (Bonn, 1991).

Geyer, Michael, 'National Socialist Germany: The Politics of Information' in E.R. May (ed.), *Knowing One's Enemies: Intelligence Assessment Before the Two World Wars* (Princeton, 1984), pp. 310–46.

Gisevius, Hans, *Wo ist Nebe?* (Zurich, 1966).

Graham, Robert A., SJ, *Vatican Diplomacy* (Princeton, 1959).

—, 'Spie naziste attorno al Vaticano durante la seconda guerra mondiale', *Civiltà Cattolica*, 1 (Jan. 1970) pp. 21–31.

—, 'La strana codotta di E. von Weizsäcker ambasciatore del Reich in Vaticano', *Civiltà Cattolica*, 2 (June 1970) pp. 455–71.

—, 'Voleva Hitler allontanare da Roma Pio XII?', *Civiltà Cattolica*, 1 (Feb. 1972) pp. 319–27.

—, 'Il vaticanista falsario. L'incredibile successo di Virgilio Scattolini', *Civiltà Cattolica*, 3 (Sept. 1973) pp. 467–78.

—, 'La Radio Vaticana tra Londra e Berlino', *Civiltà Cattolica*, 1 (Jan. 1976) pp. 132–50.

—, 'L'occhio del SIM sulla Città del Vaticano', *Civiltà Cattolica*, 4 (Oct. 1978) pp. 44–54.

Gurrey, Donald, *Across the Lines: Axis Intelligence and Sabotage Operations in Italy, 1943–45* (Tunbridge Wells, 1994).

Helmreich, Ernst, *The German Churches under Hitler* (Detroit, 1979).

Hill, Leonidas, 'The Vatican Embassy of Ernst von Weizsäcker, 1943', *Journal of Modern History*, 39, 2 (June 1967) pp. 138–58.

Hinsley, F.H., *et al.*, *British Intelligence in the Second World War*, 5 vols. (London, 1979–90).

Hoettl, Wilhelm, *The Secret Front: The Story of Nazi Political Espionage* (New York, 1954).

Höhne, Heinz, *Canaris* (Garden City, 1979).

Kahn, David, *The Codebreakers* (New York, 1967).

—, *Hitler's Spies: German Military Intelligence in World War II* (New York, 1978).

Klemperer, Klemens von, *German Resistance against Hitler: The Search for Allies Abroad* (Oxford, 1992).

Lamb, Richard, *War in Italy, 1943–1945* (New York, 1993).

Lapomarda, Vincent, *The Jesuits and the Third Reich* (Lewiston, 1989).

Lochner, Louis (ed.), *The Goebbels Diaries, 1942–1943* (New York, 1948).

McKay, C.G., *From Information to Intrigue: Studies in Secret Service Based on the Swedish Experience, 1939–45* (London, 1993).

Pollard, John F., *The Vatican and Italian Fascism, 1929–1932* (Cambridge, 1985).

Rhodes, Anthony, *The Vatican in the Age of the Dictators* (London, 1973).

Schellenberg, Walter, *Hitler's Secret Service* (New York, 1971).

Stehle, Hansjakob, *Eastern Politics of the Vatican, 1917–1979* (Athens, OH, 1981).

Weitz, John, *Hitler's Diplomat: Joachim von Ribbentrop* (London, 1992).

Zizola, Giancarlo, *Quale Papa?* (Rome, 1977).

Index

INDEX

Cass Series: Studies in Intelligence

Titles in the series include:

British Intelligence in the Palestine Campaign, 1914–1918

Yigal Sheffy, *Tel Aviv University*

Drawing on extensive British archival documentation, as well as on Ottoman and German sources, the book examines the development and efficacy of British Military Intelligence during the campaign against the Ottoman Empire in Egypt and Palestine during the war.

400 pages maps 1997
0 7146 4677 6 cloth • 0 7146 4208 8 paper

Eternal Vigilance?
50 Years of the CIA

Rhodri Jeffreys-Jones, *University of Edinburgh* and
Christopher Andrew, *University of Cambridge*

Eternal Vigilance? seeks to offer reinterpretations of some of the major established themes in CIA history such as its origins, foundations, its treatment of the Soviet threat, the Iranian Revolution and the accountability of the agency. The book also opens new areas of research such as foreign liaison, relations with the scientific community, use of scientific and technical research and economic intelligence.

256 pages 1997
0 7146 4807 8 cloth • 0 7146 4360 2 paper

Intelligence Analysis and Assessment

David Charters (Ed), *University of New Brunswick, Canada* **Stuart Farson** (Ed), **Simon Fraser,** *University Canada* and **Glenn P Hastedt** (Ed), *Editor of Controlling Intelligence*

Of the many functions carried out by intelligence agencies, analysis and assessment has received comparatively little scholarly attention. In October 1994 the Canadian association for Security and Intelligence Studies (CASIS) and the Intelligence Section of the International Studies Association (ISA) attended to this deficit by holding a special international conference on the subject in Ottawa. This volume is the product of that conference.

240 pages 1996
0 7146 4709 8 cloth • 0 7146 4249 5 paper

Intelligence Investigations
How Ultra Changed History

Ralph Bennett

Ralph Bennett, who worked for four years as a senior producer of the intelligence ('Ultra') derived from the Enigma decrypts at Bletchley Park, illustrates in this collection of reprinted essays some of the steps by which he and others developed the new type of information and in the process provides a candid glimpse of the workings of British intelligence both past and present.

216 pages 1996
0 7146 4742 X cloth • 0 7146 4300 9 paper